SPOKANE

Summer evening in Riverfront Park

Photo by Ron Swords

SPOKANE

❧ The ☙ Complete Guide to the Hub of the Inland Northwest

M. E. Buckham

JOHNSTON
ASSOCIATES
INTERNATIONAL

P.O. BOX 313
MEDINA, WASHINGTON 98039
(206) 454-7333
FAX: (206) 462-1335

Spokane: The Complete Guide to the Hub of the Inland Northwest,
First Edition
© 1995 by M.E. Buckman

ISBN 1-881409-13-9

Cover art and book design by Mike Jaynes
Production and typesetting by Kate Rose
Maps by Marge Mueller
Cover photos by Ron Swords
Interior photos by Patrice Tobler & Ron Swords

DISCLAIMER
Although diligent efforts have been made to confirm the accuracy of
information contained in this work, neither the publisher nor the author
are responsible for errors or inaccuracies or for changes occuring after
publication. This work was not prepared under the sponsorship, license,
or authorization of any business, attraction, park, person, or organization described, depicted, or discussed herein.

JASI
Post Office Box 313
Medina, Washingon 98039
(206) 454-3490 FAX: (206) 462-1335

Printed in the United States of America

Library of Congress Cataloging-in-Publication Data

Buckham, M.E. (Mary Elizabeth), 1956-
    Spokane : the complete guide to the hub of the inland Northwest /
M.E. Buckham. -- 1st ed.
        p.   cm.
    Includes index.
    ISBN 1-881409-13-9
    1. Spokane (Wash.) -- Guidebooks. I. Title
F899.S7B83   1995
917,97'370443--dc20   95-10103
                                                           CIP

iv

Acknowledgement

I would like to extend my thanks to the many individuals who shared their knowledge, insights and love of this area. Spokane and the Inland Northwest are truly products of their wonderful and giving people. My thanks also to my husband, family and friends who willingly tasted, shopped and examined while we explored the familiar and the new. And a very special thanks to Ann Schuessler and Priscilla Johnston, who made my dream a reality.

Introduction

Spokane and the Inland Northwest is an area unique in its heritage and people. This slice of Washington, Idaho, Montana and beyond was built by railroaders, ranchers, and farmers. It was crafted by men and women of vision who saw water and lots of land—and knew what the Native American tribes indigenous to the area knew: this was a good place to live.

This still holds true today. Spokane *is* a great place to live. It offers diversity, small-town charm and big-city entertainment. Pristine wilderness is a mere stone's throw away. The city is a mecca for families, retirees and students.

Spokane conjures up diverse images to many people. It's a small town on Sundays and a metropolis on Mondays, full of lilacs and a river roaring through the heart of the city. It's warm summer evenings and crisp, autumn days. It has been, and continues to be, many things to many people.

Part of Spokane's small town/big city dichotomy stems from its position as the hub of the Inland Northwest, an area encompassing 80,000 square miles (including a 36-county region with parts of Montana, Oregon, Idaho, British Columbia, Alberta, Canada and most of Eastern Washington). Nearly two million people live and work in the Inland Northwest, with their financial, retail, medical and business needs serviced by the City of Spokane.

The first settlers were drawn by the beauty and potential of the river. Its series of seven falls provided power to drive mill wheels and create lumber from trees, flour from wheat, and eventually, electricity. In its early days, Spokane's population fluctuated with the seasons. During the winter months, miners from the Coeur d'Alene Silver Valley joined lumbermen from the Pend Oreille forests to crowd Spokane's hotels. They generally stayed until spring's late Chinook winds turned the weather mild, returning then to their livelihoods.

Before the turn-of-the-century, Spokane boasted an abundance of hotels, mercantile stores and saloons—though the saloons outnumbered most other businesses. After the miners and mine-owners made their fortunes in the Coeur d'Alenes, they returned to Spokane, building elegant mansions in Browne's Addition and along the city's basalt-studded southern hillsides. The increased wealth and resulting buildings served to impress upon outsiders that Spokane was, in fact, a major city.

When the entire downtown business district burned to the ground in 1889, few residents left the area. Instead, they cleared the rubble, realigned the focus of the major business arterial from Howard Street to Riverside Avenue, and rebuilt. Within a year, 500 new structures were erected—many of them still standing today—proving the tenacity of the early town founders.

Following this turn-of-the-century frenzy of new building, Spokane entered a conservative phase, erecting solid red brick and granite buildings, in addition to rows of bungalow-style homes for families. Not until 1974, when a handful of businessmen boldly suggested Spokane as the site of a world exposition, did this entrenched little community wake up to the changing times. Using vision and foresight, the leaders of the community established "the environment" as the theme of the exposition.

Though many changes resulted from Expo '74, none was so dramatic as opening the downtown core to the roar of the river's falls. Railroad tracks, industrial warehouses and dilapidated hotels were razed. Once again, Spokanites could see and hear the Spokane River.

Today, visitors and residents, drawn by the beauty and power of the river, can stroll through a legacy of Expo '74: Riverfront Park. They come into the city to shop, conduct business, or to enjoy the sights and sounds with their children.

It is my hope that this book will help you to explore, savor and appreciate this unique city and region. This book is designed for both visitors and longtime residents, for those seeing the sights for the first time, or for those wanting to discover some of the many wonderful changes blossoming in this City by The Falls.

M. E. Buckham

Table of Contents

Chapter 5: Shopping   93

Chapter 6: Entertainment   143

Chapter 7: Of Public Interest   159

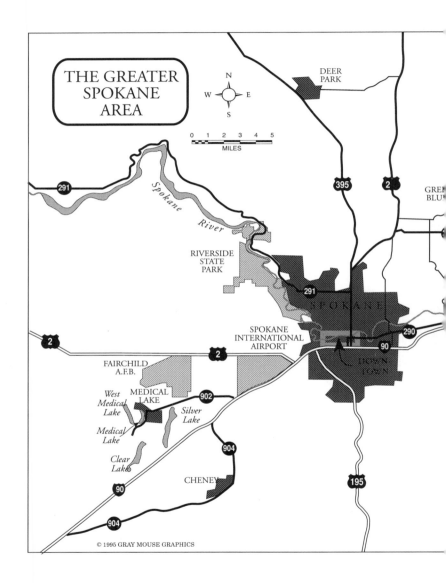

THE GREATER
SPOKANE
AREA

0 1 2 3 4 5
MILES

DEER
PARK

291

Spokane River

RIVERSIDE
STATE
PARK

395

2

GRE
BLU

291

SPOKANE

SPOKANE
INTERNATIONAL
AIRPORT

290

2

2

90

DOWN
TOWN

FAIRCHILD
A.F.B.

MEDICAL
LAKE

902

West
Medical
Lake

Silver
Lake

Medical
Lake

904

Clear
Lake

90

CHENEY

195

904

© 1995 GRAY MOUSE GRAPHICS

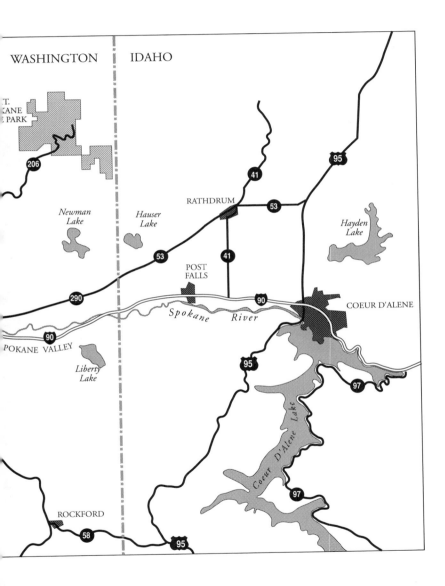

WASHINGTON | IDAHO

T.
ANE
PARK

206

Newman
Lake

Hauser
Lake

RATHDRUM

41

53

95

Hayden
Lake

53

POST
FALLS

41

290

90

Spokane River

COEUR D'ALENE

90

POKANE VALLEY

Liberty
Lake

95

97

Coeur D'Alene Lake

ROCKFORD

58

95

97

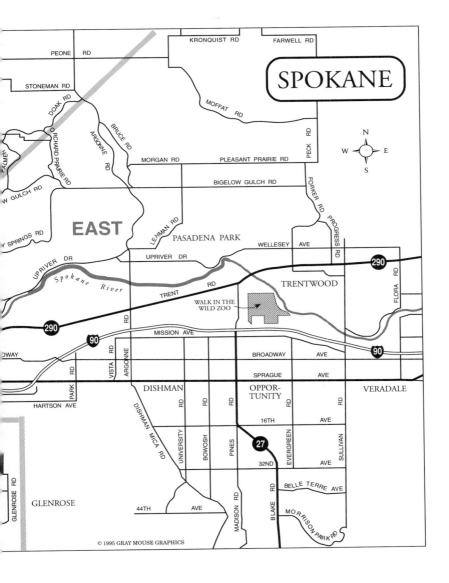

© 1995 GRAY MOUSE GRAPHICS

1

Places
to Stay

Sheraton on the bank of the Spokane River
Photo by Patrice Tobler

Places to Stay

Spokane

Spokane offers lodging to fit a variety of tastes and budgets. You can choose rooms with panoramic views of mountains, water and city lights or intimate bed and breakfast settings in turn-of-the-century homes. In 1877, the first hotel in Spokane Falls (the "Falls" was officially dropped from the name in 1891) was erected at the corner of Trent and Washington. Named the Western, it was described by contemporaries as "comfortable and commodious (with) a ladder scaling to the dizzy heights of the second floor where bear skins and buffalo hides served as beds. The one who paid his 50¢ rent first took the best in the house. It was built to accommodate people accustomed to a bare plank table without a cloth, and who were satisfied with dirt or plank floors, as long as they had a warm place to stay and a good roof over their heads."

By 1882, hotel accommodations improved, evidenced by the hiring of a woman whose weekly duties included "ironing the blankets in order to kill the lice, and thereby prevent the guests from kicking. This condition was no fault of the hotel, but our guests, traveling about the country and stopping in all manner of places, frequently collected and left these souvenirs with us."

Long gone is the heyday of Spokane hotels catering to miners and lumbermen looking for winter lodgings. Now corporate travelers and tourists vie for accommodation space.

Like other aspects of the "Lilac City," prices on accommodations have remained quite reasonable when compared to other cities around the country. In this book, rooms have been rated according to the charge for one night, double occupancy. Those hotels charging $76 and up are noted as "Expensive." Hotels and motels with rates from $46 to $75 are termed "Moderate," and those with rates below $45, "Inexpensive."

For ease of locating travel accommodations, this chapter has been divided geographically by Downtown, North, East and West. It is interesting to note that, though there are Bed and Breakfast Inns located on Spokane's south side, there are no hotels or motels. Unlike Spokane's pioneer days, when many arrived via the southern route of the Columbia River and Pullman, most of today's visitors travel the east/west I-90 corridor or the northern highways 2 and 395.

Alternatives to hotels, including hostels, bed and breakfast establishments, campgrounds, state parks and RV parks follow the hotel listings. Resorts can be found in chapter10: Outdoor Activities.

Hotels and Motels

Downtown

Expensive

Cavanaugh's Inn at the Park, 303 W North River Dr. (326-8000; 800-THE-INNS). This inn offers 402 rooms and 25 suites nestled along the banks of the Spokane River and a stone's throw from Riverfront Park and the Broadview Dairy Museum. There are two lounges and two restaurants: the more casual Atrium, situated in the main lobby beneath the towering palms, and Windows on the Season, an upscale spot with great river views. For a quiet way to entertain the kids or sooth frazzled travel nerves, enjoy the the wall-length saltwater aquarium located just beyond the main lobby fireplace. Be sure to visit the indoor/outdoor pool which is worth seeing for the rock slide alone. Sauna and steam room, exercise room and jacuzzi/hot tubs are also available. Pets are allowed. Complimentary airport transportation is available.

Courtyard by Marriott, 401 N Riverpoint Blvd. (456-7600; 800-321-2211). This hotel has 149 rooms and 12 suites, most with king-size beds. A restaurant and lounge, called the Courtyard Cafe is open for breakfast and dinner with a limited menu. There is an indoor swimming pool, jacuzzi and mini-gym. You'll find the Centennial Trail right in front of your door and a leisurely 20 minute stroll will take you either to Riverfront Park or Gonzaga University's campus. Two meeting rooms can accommodate up to 25 attendees. Complimentary airport transportation is provided.

Sheraton, 322 N Spokane Falls Court (455-9600; 800-848-9600). Built to accommodate fair visitors at Expo '74, all 370 rooms and 60 suites offer a sweeping view of downtown Spokane. Valet parking, indoor swimming pool, dry cleaning services, gift shop and beauty salon services are available. Two restaurants, the more formal 1881 Dining Room, and a lobby cafe, are on site, as are three different lounges. The 15th floor Inner Circle Lounge offers a breathtaking view in an intimate setting. JJ's lounge features live music and dancing every night, while Mingle's Piano Bar is both intimate and relaxing. Jacuzzi, sauna and exercise room are on the premises. Complimentary airport transportation is provided for guests. Deluxe meeting rooms are capable of handling from 12 to 1200.

Moderate

Best Western Trade Winds Downtown Motel, 907 W 3rd Ave. (838-2091; 800-528-1234). With its distinctive, concave shape, this motel offers 59 rooms and an outdoor swimming pool. A whirlpool hot tub is open year-round as is a weight room. Complimentary continental breakfast provided.

Cavanaugh's Fourth Avenue, 110 E 4th Ave. (838-6101; 800-THE-INNS). Equidistant from downtown, Sacred Heart and Deaconness Medical Center, this motel offers 153 rooms and three suites. It also provides a full-service restaurant and Hobart's Lounge - the best spot in town for live jazz. An outdoor swimming pool is open during the summer months. Complimentary airport transportation is available.

Cavanaugh's River Inn, 700 N Division (326-5577; 800-THE-INNS). With its river-side setting, Ripples on the River Restaurant and Lounge, and one-level design to minimize the sounds of adjacent Division Street, this is a nice spot to be near downtown, yet also feel removed from the bustle. Two suites and 240 rooms are available. Pets are welcome. An outdoor pool is open during warmer weather. Complimentary airport transportation is provided. Ask about their Cavanaugh's Cash coupons for future discounts on room rates.

Holiday Inn Express, 801 N Division (328-8505). Nine suites and 111 rooms, all with views, are built atop a 40-foot rock bluff overlooking the edge of downtown in Spokane's newest hotel. This Holiday Inn offers 100% smoke-free rooms and complimentary evening snack and breakfast. If you could choose only one hotel lobby to visit, this is the one. With its view of the city looking south and east, the marble fireplace, with a carved wood molding reminding one of an old world library, and the overstuffed wingback chairs, who needs a room? A casual dining area is situated on the north side of the reception area where you can enjoy your continental breakfast. Be sure to examine the area around the hotel sign located on Division Street. Before the advent of white men, Native Americans used this shallow impression as a campsite while fishing for salmon in the nearby river. Unfortunately, salmon have not been seen in the river since the turn of the century, and any artifacts located in the cave were long ago covered by debris.

Ridpath-Westcoast Hotel, 515 W Sprague (838-2711; 800-426-0670). Located in the heart of downtown, the Ridpath offers 315 rooms and 35 deluxe suites in two buildings spanning Sprague Avenue. Two restaurants are located in the hotel, the Silver Grill on the main floor, and the elegant Ankeny's on the rooftop. Banquet and convention facilities can accommodate groups from 10 to 1,000. The heated outdoor pool is open year-round. The hotel provides free parking for guests. Complimentary airport shuttle service is also available.

Shilo Inn Spokane, 923 E 3rd Ave. (535-9000; 800-222-2244). Across the street from PriceCostco and a short hop to the freeway, the Shilo Inn provides 105 rooms and banquet rooms equipped to handle groups up to 300. A solarium, indoor pool, spa, sauna and exercise room are available. Eagle's Nest, a full-service restaurant and lounge, offers a spectacular view of downtown, North Spokane and the Valley from its etched glass and oak setting. airport transportation is provided. Pets are welcome.

Thunderbird Inn Best Western, 120 W 3rd Ave. (747-2011; 800-57T-BIRD). Situated just off I-90 and Division Street, this 89-room motel is equidistant from Sacred Heart Hospital and the downtown business district. It has an outdoor pool open during the summer. Next door is a full-service Mexican restaurant, Rancho Chico. Complimentary continental breakfast is provided.

Towne Centre Motor Inn, 901 W 1st Ave. (747-1041; 800-247-1041). This 34-room inn is within walking distance to the downtown skywalk system. A complimentary continental breakfast complete with newspaper is provided to guests. Deaconess and Shriner's hospitals are also nearby. Free covered parking is provided for guests.

Inexpensive

Downtowner Motel, 165 S Washington (838-4411). The 42 rooms and four suites of this motel are located three blocks from City Center. Commercial, weekly and monthly rates are available.

Nendels Valu Inn, 1420 W 2nd Ave. (838-2026; 800-547-0106). Within walking distance of Browne's Addition and the Cheney Cowles Museum, this inn offers easy access to I-90, 42 rooms with a 24-hour restaurant and a heated outdoor pool. For down-home cooking, try Frank's Diner located right across the street. Truck parking and non-smoking rooms are available. Pets are allowed.

Suntree Inn, 211 S Division (838-6630; 800-888-6630). Suntree provides 80 rooms which allow pets. Free continental breakfast is included with your night's lodging, as is the use of the Jacuzzi.

Suntree 8 Inn, 123 S Post (838-8504; 800-888-6630). Pets are allowed in any of these 47 rooms located in the heart of the Davenport Arts District and downtown Spokane. Other amenities include complimentary continental breakfast and a jacuzzi.

Value Inns by Cavanaugh's, 1203 W 5th Ave. (624-4142; 800-843-4667). Value Inns has 55 rooms and seven suites with kitchen units, plus a swimming pool and jacuzzi. Conveniently located near Deaconess and Shriner's hospitals, this inexpensive motel also offers weekly and monthly rates. Pets are allowed. Airport transportation is provided for guests.

North

Moderate

Apple Tree Inn Motel, 9508 N Division (466-3020; 800-323-5796). Located near the North Division Y and Northpointe Shopping Plaza, this two-story inn has 71 rooms and 18 two-bedroom suites with full kitchens. Weekly rates are available, as are non-smoking rooms.

Best Western Trade Winds North, 3033 N Division (326-5500; 800-621-8593). Residential Corbin Park is within walking distance of Best Western's 63 rooms and two suites. There are lovely turn-of-the-century homes bordering the park. The Best Western is also close to restaurants and shopping along Division Street. Amenities include an indoor pool, whirlpool and sauna, conference room, fax and copier on site. Non-smoking rooms are available. All lodging includes a complimentary continental breakfast. Waterbeds are available upon request.

Comfort Inn North, 7111 N Division (467-7111; 800-221-2222). This is a popular overnight choice for visiting Whitworth College parents. The 96 rooms and seven suites are located near Northtown Mall and Holy Family Hospital. Outdoor pool and spa are available, as are a complimentary continental breakfast and evening snacks.

Quality Inn Oakwood, 7919 N Division (467-4900; 800-221-2222). Conveniently close to Whitworth College and Northtown Mall, this inn has 96 rooms, over 70% of which are non-smoking. Enjoy the indoor pool and spa and complimentary continental breakfast. Mattie's Restaurant next door is open for breakfast, lunch and dinner.

East

Expensive

Red Lion Inn, 1100 N Sullivan (924-9000; 800-547-8010). Just 15 minutes east of downtown, the Red Lion offers 237 rooms, 12 suites, 13 large meeting rooms and four smaller conference rooms. Rosso's Restaurant provides elegant dining with a focus on Italian cuisine, while the Coffee Garden is much more casual. Misty's Lounge offers live entertainment. Conveniently located just off the Freeway at the Sullivan exit, the Red Lion offers an outdoor swimming pool, exercise room, jacuzzi, beauty salon, gift shop, free parking, free airport shuttle and a service station.

Quality Inn-Valley Suites, 8923 E Mission (928-5218; 800-777-7355). The inn offers 91 rooms and 55 suites, including a honeymoon/romantic suite with heart-shaped whirlpool and mirrored ceiling. The Royale Suite comes with its own fireplace and the Family Suite has a fully-equipped kitchen. At least a half dozen of the suites are designed for the physically challenged. Diane's Restaurant and Lounge serves breakfast, lunch and dinner. Scheduled aerobics classes are offered. An exercise and weight room, heated indoor pool, whirlpool, sauna, sun-tanning beds, massage therapy and beauty salon are located within the motel, as is a complete business center with copier, fax and typewriter. Rooms are equipped with microwaves, bar sinks, refrigerators, hairdryers and clock radios.

Moderate

Comfort Inn, 6309 E Broadway (535-7185; 800-228-5150). These 35 rooms are situated near the Broadway Truck Stop and Spokane Interstate Fairgrounds. The inn has an outdoor pool and spa, truck parking and serves a complimentary continental breakfast.

Comfort Inn-Valley, 905 N Sullivan (924-3838; 800-228-5151). Located just off I-90 at the Sullivan exit near Spokane Industrial Park, Kaiser Aluminum Plant and Hewlett-Packard, this inn offers 76 rooms and 13 suites, some with fireplaces or jacuzzis. On site is a heated outdoor pool, hot tub and sauna. McDonalds, with a covered play area, is right next door. An espresso stop, The Espresso Shack, is just down the street. Pets are allowed. A complimentary continental breakfast is provided.

Days Inn, 1919 N Hutchinson Rd (926-5399; 800-325-2525). The inn's 92 rooms, including non-smoking accommodations, are situated just off I-90 at Argonne Road. A number of good restaurants are nearby. A complimentary continental breakfast is served to guests. Pets are allowed.

Park Lane, 4412 E Sprague (535-1626). The Park Lane's white clapboard rooms with brown trimming look much as they did when the first units in the U-shaped complex were constructed in 1939. Close to the Spokane Fairgrounds, the motel has 28 rooms, 10 suites and 30 RV hook ups. Pets are allowed. Complimentary breakfast is provided. Airport Park and Fly shuttle service is also available.

Spokane Valley Super 8, 2020 N Argonne (928-4888; 800-800-8000). These 189 rooms and two suites are located just off I-90. There are a half dozen restaurants nearby, including Burger King, Wolffy's Rockin' 50s Hamburgers and the Longhorn Barbeque with its great ribs and full course meals. The motel welcomes pets. Complimentary breakfast is provided.

Inexpensive

Carroll's Motel, 1234 E Sprague (534-0669). Located near Playfair, you'll find 16 rooms and two suites. Carroll's provides free local calls from your room. Daily and weekly rates are available and pets are allowed.

Red Top Motel, 7217 E Trent (926-5728; 800-447-8202). Millwood, Felts Field and Walk in the Wild Zoo are just a short drive from these 27 rooms and six jacuzzi suites. There's also an outdoor pool. Pets are welcome.

West

Moderate

Hampton Inn, 2010 S Assembly Rd (747-1100; 800-HAMPTON). Fifty percent of the hotel's 131 rooms and 11 hot tub suites are designated non-smoking. Five minutes from downtown and the airport, the Hampton is located just off the old Sunset Highway. Migratory wildfowl still visit the marshy area just in front of the main door. The indoor pool and spa are open 24 hours. Meeting and board rooms are available with fax and copier service, and there are computer jacks in all rooms. A deluxe complimentary continental breakfast is provided early in the day, while a deli near the front check-in area offers a light menu for lunch and dinner. There is an exercise room and children under 18 stay free with parents. Free 24-hour airport shuttle service.

Holiday Inn West, 4212 Sunset Blvd. (747-2021; 800-272-6232). Many of the inn's 136 rooms offer panoramic views of the city and valley. Indian Canyon Golf Course is nearby and public tennis courts are across the street. The middle band of the Spokane Indian tribe used the Indian Canyon area for their winter campgrounds, and pre-freeway auto traffic passed this way on Sunset Highway. The restaurant and lounge offer an impressive view of the city, especially at night. An outdoor pool is open during the summer months. Complimentary continental breakfast. Free airport shuttle service.

Ramada Inn, across from Spokane International airport (838-5211; 800-272-6232). These 167 rooms and nine suites include four Executive Suites, each with a private swimming pool. The Presidential Suite is complete with living room, dining area, fully-equipped kitchen and whirlpool. Remington's Restaurant is casually elegant and the Solarium offers exhibition cooking six nights a week at the Seafood/ Oyster Bar. A walk across the street takes you to the airport lobby, which makes this a convenient spot for business meetings and visitors arriving by plane. Indoor and outdoor pool, weight room, spa and tanning saloon are all available to hotel guests.

Friendship Inn-Spokane House, 4301 W Sunset Highway (838-1471; 800-424-4777). Located just off of Sunset Highway, once the main thoroughfare into Spokane, this inn is known to locals as The Spokane House. Its 89 rooms and ten suites include non-smoking rooms. Enjoy the beautiful view from the Spokane House restaurant and lounge or spend some time in the outdoor pool, sauna and spa. Pets are allowed. A complimentary continental breakfast is provided.

Super 8 Motel, 11102 W Westbow (838-8800; 800-800-8000). This motel, near the Holiday Inn, tennis courts and the Indian Canyon Golf Course, offers 80 rooms and two suites. It also provides an indoor pool and complimentary continental breakfast. Pets are allowed.

Inexpensive

Boulevard, 2905 W Sunset Highway (747-1060). Here you'll find 15 newly remodeled rooms in a Swiss Chalet setting. You're near the freeway, Spokane Falls Community College, Spokane International airport, Cemeteries and Airway Heights. Be sure to take a stroll through Finch Arboretum, which is within walking distance. The Boulevard also has an outdoor pool.

Cedar Village Motel, 5415 W Sunset Highway (838-8558). The Cedar Village contains 28 rooms located within two miles of the airport. They provide free airport shuttle service while you leave your car at the motel. Pets are allowed. Weekly rates and kitchenettes available.

Hotel Alternatives

Spokane is home to two of the state's top three hospitals, with 30% of their admissions coming from residents outside Spokane County. Combine this draw with major industries, such as Boeing, Kaiser and Itron, and you'll find a number of visitors who are looking for more than temporary lodging. For those planning on a longer stay in the Lilac City, you may want to consider one of the following options:

Solar Estates, 1832 S Lawson, Airway Heights (244-3535), or E 20 Pinecrest Road (468-1207). At Solar Estates, the corporate traveler on assignment to the Spokane area, or the person looking for deluxe accomodations, can find reasonable, comfortable lodging. Each contemporary unit is fully furnished down to the towels, dishes, cookware, microwave, iron and coffee pot. A jacuzzi bathtub is a nice feature in each unit. Weekly maid service. Rentals are arranged on a monthly basis.

Wolff Lodging, 9016 E Indiana (922-1600; 800-528-9519). Ten properties, including apartments and condos, are located downtown, in the South Hill, the Valley and the Northside. They come fully equipped with cookware, linens and bedding. Weekly maid service. Except for the Cooper George apartment building, all locations are contemporary buildings which offer one- and two-bedroom designer-decorated accommodations. The management team works to anticipate your every need. A number of major corporations are among their satisfied clients. Since most units rent monthly or weekly, nightly lodging is subject to availability.

Hostels

Spokane Hostelling International, 930 S Lincoln (838-5968). Located 10 blocks from the city's center in a tree-shaded area of residential homes, the hostel has 22 beds with dormitories for men and women, as well as family and couple's rooms—all on a space-available basis. Along with cooking facilities and hot showers, the hostel offers common areas for relaxation, outdoor recreation areas, laundry and off-street parking. No smoking, alcohol or pets are permitted. No credit cards accepted. Reservations are recommended.

Bed and Breakfasts

To stay at a bed and breakfast is an interesting alternative to conventional hotel and motel lodging. Whether you choose a contemporary home close to attractions you wish to visit, or a turn-of-the-century house filled with whispers of a by-gone era, relaxing in a private home offers a close look at the community and its residents. Hospitality, an insider's knowledge of sights and events, full or continental breakfasts and the individual personality of your hosts all enhance a visit to the Lilac City.

Spokane bed and breakfast rooms average $60 to $70 a night, double occupancy, although some rooms can run as high as $98 and others are less than $50. If you have particular dietary needs or other concerns, such as allergies to home pets, feel free to contact your host directly or use Spokane's Bed and Breakfast Reservation Service.

Spokane Bed and Breakfast Reservation Service, 627 E 25th (624-3776). Let Pat Conley help you select the perfect accommodation from one of the dozen area homes most suited to your needs and desires. She handles listings in Spokane, Coeur d'Alene, Seattle, Canada and points in between. Choose from gracious Victorian, spacious contemporary or scenic mountain homes. Pat will also place reservations for you at no charge.

The Cobblestone Inn and Bakery, 620 S Washington (624-9735). Located in a home built in 1900 by a banker named Corbitt for his young bride, the Cobblestone features original parquet wood floors, stained-glass windows, and two second-floor rooms for guests. The Paris Room has a private bath and bay window, while the Roubaix Room has two queen beds, private bath and bay window. Both are non-smoking. Downstairs is the public bakery operated by owners and innkeepers Matt and Robin Doval. You can relax in the ambiance of this lovely home while sipping an espresso drink and nibbling on freshly baked pastries. It doesn't get any nicer than this. Breakfast includes fresh baked pastries and breads. And you're only a walk away from Sacred Heart Medical Center.

Fotheringham House, 2128 W 2nd Ave. (838-1891). Located in the heart of historic Browne's Addition, this lovingly restored home was built in 1891 and named after the first Mayor of Spokane, David

Fotheringham House bed and breakfast in Spokane's Browne's Addition
Photo by Ron Swords

B. Fotheringham. Crafted in the Victorian style, it features hand-carved woodwork, tin ceilings and an open carved staircase. Antiques from the mid-to-late 1800s furnish the three guest rooms. One room offers a private bath, the other two share a large full bath.

Spokane's oldest park, Coeur d'Alene Park, is located across the street, as is one of the city's most elegant restaurants, the Patsy Clark. Just walking the tree-lined streets in the neighborhood is a vacation. The home is non-smoking and not suited for children under 12. Don't miss trying the trademark Fotheringham House hazelnut coffee with your breakfast.

Hillside House, 1729 E 18th (534-1426 days; 535-1893 nights/weekends). Choose either the Blue Room or the Lace Room for your stay on Spokane's lower southside. An outside deck surrounded by trees and the antique furnishings throughout the house make this a pleasant and home-like environment for the whole family. Wooded Lincoln Park is a short walk away. Children accepted. Airport pickup can be arranged. This is a non-smoking home.

Love's, 31317 N Cedar Road, Deer Park (276-6939). Only 20 minutes north of Spokane is an 1886 reproduction Victorian home complete with homemade quilts and country antiques. Bill and Leslie Love invite their guests to roam their lovely garden, relax in a private hot tub and use groomed trails for cross-country skiing. The Loves have also hosted weddings, receptions and meetings in their storybook home. airport transportation is available.

Marianna Stoltz House, 427 E Indiana (483-4316). Built in 1908, this classic American foursquare home is listed on the local register of historic landmarks and is situated on a lovely tree-lined street five blocks from Gonzaga University. A wide, wrap-around veranda invites guests to enjoy a summer's evening. The lower level's spacious parlor, dining and sitting rooms are decorated with oriental rugs and period antique pieces. Four bedrooms, some with private, others with shared baths, are located on the second floor. Old family quilts and lace curtains create a comfortable yet romantic atmosphere. Breakfast specialties include the Stoltz House Strada, puffy Dutch pancakes with homemade apple syrup or Peach Melba Parfait. This is a non-smoking establishment.

Oslo's, 1821 E 39th (838-3175). Owner Aslaug Stevenson provides her guests with a relaxing Norwegian atmosphere in a contemporary South Hill home located 15 minutes from downtown. Born and raised in Norway, Aslaug enjoys sharing her native ethnic recipes and love of gardening. As a landscape designer and master gardener, she's a font of knowledge on local horticulture. A large terrace overlooks Aslaug's gorgeous gardens. Susy, a friendly pug dog, is the home's official greeter and is guaranteed to bark until petted when you arrive, and whine when you leave. Scandinavian cuisine is available for breakfast. There are no accommodations for children under 12. This is a non-smoking environment.

The Spokane Room, 15405 N Edencrest Dr. (467-9804). Owner Dede McKay is a professional artist and her husband Bob an avid gardener. Their Northside home is near Wandermere Golf Course and not far from the Little Spokane River. They offer a single room with queen-size bed, private bath and deck overlooking the garden. It is a non-smoking accommodation.

Waverly Place, 709 W Waverly Place (328-1856). Constructed in 1902, this gracious Victorian home was one of the first homes built on Corbin Park. Originally a Native American race course, the park still retains its oval shape and is named after early Spokane Railroad and Empire builder D.C. Corbin (who built his own race track on the site). Spacious guest rooms have both private or shared baths. The full gourmet breakfast may include Swedish pancakes with huckleberry sauce or sunrise tomatoes and kringla.

Places to Stay
Outside Spokane

The city of Coeur d'Alene in Idaho, is only 30 minutes east of downtown Spokane. As a result, city, county and state lines blur when choosing lodging accommodations. For Spokane residents, a stay in the "City by the Lake" offers a relaxing break. For travelers, it's often easier to find accommodations in outlying areas during annual events, such as Bloomsday, when Spokane lodgings are booked a year in advance. Here are several options east of Spokane.

Hotels, Motels and Resorts

Expensive

The Coeur d'Alene, A Resort on the Lake, 2nd and Front streets (208-765-4000; 800-688-5253). Copper towers reflect the sunshine off adjoining Coeur d'Alene Lake and hint at the reason this spot has been recognized by *Condé Nast Traveler Magazine* as one of America's top mainland resorts. With 338 units, 13 condos and an additional 90 rooms planned in an expanded area east of the current main building, this landmark hotel is a popular destination spot. An attached marina with wrap-around boardwalk, and a 3,000-square-foot penthouse suite complete with glass bottom swimming pool are only a few of the unique attractions of the Coeur d'Alene. An 18-hole golf course features the world's first floating green which is repositioned nightly to give golfers a new challenge daily.

Three restaurants are located within the resort, two at water's edge and the elegant Beverly's on the seventh floor. Thirty boutiques and gift stores are situated either within the main lobby or adjacent to the hotel. Coeur d'Alene city beach is only a short walk. To say the Coeur d'Alene is an experience unto itself is an understatement.

Templin's Resort, 414 E 1st, Post Falls, ID (208-773-1611; 800-283-6754). Located midway between Spokane and Coeur d'Alene, this is a great spot to take advantage of activities in both cities. Its 167 rooms and six suites are nestled along the Spokane River just off I-90 in Post Falls. Templin's is the only Idaho hotel to earn recognition as an outside wildlife viewing site. Take advantage of the chance to spot a diving osprey from the comfort of the restaurant, Mallard's, or from the new 10,000-square-foot conference center which can accommodate up to 800 attendees. At night, Mallard's lounge offers live entertainment and dancing. During the day visit the hotel's indoor pool, sauna, spa and fitness center or gift shop. For a special treat, take a riverboat cruise or rent your own boat, canoe or pontoon boat.

Moderate

Pines Resort Motel, 1422 Northwest Boulevard (208-664-8246). This motel, located between I-90 and Coeur d'Alene Lake, offers 65 rooms and two bedroom suites. A full-service restaurant and lounge is part of the motel complex. There's also an indoor pool, jacuzzi and heated outdoor pool. Pets are allowed.

Shilo Inn, 702 W Appleway (208-664-2300; 800-222-2244). Located just off I-90, this hotel offers 134 rooms with 75% of them non-smoking and four kitchen units. They have an indoor pool open year-round, fitness room, steam room, spa and sauna. A number of fast food restaurants are within a five block radius. Pets are welcome. Complimentary continental breakfast.

Bed and Breakfasts

Gregory's McFarland House, 601 Foster, Coeur d'Alene, Idaho (208-667-1232). All five bedrooms in this home built in 1905 offer private baths with claw-footed tubs as well as showers. This is only a sample of the ways owners Winifred, Stephen and Carol Gregory have combined the nostalgia for antiques with the comfort of modern amenities throughout their home. While a VCR and complete movie library awaits you in the entertainment room, an antique table which traveled around the Horn from England to San Francisco and has been in Winifred's family ever since, stands in the dining room. By all means, spend time in the glass conservatory which overlooks the private rear garden and is decorated in white wicker and shades of pink. It's no wonder guests keep flocking back.

The Roosevelt Inn, 105 Wallace, Coeur d'Alene, Idaho (208-765-5200; 800-290-3358). Larger than a traditional bed and breakfast, yet not forsaking the pampering and charm of a smaller establishment, this 1905 school house was named in honor of Vice President Teddy Roosevelt's visit to the Coeur d'Alene and Spokane area. In German, the name "Roosevelt" means "rose field" and the theme of roses is incorporated throughout the 22 rooms. Leaded-glass windows in the parlor and dining room sport roses, the carpet is a dusty rose shade and even the bed covers and curtains contain rose motifs.

Owner John Marias, an emigrant from Hungary, rebuilt the school's steeple which blew down in a wind storm in the 1950s. After quite a hunt, he also located the school's original silver bell which now hangs in front of the Inn. All rooms are furnished with turn-of-the-century antiques, many of them imported from Europe. Some come as two-bedrooms suites. After a day at the Roosevelt, you'll wish school would never end.

Campgrounds, Resorts, RV and State Parks

When the smell of a burning campfire beckons, or you feel the urge to study a night sky filled with stars, it's time to pack the tent and head to the great outdoors. The Spokane area offers a broad range of camping experiences to suit the experienced and inexperienced overnighter. Whether your idea of roughing is back-packing over trails to set up a campsite, or pulling up your RV to a clean and well-maintained facility, you'll not have far to travel.

With Eastern Washington's long, hot summer days and cool nights, camping is more than an alternative to traditional lodging. It's an adventure enjoyed by many residents and visitors alike.

For the purposes of this guide book, prices are listed for those locations offering camp sites only. The price of RV hookups and cabins can vary depending on the time of year and amenities requested. Your best bet is to call ahead for the latest cost information and reservations, especially during summer's busy season.

Alpine Campground, I-90 Exit 293, 18815 E Cataldo, Greenacres (928-2700). At Alpine, just 13 miles east of Spokane, you'll find RV hookups and 30 tent spaces. Amenities include showers, laundry, grocery, picnic tables, a recreation room, coin games, a heated swimming pool, basketball hoop, playground, badminton, horseshoes and volley ball. Alpine is open all year and pets are allowed. Credit cards are accepted.

Beaver Creek National Recreation Site (208-245-2512). Upper Priest Lake offers this site for 20 tents and, for larger groups, one 30-person site. Reservations are recommended for the group site, with a $30-per night fee. Single sites are $5 per night.

Blue Lake Resort, Hwy. 17, Coulee City (632-5364). Located on the south end of Blue Lake, this family-oriented resort offers modern cabins, full RV hookup sites, tent camping and a store.

Colville National Forest, Lake Gillette (684-4557). Located near the Pend Oreille River are 43 tent and trailer sites. This campground gets busy on weekends, so call ahead for reservations. Cost is $6 per night or $7 for preferred sites.

Coulee Lodge Resort, 33017 Park Lane Road NE, Coulee City (632-5565). Open April through October, the Coulee Lodge has cabins, RV hookups and tent sites. This resort is situated on small, quiet Blue Lake.

Coulee Playland Resort, Hwy. 155, Electric City (633-2671). You can find restrooms, hot showers, phones, a laundry, mini-store and boat rentals at this tent and RV resort near Grand Coulee Dam.

Deer Lake Resort, 3908 N Deer Lake Road, Loon Lake (233-2081) With 195 acres of forestland spread before you, it's easy to loose track of time at this family-oriented resort, located 35 miles north of Spokane. Besides tent sites, tepees and RV sites, amenities include a large picnic area, volleyball court, boat docks, laundry and shower facilities.

Diamond Lake Resort, 325231 N Hwy. 2, Newport (447-4474). Spring-fed Diamond Lake is stocked with rainbow and cutthroat trout for the April through October fishing season. Winters, the lake freezes and is used by cross-country skiers. During the May through October camping season, the resort rents eight cabins with kitchens and baths, RV sites and campsites. A day-use picnic area charges $2.50 per person. The boat launch costs $5 round trip. Some cabins are also available in winter.

Emerald Creek Campground (208-245-2531). Rockhounders hot on the scent of garnets will love this 18-tent/trailer site located 25 miles south of St. Maries, Idaho. India and Idaho are the only two places on earth where star garnets—the Idaho State gem—are found. Digging permits are available at the digging site, $10 for adults and $5 for kids 14 and under. Ask for directions at the campground to the nearest digging site. Fees are $6 per night.

Farragut State Park (208-683-2424). Only a hop, skip and jump from Coeur d'Alene, Farragut offers 90 tent/trailer sites; 45 with water and sewer hookups. Lake Pend Oreille skirts the Park, and Silverwood Theme Park (see Chapter 7: Of Public Interest) is minutes away for a change of pace. Cost is $9 per night, or $12 for sewer and water.

Jump Off Joe Lake Resort, 3290 Jump Off Joe Road, Valley, Washington (937-2133). Many seniors stay for weeks once they reach this quiet, pine-studded resort 35 miles north of Spokane. The resort has 16 full RV hookups and two pull-thrus, plus three cabins. Hot showers, restrooms and laundry, a boat dock and launching ramp provide easy access to the lake.

KOA Campground, 3025 N Barker Road (924-4722). At this KOA Campground you'll discover full RV hookups, tent space and cabin rentals. Amenities include 20- 30- and 50-amp electric service, showers, laundry, grocery store, swimming pool, cable TV, and a recreation hall. Open all year. Weekly and group rates are available, and credit cards are welcomed.

Lake Roosevelt National Recreation Area (725-2715). Just 22 miles north of Davenport, this camping area near historic Fort Spokane offers more than 100 sites in six different campgrounds— three are drive-in and three are boat-in only. Availability is based on a first-come, first-served basis. Fees are $10 per night.

Lyons Ferry State Park (646-3252). This park is near Palouse Falls and the Snake River. There are 50 standard sites. Fees are $8 a night with an additional $4 per extra vehicle.

Marshall Lake Resort, 1301 Marshall Lake Road, Newport (447-4158). This large, shady tree-covered campground has RV sites, modern and semi-modern cabins and rooms offered by the day, week or month. In the summer months, you can enjoy swimming, hiking and horseback riding. During winter, cross-country skiing and snowmobiling are popular activities.

Mt. Spokane State Park, Rt. 1, Box 336, Mead (456-4169). Five thousand feet above sea level, and seven miles from the park entrance, lies a twelve-site campground. This park is not recommended for large RVs. Restrooms, drinking water and picnic tables are provided. The mountain is well suited to all-season activities, with horseback-riding trails, hiking, cross-country skiing, snowmobiling and sledding. Huckleberry picking is a fall highlight. Cost is $10 on a first-come, first-served basis.

Park Washington/Ponderosa Hill, 7520 S Thomas Mallen Road (747-9415; 800-494-7275, ext. 801). Look for big rig pull-thrus (43 sites), as well as an exclusive tent and small RV area (48 sites), at this campground with its own security gates. There are also 18 acres of Ponderosa pines to shade most of the 120 RV hookups and 20-, 30- and 50-amp service for telephone and cable TV. A fax machine is also available. The park is adjacent to the Fairways golf course. Open all year. Daily, weekly and monthly rates are available and credit cards are accepted.

Peaceful Pines, 13315 W SR-904, Cheney (235-4966). Only 1.5 miles from Eastern Washington University, this campground and park is set in a circle of lawn and trees. Ten sites with full RV hookups and 16 sites with electricity and water are available. Picnic tables, BBQ and hot showers are a few of the other amenities. There are nine lakes within 15 miles of the camp. Cheney City Park is less than three miles away. The campground is open all year.

Priest Lake State Park (208-443-2200). This is a great spot for late-summer huckleberry picking. The two sites, called Indian Creek and Lionhead, have 70 tent/trailer spaces; 58 electricity and water hookup sites and 12 electricity, water and sewer hookups. Indian Creek fees are $9 per night. Lionhead charges $8 and has spaces for tents only.

Riverside State Park (456-3964). Only 15 minutes from the center of the city, you'll discover 110 overnight camping sites nestled along the banks of the Spokane River in a natural area of basalt rocks and ponderosa pines. No full hookups are available, though there is a washroom and shower facility, pay phone, kitchen shelters and dump station for RVs. Be sure to cross the rope suspension footbridge originally constructed by the CCC during the Great Depression. Kids and adults love traversing the swinging span, particularly during spring's water run-off when the river is especially turbulent. The area is dotted with well-traveled hiking trails and horse paths. Cost is $11 per night.

Sun Lakes State Park (632-5583). This 175-tent/trailer campground is only seven miles south of Coulee and lies in close proximity to Dry Falls and Steamboat Rock. There are 18 full utility sites. Cost is $9 per night or $12 for sewer and water hookup.

Sutton Bay Resort, Newman Lake (226-3660). This family-oriented resort is located only minutes from Spokane. A sandy beach contains a log-enclosed swimming area. The fishing dock juts out into a lake stocked with rainbow trout, bass, crappie and perch. Cabins, camping and trailer spaces are rented by the week, month or season.

West Medical Lake Resort, Medical Lake (299-3921). The fishing is great at this resort with RV hookups. Fishing season runs from April 1st through July 6th, then again from September 1st through the 30th. The resort has a fishing dock, and you can rent boats, barges, motors and moorage.

Williams Lake Resort, 18617 W Williams Lake Road, Cheney (235-2391; 800-274-1540). Rainbow and cutthroat trout attract anglers to this 320-acre lake. The resort offers 90 seasonal or permanent spaces, plus 60 RV hookups with power and water. Tenting spots, a picnic area and playground are also available, as is a restaurant, grocery store, showers, boat launch and sandy beach for swimming. Don't miss owner Sandy Klink's famous homemade pies for sale at the restaurant.

2

Transportation

Three bridges over Latah Creek

Photo by Ron Swords

Transportation

Transportation has long played a pivotal role in the development of Spokane and the Inland Northwest. Founding father James Glover staked his fortune on the belief that one day railroads would criss-cross the little hamlet hugging the thundering falls. In 1881 when the first Northern Pacific locomotive steamed into town, transportation forever altered the small town of Spokane Falls.

Though the 155-foot Northern Pacific Clock Tower, erected in 1902, still stands at the heart of downtown Spokane, and trains rumble across elevated tracks through the city's center, railroads have given way to other modes of transportation in the Inland Empire.

Freeways and City Streets

Spokane is very much an automobile city now, with only 4.3% of the total county population walking to work and less than 1% biking to their place of employment.

I-90, the interstate freeway, which links the city and valley, is the major east-west route and all primary north-south arterials feed into it. Flooding glacial waters thousands of years ago carved the low lying area I-90 follows. Basalt bluffs, left standing after the waters receded, flank its route.

Division Street, which divides into state highways 2 and 395 north of the city, carries the majority of northbound traffic—about 32,000 cars a day. While the city has waged a war for years to create a north/south freeway to lessen the load on Division Street and other arterials, the closest they've come to easing the congestion is creation of the Ruby Street couplet. This street, located just east of Division, will eventually carry all traffic heading north, while Division will handle all south bound traffic. The first phase was completed in July of 1994, and construction will continue in stages until completed.

Until about 15 years ago, the growth of Spokane followed the easiest geographic route for expansion: east toward the Valley. Now commuters struggle with overburdened arterials in their quest to reach new subdivisions built north and south of the downtown area. It's wise to be aware of congestion along these routes during rush hours, or if summer construction projects block traffic along these corridors. Significant northbound routes in the city include Hamilton, Monroe, Freya/Market and the Maple/Ash corridor. Southbound arterials include

Monroe, Grand, Southeast Blvd and Thor/Freya. North/south arterials traversing the Valley include Park Road, Argonne, Pines and Sullivan. Sprague parallels the freeway as an alternative east-west route.

Fortunately for most Spokane residents, the distances between work and home is still not plagued by the congestion one sees along I-5 or California freeways. Though, as in all metropolitan areas, the primary arterials and freeway are busy during morning and evening rush-hour traffic.

From the first mud-churned path winding along the Riverside, the Spokane River divided north from south and Howard Street divided east from west. But in 1891, the dividing lines became Division for east and west and Sprague for north and south. This system remains in place today.

The one-way streets of downtown Spokane pose a challenge to visitors and locals alike. On-street parking in the core is now free, but a two-hour time limit is strictly enforced. The issue of free parking is constantly debated, so in the future you may see metered parking throughout downtown, including the core. Plenty of street-level lot-parking is available throughout the area, while the Parkade Plaza (entrance on Main), Riverpark Square (entrance on Post) and City Ramp (entrance on Stevens) are three tiered-parking ramps. Check with these and the other lots for a list of promotional discounts provided by certain retailers and select restaurants. In exchange for your patronage and shopping dollars, you'll be issued free tokens for parking.

Air

As you travel to or from the Spokane International Airport, located seven miles west of downtown Spokane, keep on eye out for sheared basalt formations along the side of the road. When melting glacial waters met volcanic flow from the Cascades hundreds of thousands of years ago, these distinctive columnar shapes were created.

Though much more modern than the surrounding geological formations, the Spokane International Airport's main terminal, with its radiating arms and stucco exterior, is as recognizable to Spokanites as the basalt outcroppings. The main terminal was constructed in 1965. In 1993 alone, over 2,330,000 passengers passed through its spacious central hallway.

The airport contains a number of services in the main terminal, and the commute between annexes is only a short walk. In the main concourse is a full-service restaurant and cocktail lounge, open seven days a week from 5 a.m.-10 p.m., as well as a gift shop, also open seven days a week 5 a.m.-10 p.m.. Satellite snack bars are on each concourse and are open during regularly scheduled flights. A barbershop with shoe shine service, is situated just past the security checkpoints as you disembark and is open Monday through Friday 6:15 a.m.-5 p.m.

All the airline ticket outlets and major rental car companies are represented on the entry-way level of the airport terminal.

Glance up above the escalator leading from the parking garage skywalk to see an early piece of welded sculpture by well-known area artist Harold Balazs.

Along the entry level, you'll find Global Travel Agency and the Foreign Exchange (624-6119). Both are open Monday through Friday 5:30 a.m.-9 p.m., Saturday and Sunday 9 a.m.-5 p.m. The Foreign Exchange handles Canadian and Japanese currency only. It's recommended that you call ahead and check availability for purchasing large dollar amounts in Canadian currency or any amount in yen. It's not necessary to call if you wish to sell.

Airport Parking: Five levels of indoor parking (14,075 stalls) and an outdoor lot are located directly across from the main airport terminal. The same rate applies whether you park outside or indoors, and parking is permitted for up to 60 days without prior arrangement. Rates charged for parking start at one dollar per hour with a maximum rate of $4.50 daily, $22.50 weekly and $67 monthly. Cash, local personal checks and travelers checks are accepted for payment, but no credit cards. If you're in need of a jump start or air for your tires, a call on one of the aid phones will bring assistance free of charge.

There is no scheduled airport transit service to or from the airport, however most major hotels offer shuttle transport or the following companies may be of assistance:

Airport Shuttle Service, P.O. Box 392 (535-6979). Door to door service in the Spokane/Cheney/Coeur d'Alene area. Reservations are requested with a 24 to 48 hour lead time, otherwise there may be a wait until service is available. Rates are based on travel locations with an average rate from the airport to downtown of $7 and to Coeur d'Alene for $32, both one way for a single adult. Group rates are available, and children under 12 travel free with an adult.

Skylink, 1675 W Appleway, Coeur d'Alene, Idaho (800-2-SKYLINK). This is the best bet if you're traveling directly from the airport to Coeur d'Alene. Rates are $15 one way for an adult. Group and child discounts are also available. Keep in mind though that you're dropped off at the Skylink office building located near the I-90 freeway. An additional $4 to $5 cab service fee might be required to get you where you want to go within downtown Coeur d'Alene. For an additional fee, Skylink will transport you door-to-door. Reservations are required with three to 24-hour lead time. Up to 14 shuttles run every day except Saturday.

Scheduled airlines serving Spokane:
Alaska Airlines 800-426-0333
Delta Airlines 800-221-1212
Horizon Air 800-547-9308
Northwest Airlines 800-225-2525
Southwest Airlines 800-435-9792
United Airlines 800-241-6522

Bus

Greyhound, 1125 W Sprague (624-5251). Located in the Amtrak Station at Bernard and Sprague, the Greyhound Bus service is the largest operation of its kind in the area. As the ticket agents will tell you, "we travel almost everywhere," and they do. The ticket office is open about 18 hours a day with a schedule available by calling the number listed above.

Empire Lines (624-4116). Serving Spokane since 1939, Empire Lines offers scheduled trips to western Washington and southern Canada, with all routes traveling through Wenatchee. They also provide chartered services.

Rail

After the devastating 1889 fire, the Northern Pacific Railway Company decided to move their depot away from the congestion of Spokane's city center to a site along the edge of town. By January of 1891, the pressed brick building, with its decorative granite trim, was opened for traffic. Major renovations have been made to this original structure, where rail and bus terminals are now combined beneath one roof. The building is designed to look much as it did during the 1920s, the heyday of passenger train traffic in the Inland Empire.

Today, Amtrak passenger trains leave Spokane on the Empire Builder running out of Chicago. In Spokane, the route splits with trains heading west for both Seattle and Portland. Many Spokanites find travel by rail both affordable and a pleasant travel alternative in spite of the fact that all trains departing Spokane leave after midnight. There hasn't been daylight service in town for over 25 years. For Amtrak reservations call 800-872-7245. A printed travel guide with detailed information is available at the terminal office during regular business hours.

Metropolitan Transportation

Spokane Transit Service (STA)

Outside of individual cars, Spokane's major public transportation is via bus. While most of the 137 Spokane Transit Authority (known as STA) buses are a distinctive blue, green and white, keep an eye open for the one decorated with Bloomsday runners, or the distinctive black and red bus promoting the drug awareness program Project D.A.R.E.

A glass, steel and brick structure, called the Plaza, is located at Riverside and Wall. This is the main terminal to catch and transfer buses, and its two floors house an international food court, police substation and centrally located Bus Shop. Even if you don't plan on riding a bus, be sure to stop and take a peek at the Plaza's atrium lobby with its tall trees and water feature which highlights a sculpture by local artist Ken Spiering.

In the downtown core, information regarding routes and scheduled departures is posted at periodic kiosks. For quick route and schedule information via phone, call 328-RIDE or TDD-456-4327.

Exact change, tokens or a pass is required to travel STA buses. Fares are the same on all routes and free transfers should be requested when you board your first bus. The cost for a ticket for riders from 6 to 65 years old is 75 cents. Children 5 and younger travel free with an adult. Reduced fare cards are available for people over 65, those with a qualifying disability or individuals who have a valid Medicare card. An STA photo I.D. card is issued to those who qualify and must be shown to ride for 35 cents.

The exception to these fees is the two shuttle routes; one serving the lower south side and hospitals (Bus #26) and the other shuttling riders between parking sites at the Coliseum and downtown (Bus #27). Both these routes cost 35 cents. Paratransit service is also 35 cents. Passes may be purchased on a monthly basis only and sell for $25 for adult, $19 for youth 6 to 17, $12.50 for reduced fare. A special College Quarter Pass is available for registered college students for $60.

STA offers customers two city locations to buy tokens and passes, obtain the most current schedules and maps or even find correct change: The Plaza at Riverside and Wall and The Bus Shop, Too at the Spokane Transit Facility 1229 West Boone Avenue. Both sites are open weekdays 7:30 a.m.-5:30 p.m., Saturday 10 a.m.-5 p.m. and Sundays noon-5 p.m.

In the Valley, at the Transit Center located at East Fourth Avenue and South University Road, you can purchase passes from 11:30 a.m.-6 p.m the first and last weeks of the month.

In June of 1994, 30 STA buses began a one-year program to test the use of bike racks on buses. These selected buses operate on nine routes which cover most of the service area. They do require the display of a permit (testifying to the completion of a short safety class) before a cyclist can use them. The good news is that your bike rides free.

Other special services offered by STA include a paratransit service for physically challenged passengers, which is either door to door or curb-side depending on your needs (328-1552), and a Vanpool/Rideshare program (326-7665) designed to cut back the number of single-rider vehicles on the road.

Handy STA Numbers:
Routes and Schedules: 328-7433
Hearing Impaired: 456-4327

Taxis

Unlike hailing a cab in vintage 1940 movies, getting one in downtown Spokane is not as easy as whistling and waving, however, they are available. The simplest way is to head for a major hotel where the front desk will call one for you. During the day, there are also several stations with waiting cabs: near or at the Ridpath Hotel, Sheraton, Parkade Plaza, Burlington Coat Factory, The Onion and the bus stations. At night, the only waiting cabs are in front of the hotels.

Major Dispatchers:
Inland Taxi (326-8294)
Spokane Cab (535-2535)
Yellow Cab (624-4321)
United Cabs (534-4708)

Limos

The yellow pages list over 14 limousine services in the Spokane area. One of the oldest companies offering the ultra-stretch car for seven and 10 passengers is Luxury Limousine (927-2200). Embassy (325-5932) has the only wide-body limo in town. They also offer a Christmas light tour (2-hour minimum) which makes an unusual gift or romantic treat. Happy Hog (535-6930) sports a six-passenger, pearl-covered pink Lincoln. Australian Limousine Service (924-9232) will not drive you Down Under, however they do have a 10-passenger limo and are licensed and insured for both Washington and Idaho.

Special Occasions

For a romantic get away or a re-creation of days-gone-by, why not consider a horse and buggy ride? Carriages For Hire, Route 1, Box 165, Elk, Washington (292-8696) offers three different horse and buggy combinations for hire. Owners Mary and Harley Medeiros will supply the driver, complete with period costume if you wish, decorate their buggies to compliment a color theme and, best of all, will clean up after their "horse" powered vehicles.

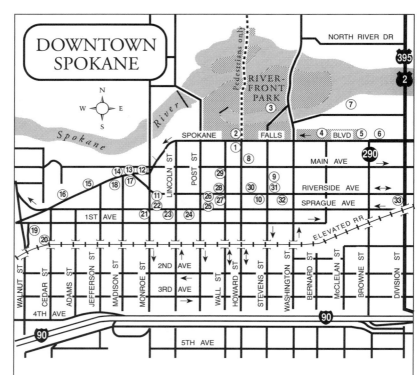

1. James N. Glover original trade store
2. Riverfront Park–Charles Looff Carousel
3. Northern Pacific Clock Tower
4. Opera House
5. Convention Center
6. International Ag Trade Center
7. Centennial Trail
8. Bennett Block
9. Levy Building
10. Fernwell Building
11. Spokesman Review Building
12. Spokane Club
13. Chamber of Commerce
14. Elks Club
15. Masonic Temple
16. North Coast Life/Smith's Funeral Home
17. Catholic Diocese Chancery Building
18. Our Lady of Lourdes Catholic Cathedral
19. Carnegie Library
20. Eldridge Building
21. Fox Theatre
22. Chronicle Building
23. Metropolitan Performing Arts Center (the Met)
24. Davenport Hotel
25. Peyton Annex
26. Peyton Building
27. Plaza-Transit Center
28. Sterling Savings and Loan Bank
29. Crescent Court
30. Sherwood Building
31. U.S. Bank/Old National Bank Building
32. Paulsen Building
33. Spokane Marketplace

3

Sightseeing

Spokane skyline at twilight

Photo by Ron Swords

Sightseeing

When people refer to "Spokane," they often include the Spokane Valley and areas of Spokane County in their descriptions. For many, they are one and the same. The city of Spokane encompasses 180,800 people and is considered the most populous northern city in the United States, including Alaska. Approximately 90,000 residents live in the Valley area, which includes the small communities of Greenacres, Millwood, Veradale, Opportunity and Otis Orchards. Over 374,000 residents live in Spokane County.

Numbers aside, Spokane is the sum of all its varied components, with the various areas of the city and county possessing unique differences.

It's easy to find your way around Spokane, once you understand how the city is laid out. Street addresses are divided geographically with Division Street literally dividing the city into east and west and Sprague separating northern streets from southern ones. For ease of direction, it's important to realize all avenues run east and west, while all streets run north and south. Numerically named streets such as 12th or 29th are located only on the south side of the city and valley.

For the first-time visitor or even a resident escorting guests around the city, the best place to begin is at the *Spokane Regional Convention and Visitors Bureau,* 926 W Sprague (747-3230) open Monday through Friday 8:30 a.m.-5 p.m. and Saturday 8 a.m.-4 p.m. During the summer months, the Bureau is also open on Sundays 9 a.m.-2 p.m.

The Bureau offers free maps and brochures, detailing area restaurants, golf courses, historical sights and more. Don't miss the series of Day Tour maps the Bureau produces. You'll also find The Spokane Arts Commissions Calender of Events here as well as free local publications such as *Family Magazine* and *The Inlander.* Volunteer staff members love to share their knowledge of the city, and they'll make sure your visit is a memorable one.

Visit the *Spokane Chamber of Commerce,* 1020 W Riverside (624-1393) or the *Spokane Area Economic Development Council,* 221 North Wall (624-9285) for economic and statistical information concerning Spokane-based businesses and industry, plus general area facts.

Stop by the *Spokane Valley Chamber of Commerce,* 10303 East Sprague (924-4994) for free pamphlets, brochures, maps and literature pertaining to the Valley.

A number of bus tours of the city can be arranged through private tour companies. *KariVan Tours* (489-8687) sports a lilac bus for its guests. Groups of ten or more interested in tours should contact *Group Coordinators,* 2805 W 17th (455-4354) for event planning, tours and other convention services.

For ease of exploration, this guide divides the city into large geographic quadrants. Each area contains unique sights and a different feel. Enjoy the diversity which is Spokane and its environs. For information about public art and galleries, see Chapter 7: Of Public Interest.

One of the best ways to see downtown Spokane is on foot. With outdoor art tucked away in courtyards, gargoyles gracing arched entryways, art deco motifs and history around every corner, it's well worth the slower pace and closer examination made possible by walking.

Downtown

At one time, the heart of early downtown Spokane Falls was centered at the corner of Howard and Spokane Falls Boulevard (then called Front Street). James Glover built a trade store on this site in 1873, after buying the land rights of two homesteaders, Scranton and Downing, along with their under-sized lumber mill. He anticipated that the railroads would come, along with settlers drawn to the river's beauty and the city's potential. He was right. One-hundred years later, Riverfront Park was created on this same spot to host Expo '74.

Riverfront Park, often called the jewel of Spokane's downtown core, combines green rolling hills with vistas of the upper, middle and lower falls of the Spokane River. Where early day town fathers once fished for migrating salmon, you can now ride a gondola over the churning white water, most impressive during its spring run-off. A five-story movie theatre, working turn-of-the-century, handcarved Carrousel, a gift shop and Science Center all compete for visitors' attention within the park's 100 acres.

Notice the *Great Northern Clock Tower* situated in the center of the park. Built in 1902, this is all that remains of the Great Northern Railroad Depot, which operated on this site from 1902 until 1971. Today the tower is a symbol of the merging of old Spokane, built by the power of the railroads, with new Spokane, developing since Expo '74. The clock tower is still wound by hand every week.

The green belt facing the tower is the site of many annual events, including **Kids Day, Neighbor Days, Pig Out in the Park** and the **4th of July Royal Fireworks Concert** to name a few. (See Annual Events, Chapter 12.)

Adjacent to Riverfront Park is the **Opera House,** its windows reflecting the calm serenity of a placid stretch of the Spokane River. This elegant, 2,700-seat legacy from Expo '74 is used by the Spokane Symphony, traveling road shows, concerts, stage productions, convention groups and lecturers. Across the connecting breezway, you'll find the **Convention Center.** Created as part of the State of Washington's participation in Expo '74, the Convention Center's 40,000 square feet of exhibit space allow banquet seating for up to 3,000 people. It's also the setting for many concerts and the home, boat and garden shows. Attached to the Convention Center is the **International Ag Trade Center.** Built in response to increased convention space demands, the Ag-Trade building hosts many conferences and meetings from agricultural trade shows to recreational vehicle shows.

On the Looff Carrousel in Riverfront Park

Photo by Ron Swords

Between these buildings and the river runs the *Centennial Trail*. Though not yet completed, the finished trail will follow the river a total of 39 miles from the old Spokane House fur-trading post to the border of Idaho. Today, the trail begins in Riverfront Park and meanders along the river's edge to the state line. A number of historic landmarks dot the trail. Most of its paved path runs 12-feet wide to accommodate bikers, runners, walkers and skaters. Traversing it is one of the most popular ways to enjoy the beauty of the river all year round.

From "new" Spokane to "historic" downtown is as simple as turning a corner. Modern office complexes stand side by side with buildings erected over 100 years ago. When 32 blocks burned in the Great Fire of 1889, Spokane began a construction boom that left its imprint well into the 1970s, when many of these buildings were razed to make way for Expo '74.

Excellent examples of the pre-turn-of-the-century architecture include the *Bennett Block*, corner of Howard and Main, which was built by and named for the son-in-law of founding town father, Anthony Cannon. The *Levy Block*, on Stevens between Main and Riverside, is an 1889 building constructed before the use of steel reinforcements. The *Fernwell Building*, at the corner of Riverside and Stevens, illustrates the way steel construction allowed architects to expand both the lower level, flooding it with light, as well as building taller structures without fear of collapse.

While many of the earliest and grandest buildings were built on Howard Street, two major obstacles hampered the growth of this thoroughfare. North, the river-blocked building, while south, ten sets of railroad tracks choked horse-drawn traffic on a regular basis. Thus, when the rubble was cleared from the 1889 fire, the focus of the city shifted, turning east to expand along Riverside Avenue.

Standing at the corner of Howard and Riverside, looking west, you'll notice the landmark *Spokesman Review Building*. Dedicated in 1891, this turreted structure was the tallest building in town for nearly ten years. In 1896, newspaper owner William H. Cowles brought his bride to live in the sixth-floor penthouse. Today, Cowles' great grandson publishes the *Spokesman-Review*, which, under different names, has been the major newspaper in Spokane since 1883.

The Spokesman Review Tower, though no longer used as living or business quarters, has long been recognized as an architectural landmark that divides the city. East of Riverside lies the business section of downtown. For many years, the most prominent social clubs and homes lay to the west. As families moved to the suburbs, away from the heart of downtown, social organizations and clubs followed. But for many years, the elite locale for the social set was associated with the crescent of adjoining buildings which front west Riverside.

The first building in the crescent is the *Spokane Club*. The club was organized in 1890 as a male bastion for business purposes. In 1910, Kirkland K. Cutter designed and built the graceful building located at the corner of Riverside and Monroe. It still boasts the second largest private library in the state and is open to club members and their guests. Next door is another Kirkland Cutter building, the *Chamber of Commerce*, with masks of Native American chiefs gracing its columns. The *Masonic Temple*, erected in 1905, was enlarged in 1925 to architecturally harmonize with the *Elks Club* directly to the east of it. For many years, *Smith's Funeral Home* was the last in the sweep of this social crescent.

In the 1980s, the *North Coast Life Insurance Company* purchased Smith's Funeral Home and the Elks Building next door, and updated both while retaining most of their original exteriors. In 1923, Great Northwest Life Insurance Company built its headquarters across the street at 1023 W Riverside. The newspapers of the time described it as the "best money can buy." Today, the *Chancery for the Catholic Diocese* inhabits this Italian Renaissance Revival building. Next door, *Our Lady of Lourdes,* begun in 1902, serves as the Cathedral of the Spokane County Diocese. The interior of the Cathedral has undergone major renovations, with little remaining of the original wood and marble work. All these buildings along the western Riverside crescent are registered as a National Historic district.

A little further west, at the intersection of Riverside and 1st, stands the *Carnegie Library*. The library was built in 1905, on land donated by John Finch of Finch Arboretum fame. It's the cornerstone of the renovation of the 1st Avenue neighborhood. Since its earliest days, the area between the Browne's Addition residential area and the downtown business district, now known as the 1st Avenue neighborhood, was made up of auto dealerships and apartments.

In 1925, the *Eldridge Building,* 1325 W 1st, opened as the largest automobile showroom in the state. Today it houses an eatery and office space. The original tile flooring of the auto dealership is still visible. A number of antique shops and small gift shops are located at the west end of 1st Avenue near the Eldridge.

As you walk east along 1st Avenue, you'll notice many 1930s art deco buildings and motifs grimy and in need of paint. These buildings have been sadly neglected over the last 50 years. When you reach the preserved *Fox Theatre,* 1005 W Sprague, you'll be able to discern more clearly the patterns and colors of the art deco architectural era. The streets were jammed at the Fox's 1931 grand opening and, until 1975, its opulent interior remained unaltered. Now it houses three smaller movie theatres.

Across the street from the Fox is the cream terra cotta and polished granite **Chronicle Building,** erected to house the offices of the *Spokane Chronicle,* the evening paper. The paper has since merged with the *Spokesman-Review* which now owns and operates the building. The building is still open to the public, and the rich detailing of marble, stained glass and carved woodwork in the entryway are well worth a closer look.

The **Metropolitan Performing Arts Center** (the Met), lies just east, at 901 W Sprague. This historic building was erected in 1915 as one of the first motion picture theatres in Spokane. Today, ballets, concerts and other forms of live entertainment fill the stage, carrying on its 80-year history of providing pleasure to the community.

Across the street from the Met is *The Davenport,* another grand building of historic significance, considered by many to have been the finest and most elegant hotel in the west.

An early entrepreneur, Louis Davenport, arrived in Spokane with less than two dollars in his pockets and went on to create a hotel known world wide. He began by hauling rubble from the charred remains of buildings burned in the 1889 fire, soon making enough money to establish a restaurant in a flapping canvas tent called the Waffle Foundry. His was not the only business housed in a make shift structure. Most resided in tents until post-fire replacement buildings made of brick and iron were erected.

In 1893, Louis hired the most prominent architect of the era, Kirkland K. Cutter, to design his restaurant. He called it the Italian Gardens. Erected at the corner of Post and Sprague, its mission-style exterior, with white stucco walls, red tile roof and distinctive tower, contrasted dramatically with the predominantly red brick downtown buildings.

By 1914, Davenport had bought the entire block on Sprague Avenue. It was here the elegant Davenport Hotel was opened. The establishment catered to such illuminaries as Jack Dempsey, Clark Gable, Charles Lindbergh, the Emperor of Ethiopia and Mahatma Gandhi.

Louis Davenport sold his hotel in 1945, but it stayed open another 30 years. Gone are the singing birds in the lobby, the spray of water splashing in the central foyer and the crackling fire in the lobby's fireplace which burned continuously. But you can still enjoy the hotel's elegance at tea dances on Friday evenings, or you can book one of the many ballrooms for a special occasion.

If you head north from Sprague on Post, you'll see the *Peyton Building and Annex*. The two-story annex fronts Sprague Avenue and was built to house a billiard parlor on the second floor and a bowling alley in the basement. At one time an indoor golf course and speak easy were also housed here. *The Peyton Building*, at the corner of Post and Riverside was originally two buildings with additional stories linking them together.

The difference in architectural styles is an interesting facet of the Peyton buildings. The Romanesque revival-style, fronting Riverside, with its arched windows and columnar lines, contrasts with the Chicago commercial-style on Sprague, a forerunner of today's modern skyscrapers.

Standing once again on Riverside, facing east, you'll notice two of the newest editions to Spokane's downtown skyline. On the south side of Riverside and Wall is the *The Plaza*, a glass and steel structure housing the Spokane Transit Authority's bus terminal. This is the main location for boarding and transferring on city buses. Its two floors house an international food court, police substation and smaller shops. On the northern corner of Riverside and Wall, you'll notice the *Sterling Savings and Loan Bank*. This building's tower combines height with an eclectic Greco-Roman style architecture and vies with the Review tower as one of the two prominent spires fronting Riverside.

Directly north of the Sterling Savings and Loan Bank building at Wall and Main, is the *Crescent Court*. In 1889, a small mercantile company opened its doors. Its name was chosen for the "crescent" curved angle of Riverside street. The day after its opening, every building in downtown Spokane burnt to the ground, except for The Crescent. It was an auspicious beginning for this landmark retail store. In later years, Frederick and Nelson bought the business, though local residents still referred to it as The Crescent, even after Frederick and Nelson closed its doors in the 1980s. In 1994, The Crescent re-opened, this time as the *Crescent Court,* a series of small retail shops, restaurants, a convention area and ballroom.

Outside the Crescent Court on Wall Street is a two-block pedestrian mall, a meandering cobblestone path lined with flowers, old-time street lights and benches. Wall Street was once called Mill Street for the mills anchoring the Spokane River's northern edge. Today you can catch public transportation to the free parking area on the north side of the river near the coliseum.

If you stroll Riverside east from the Crescent Court, you'll find the *Sherwood* building at 510 W Riverside, where architect Kirkland K.

Cutter added gargoyles and griffins to the Chicago-style building. See if you can spot Quasimodo over the arched entryway.

The *U.S. Bank Building* at 422 W Riverside was originally known as the *Old National Bank Building*. A national competition in 1911 sponsored by the bank elicited the talents of noted Chicago architect Daniel Burnham to design the structure. Despite the need to ship the steel beams by rail and haul most of the materials to the site by horse and wagon, the building was constructed in only 10 months and is considered an example of the pure Chicago School architectural style. Compare this style, using a steel skeleton for the structure, terra cotta facing, windows filling a large portion of the facade and the pattern of intersecting lines which dominate the building, with the earlier style Romanesque revival-style architecture of the *Fernwell Building* one block west. It's easy to see why the Chicago style was the forerunner of the 20th-century steel and glass skyscrapers we know now.

Across the street on Riverside, you'll find the *Paulsen Building* and the *Paulsen Medical and Dental Building*. August Paulsen worked as a cook in the mining fields of Idaho. For eight long, hard years, he and his wife and several partners scraped away in the evening hours at a hole in the ground looking for silver. What they found was lead. In a rags to riches story proving hard work does pay, in this case because of what happened to lie underground, Paulsen's hole became the Hercules Mine, one of the richest in Northern Idaho.

Taking his newly earned wealth, Paulsen commissioned two architects to create the "best 11-story office building money could build." Thanks to the invention of the hydraulic lift he built Spokane's first skyscraper. Twenty years later, in 1929, Paulsen built the Medical and Dental Building, creating another first, a setback skyscraper. Built with structural stone overlayed by a terra cotta exterior, the building used a series of steps, called setbacks, to give it the look of a feudal castle.

If you scan the top floor of the structure, you'll notice evergreen shrubs. A penthouse was erected on this floor, and it's still used by the Paulsen family today.

The *Spokane Marketplace*, open Wednesdays and weekends, is part of the downtown core. Here, you'll enjoy the sweet, spicy smell of garden-grown basil intermingled with the aroma of fresh-baked bread. Since 1991, the market has grown from 63 vendors and 17,000 customers to roughly 200 vendors serving more than 300,000 people. For many years the market was located at the corner of Riverside and Division, though its final home is in transition. For directions and specific information about the hours and events, call the central office (482-2627). The Market is open May through October.

West

West of the city's core are the mansions of millionaires and fields of early-day battles between the U.S. Army and area natives. You can easily tour this section by car in less than a day. However, a walking tour of the *Browne's Addition* area is both interesting and enjoyable.

Directly west of the downtown business district is Browne's Addition, one of the city's oldest and most elegant neighborhoods. Named after early pioneer J.J. Browne, it houses many lavish mansions, most built between the 1880s and 1890s. Today, there are also apartment complexes and smaller single-family dwellings lining the tree-shaded streets.

To reach Browne's Addition from downtown, follow 2nd Avenue west. Homes of particular note include the *Glover* at 1725 West 1st. Originally built and owned by town founder, James Glover, in 1881, the house stood at the corner of Riverside and Stevens. After the great fire of 1889, this structure of hand-hewn timbers and hand-wrought nails was moved to its present site. Note the unique chimney design with stained glass windows between the flues.

The Amasa B. Campbell House at 2316 W 1st Avenue was donated to the Eastern Washington State Historical Society by Campbell's daughter, Helen Campbell Powell. This 1898 home, now part of the Cheney Cowles Museum, offers a wonderful glimpse into the life style of the wealthy mine owners. Admission to the Campbell House is included in the admittance fee to the museum. Admission is $3 for adults, $2 for children and seniors. On Wednesdays, admission is half price until 5 p.m., then free until closing. Open Tuesday through Saturday 10 a.m.-5 p.m., Wednesday 10 a.m.-9 p.m., Sunday 1 a.m.-5 p.m. Register at the museum's front desk, where you'll be issued an official "calling-card" for the next tour through the house.

In old Spokane, there was a great deal of social rivalry between the ladies of Browne's Addition and those who lived along 7th Avenue (the Hill). The ladies who lived in the mansions on "the Hill" did their calling Thursdays, while the ladies who lived in the mansions in Browne's Addition returned the visits the following Wednesdays. The Louis XV reception room of the Campbell House, with its silk moire wallpaper, marble fireplace and golden ornamentations, is still just as it was when Mrs. Campbell received her visitors.

Both Amasa Campbell and John Finch, whose 18-room *Finch Mansion* is located at 2340 W 1st, made fortunes in the Coeur d'Alene mines. Finch's Grecian-revival residence once included mahogany pillars, gold-leaf furniture and a private art gallery. It is currently an apartment building.

First Avenue becomes Poplar Street in front of the Finch mansion. Follow Poplar one block until you arrive at Pacific Avenue. The apartment complex at the west end of Pacific Avenue covers what was once the local *Chinese Cemetery*. Many an elaborate funeral procession, led by mourners carrying flutes and fluttering banners, filed down Pacific Avenue to this site. The graves here were piled high with plates of roasted chicken and duck to help feed departed spirits and set next to lighted josh sticks. Since it was believed a spirit would wonder forever if not buried upon Chinese soil, all these graves were exhumed over the years, and the remains returned to China.

Between Browne's Addition and the Spokane River is another charming neighborhood, *Peaceful Valley,* originally settled by Finnish and Scandinavian emigrants. You can still see the small dwellings called "shotgun houses." The name came from the way they were constructed, with one room behind the other. The idea was you could shoot a shotgun through the front door and the bullet would fly straight through the back door.

Driving west from Browne's Addition, you'll pass high above Latah Creek. Both I-90 and Highway 2, known as Sunset Highway, cross Latah Creek just above where the creek joins the Spokane River. For many years, Sunset Highway was the main route into Spokane from the west. Stop at the Holiday Inn West Motel or Friendship Inn-Spokane House Motel at the crest of the Sunset Highway hill where the view of the city and valley at sunset is spectacular. Just after you cross the Latah Creek Bridge and begin the climb up Sunset Highway, you'll find *Finch Arboretum*. It's well worth a stop, especially in the spring, when the lilac, azalea and rhododendron bushes, cherry, plum and crabapple trees bloom. A stop in the fall is nice too, when the maple, hawthorn and oaks shed their leafy finery. Even in the dead of winter, the mile-long strip of lawns and trees has a quiet, majestic beauty all its own.

As you continue west along Sunset Highway, you'll pass an area known as *Garden Springs*. Natural springs flow close to the surface here, including Garden Springs Creek, which gurgles through Finch Arboretum. A handful of businesses and homes are nestled among the basalt cliffs of Garden Springs.

The community of *Airway Heights* clusters on either side of Highway 2 as it continues west. This area is home to ethnic eateries, such as the House of Seoul and the Asian Restaurant, and traditional restaurants like the Buckhorn, Longhorn Barbecue and Savage House Pizza Parlor serving down-home cooking.

Located just 12 miles west of Spokane along Highway 2 is the *Fairchild Air Force Base*. Since Fairchild was established in 1942, this 10,000-acre facility has become one of the top three employers in the county, making an economic impact in the region of over $400 million a year. An Air Force Survival School is located at Fairchild, as is the Washington Air National Guard.

Across the highway from the entrance to Fairchild is a marker commemorating the *Battle of Spokane Plains*. In September 1858, Colonel George Wright subdued the only serious uprising between area tribes (Palouse, Coeur d'Alene, and the middle band of the Spokan Indians) and the encroaching white settlers. Later, a fort was named in Colonel Wright's honor. Seventeen of the 23 officers who served with him in the battle went on to become generals in the Civil War.

Continuing west along Highway 2, you'll cross Deep Creek, carved into existence thousands of years ago by glacial activity. You'll pass by rich, rolling farmland and small, agricultural communities like Reardon, Davenport and Creston.

North

North of the city, are some of the newest housing subdivisions. This area also contains one of the oldest geological formations in the area, Mt. Spokane. While now the drive from downtown Spokane to Mt. Spokane is an easy 30-minute trip, crossing the Spokane River was not always as easy as it is today. The first white settler on the north side, Colonel David P. Jenkins, built a home in 1879, at 820 W Mallon. He had to row back and forth across the river to reach his downtown law practice.

Though not the first bridge built across the river, the *Monroe Street Bridge* has long remained one of the most prominent architectural features of the downtown landscape. The first bridge, a rickety, wooden structure, burned to the ground in 1890. A second bridge, built of steel, became so shaky over time that employees of the local trolley-car company would remain at each end of the bridge when the trolley passed over. Their job was to shout a warning if the bridge looked ready to fall.

The current bridge was built in 1911 and was the longest concrete arch structure in the United States. In order to scale the structure down to a more human scope for pedestrians who walked across the bridge, architect Kirkland K. Cutter fashioned a cement balustrade and arched passageways atop the bridge. The mere bulk of these additions, still visible today to those who drive and stroll across the bridge, give a sense of permanence and stability missing from many more sleek and unadorned modern structures.

Once you cross the bridge, travel northwest. You'll see the beautiful and unique **Spokane County Courthouse**. This Renaissance-style structure was erected in 1895 on land donated by Colonel Jenkins. It was modeled after two famous 16th-century French chateaux. The detailed exterior, festooned with decorative arches, wreaths and ornamental brickwork, is a delight to the eye. At night, the central tower is lit and resembles a fairy-tale castle. Near the south entryway, you can still see two small hitching rings embedded in the sidewalk, another reminder of days gone by.

The courthouse is the cornerstone of a series of city and county municipal buildings. Of note is the **Spokane County Jail**, just north of the courthouse, and the **County Health Building**, further south. West of the courthouse, at 1843 W Broadway, is the first brick home ever built on the north side of the river. As you continue west on Broadway, you'll note many turn-of-the-century homes. This is one of Spokane's older neighborhoods, with a history as rich and varied as the architectural styles. Broadway eventually joins Summit Boulevard, which winds above the Spokane River. The oldest continuously lived-in house is located just off Summit at 1735 W Point Road. Though the home, which is occupied, has been remodeled several times, the walls of the original slab hut, built in 1872, still remain today.

If you start at the Courthouse and travel east on Broadway instead of west, you'll reach the parking lot of the **Flour Mill**. From its opening in 1895 until its closure in 1972, this mill ground the area's wheat. Today it houses a series of specialty shops and restaurants. A walk through the restored interior is a charming break from the modern-day world. Just north of the Flour Mill is the new **Spokane Veterans Memorial Coliseum**.

This $55-million building hosts a variety of events and can hold up to 12,500 spectators. The coliseum is home to the Spokane Chiefs Hockey team, the State B Basketball tournaments, and a number of major sport and entertainment events. A 50- by 20-feet scoreboard, giant video screen and 14 luxury suites ring the oval stage area of the arena.

Back to Monroe Street, head north, and you'll pass a variety of small retail shops and businesses as you head to Northwest Boulevard. This angled, five-corner intersection was once a wagon road. Head west on Northwest Boulevard until you reach Maple, then veer north. One block west of Maple, at the corner of Euclid and Ash, is **Drumheller Springs**. This spring, still bubbling today, was once a stopping place along the old Indian Trail between the Spokane River and the Spokane House Trading Post. The water was so fresh that town founder Anthony Cannon had a supply of barrels filled and freighted by wagon to his home on a weekly basis.

Just above the springs is the site of the first schoolhouse in the area. Opened in 1870 by Chief Spokan Garry, it served members of the Spokan Indian tribe until 1875. Garry acted as an important intermediary between his people and the white settlers in the area, and today a number of municipal buildings and a park bear his name.

Further north on Maple, the street intersects with Wellesley Avenue. West on Wellesley brings you to the *Joseph A. Albi Memorial Stadium* (called the Joe Albi Stadium by locals) and the *Veterans Administration Medical Center.* Joe Albi Stadium boasts 35,000 permanent seats and is used for local high school and college football games.

Returning to Maple, you'll pass through residential neighborhoods whose architectural styles exemplify the growth of Spokane. There are cottage-style bungalows, post-World War II housing tracts, ranch style homes and newer neo-Victorian family dwellings. Until the 1940s, Wellesley Avenue delineated the northern edge of the city's housing developments. From the 1950s through the 1970s, homes filled the area between Wellesley and Francis.

Maple Street merges into Country Homes Boulevard just beyond the intersection at Francis Avenue. Starting in the 1970s, home building expanded north along this very route. The *Little Spokane River*, once considered part of the heart of farmland, is now flanked by row upon row of new homes.

Though homes line its banks, many species of wild life make Little Spokane River their home. Beavers, muskrats, heron, deer, ducks, over 100 species of birds, trout and other fish live here. This is the only surviving river in the state of Washington whose natural route has not been diverted, altered or dammed for encroaching growth and development.

You'll cross over the Little Spokane River if you continue on Country Homes Boulevard to Division Street. Here the two roads meet and divide at an intersection known locally as the North Division "Y." From this point north, you'll travel on either Highway 2 to Colbert, or Highway 395 to Deer Park. If you take Highway 2, you'll soon find yourself at the cutoff to the Day-Mt. Spokane Road.

Mt. Spokane is one of the oldest land formations in the area. Visitors to the mountain's summit are rewarded with a panoramic view encompassing two countries (Canada and the United States), three states (Washington, Idaho and Montana), two mountain ranges (the Selkirks and the Coeur d'Alenes) and eight lakes (Spirit, Pend Oreille, Priest, Hayden, Coeur d'Alene, Liberty, Loon and Newman). Bobcats, coyotes, porcupines, black bear, moose and three species of deer can be seen in the 13,000-acre state park surrounding the mountain. A favorite spot to stop and enjoy the view is *Vista House*, located near the end of the Day-Mt. Spokane Road. A 25-yard hike will bring you to this rock structure originally built as a fire lookout. It still looks right at home among the rock outcroppings and pine trees bracketing the 5,881-foot summit.

By returning to Spokane via Market Street, you'll cross through an area now known as *Hillyard*. The railroad yards were created by railroad magnate Jim Hill in 1892. Today the area on Market between Francis and Wellesley avenues is a mecca for antique lovers. You can easily spend a day wandering through small stores offering every type of collectible. The neighborhood is also known for its murals illustrating historical events of Hillyard. Look for one such scene depicting the area's railroad background on the corner of Market and Wellesley.

South

Like most of the city, a tour of the south side is best accomplished by car, but don't forget to stop and stroll through some of the town's loveliest parks and older neighborhoods. You can still see several of the elegant turn-of-the-century mansions which once dotted the basalt cliffs of Spokane's lower south side. Many of these classic structures are well worth a drive by.

The Corbin House, at 507 W 7th, now the site of the city's Parks and Recreation Department Art Center, was built for railroad tycoon Daniel C. Corbin. It is said that Corbin was so punctual, locals set their pocket watches by his five-o'clock-sharp departure from the office every evening. Corbin was also known for his frugality, which is evident in the interior of his home. Rich detailing was eschewed in favor of simple doorknobs and plain wood moldings. By today's standards, both look quite elegant. In the 1960s, a road, Ben Garnet Way, was constructed to make access to the south side of the city easier. Unfortunately, it destroyed Corbin's carriage house and altered the look of the area by carving a chunk out of once impassable basalt cliffs.

Following 7th Avenue west, you'll find the home of *F. Lewis Clark*, located at 701 W 7th Avenue. The half-timber and stucco exterior of this English Tudor home contrasts sharply with Corbin's more austere Georgian-style abode. Both residences were designed by Kirkland K. Cutter.

Clark made one of his fortunes in mining. He cleared 13 million, non-taxable dollars in one deal alone. His other wealth came from milling flour, as well as railroad and real estate investments. In his free time, he hobnobbed with European royalty, sailing his 105-foot yacht, the "Spokane," with King Edward of England and Kaiser Wilhelm of Germany.

In 1929, the Clark home was donated to the Catholic Diocese of Spokane as a girls' school and for over 50 years served as classrooms for Marycliff High School. Today the house is used as office space.

Next door to the Clark mansion at 815 W 7th stands the *Austin Corbin Home*. Austin was the son of Daniel Corbin. He built his southern colonial-style home in 1898 for the then unheard-of sum of $65,000. One stairway in the house was built specifically to accommodate musicians who played at the lavish parties thrown regularly by the Corbin family. In 1945, the home was donated as a convent for the Franciscan Sisters who taught at Marycliff High School. When the school closed in 1979, the structure became an office building.

Another grand home, now a restaurant, is the *Glover House*, located at 321 W 8th Avenue. Built for town founder James Glover in 1889, it boasted many firsts in the area. It was the earliest home built beneath the rock cliffs and one of the original residences designed by Kirkland Cutter to win the seal of approval among the area's socially elite. It was also the first home in the city to boast indoor bathrooms. The 22-room home contained a two-story entry hall and central heating.

The home passed out of Glover's hands when he lost his fortune in the Panic of 1893. Today, *Adolfson's* restaurant is housed in the mansion. To tour the house, contact the restaurant staff.

Above these homes, just off Ben Garnett Way on South 13th Avenue, is tiny *Cliff Park*. This is the city's highest point and provides an unparalleled view of downtown, Mt. Spokane to the north and, in the far distance, peaks of the Canadian Selkirk Mountains.

Directly east of Cliff Park is the *Sacred Heart Medical Complex*. Sacred Heart was founded by the Sisters of Providence in 1887 and is the third largest employer in the county. Over 30% of the hospital patients come from outside Spokane County. Sacred Heart continues to grow and expand, and now includes a Cancer and Research Center, Heart Institute and Neonatal Intensive Care Center.

Traveling south along Grand Boulevard from Sacred Heart, you'll see the inspiring Gothic *Cathedral of St. John the Evangelist*. The structure is easily recognizable from a distance, and is truly a sight to be admired up close. Construction on the cathedral began in 1925, and took nearly 28 years to complete. The building combines a typical English Gothic-style cathedral with French influences. The exterior stone was quarried near Tacoma, Washington, and the interior sandstone came from Idaho. Interior wood beams are of solid California redwood, some up to 257 feet long.

One of the many unique features of the Cathedral is the the 40-ton carillion made of 49 cast bells. The largest bell, Big John, weighs 5,000 pounds. A series of free carillion concerts are held every Thursday evening in August. Performances feature guest musicians from around the world. You can listen to the carillion played Thursdays at noon and Sunday mornings at 9:30 throughout the year.

Tours of the Cathedral are available Monday, Tuesday, Thursday and Saturday, noon-3 p.m. Special group tours can be arranged by calling the Cathedral office (838-4277) or stopping by the bookstore and gift shop, which is open Monday through Friday, 10 a.m.-3 p.m.

Nearby is *Manito Park*. Early day residents once trudged uphill on foot to reach this 90-acre park at Grand Boulevard and 17th Avenue. Today you can eliminate the trek by driving.

Manito Park offers a variety of attractions and is popular with visitors and residents alike. A natural, spring-fed pond, once reaching from Grand to its current shores on the lower south western edge of the park, is home to migratory wildfowl throughout the year. This is a favorite spot to feed ducks, geese and resident swans. During the winter, many people brave the frozen surface for a brisk game of ice hockey.

The park has under gone many transformations since it was originally designed by the Olmstead Brothers (who also layed out New York's Central Park). Today there are seasonal flower beds at several locations within the park. The Joel E. Ferris Perennial Beds, the Rose Garden with over 1,500 varieties of roses, the formal Duncan Gardens with its ever-changing display of annuals and the Japanese Garden with its rippling waterfall are a few of the eye-catching attractions you'll enjoy in this park.

See if you can find the old-fashioned water trough along the park's eastern border, located next to Grand Boulevard, it's one of only two remaining in the city. After the strenuous pull up Grand, early day wagoneers paused at the trough to water and rest their horses.

If you continue traveling south on Grand Boulevard until you reach 29th Avenue, and then head west, you'll arrive at *High Drive*. This is a scenic road overlooking Latah Creek and the modern Palouse Highway leading south to Pullman. When you view the creek bed below from this distance, it's easy to see how glacial activity formed it. If you continue south along High Drive to 57th Avenue then east, you'll connect with the *"Old Palouse" Highway* and the area known as Moran Prairie.

This thoroughfare, built in 1910, was the first modern highway to reach Spokane. At the time, most of the traffic from coastal cities like Seattle and Portland arrived via steamer, traveling over the Columbia River, through the port of Lewiston and across the rolling hills of the Palouse. The "Old Palouse" Highway leads south into the richest wheat-growing country in the world. It's well worth a day's time to visit the small farming communities of Rosalia, Tekoa, St. John's and Colfax.

Go back to 29th Avenue. This is one of only two thoroughfares which traverse east/west all the way across the southside of Spokane (the other is 57th Avenue) and is considered dividing line between old and new Spokane. Between 29th Avenue and downtown are older neighborhoods. South of this busy street are a number of housing subdivisions built since the 1970s.

Further south and east of these tracts of newer homes are *Browne's and Tower Mountains*. Browne's Mountain was named for J.J. Browne, early town founder. After Mr, Browne lost most of his wealth in the financial panic of 1893, he retired to the solitude of a country home located near the mountain. Today, new homes dot the mountain's slope. Tower Mountain was named after the series of television and radio antennas which grace its peak. Their glowing red beacons are a familiar sight on Spokane's night-time horizon.

The Olmstead Brothers, who planned the lovely Manito Park, also designed a number of streets between 8th and 29th avenues. The result is beautiful—residential homes built along tree-lined streets, which dead-end into basalt cliffs or other natural obstructions. Take the time to enjoy such streets as Rockwood Boulevard, Overbluff Estates and, lower on the south side, Altamont Boulevard. Many south-side neighborhoods, still have cobblestone streets. The thick, reddish brick gave horse hooves traction, especially during the snowy winter months. A few places to see these streets are at South Howard between 21st and 23rd, West 5th Avenue at Jefferson to Adams and at 6th Avenue and Cedar.

Altamont Boulevard, a kidney-shaped street between 9th and 13th avenues, was once a Native American horse-race track. Today, it's lined with giant maples and beautiful turn-of-the-century homes. It's also located only blocks east of *Perry Street*.

Perry is a north/south thoroughfare dotted with neighborhood shops catering to special-interest groups. Some of the stores you'll find are Gertrude's German Deli, Talexia Ethnic Beauty Supply and the Windmill Coffee Shop. Just south of where Perry Street meets Southeast Boulevard is a set of steps linking the upper south-side of homes along the basalt bluffs with the lower south side homes. Kids of all ages have always enjoyed this remnant of days when walking took precedence over driving. Take a few moments to stretch your legs here, as it also affords a great view. It's an easy walk for everyone.

East

East of downtown Spokane is the *Valley*, an area of residential homes, farmland and businesses. The Valley is really a number of separate, small communities and unincorporated areas. For many years, the Valley plain has been covered by lush farmland and spreading orchards. It wasn't always so fertile.

Tens of thousands of years ago, glacial waters sluiced through the Valley, carving a channel between basalt scablands. One flood broke from an ice dam near present day Missoula, Montana. Reputed to be the largest flood known to man, this raging water rushed through the area at over 60 miles an hour and over 2,000 feet deep. This, and other floods, deposited layers of granite ranging from fist-size to man-high boulders throughout the area.

Today, we can see these rounded granite rocks used in the building of many early Valley homes and businesses. Look for their incorporation in the *Veradale Water Power Building*, located on Evergreen off Sprague Avenue. The building is shaped like a castle. You can see other, larger granite boulders wedged into the hillside near the Walk in the Wild Zoo off Pines Road and Interstate 90.

Vera Water Power Castle in the Valley
Photo by Ron Swords

The Spokane Aquifer was created by these boulders. Water sieved through this gravel-like material, flows below the surface and supplies the drinking water for almost 400,000 people in the Spokane and Northern Idaho area. These smooth river-shaped rocks also contributed to the growth and texture of the settlement in the Valley area.

Early settlers who came seeking the rich soil of the Palouse area, a few miles south of the Valley, were dismayed to discover gravelly soil here. Thwarted in planting wheat, farmers tried to establish orchards, though with little early success.

Undismayed by the rocky soil, A.T. Dishman, an early pioneer, moved to the sunflower- and bunch-grass covered Valley in 1889. He began quarrying thousands of tons of granite from the area into Spokane to replace the buildings destroyed by the great fire of 1889. The quarry area is still known as *Dishman Hills*.

Dishman then went on to create the town of *Dishman* at the corner of Argonne and Sprague. The early town included a hotel, post office, store, roller-skating rink, dance hall and rodeo grounds. In 1938, the Dishman Theatre was created, bringing movies to the Valley for the first time. The theatre still stands at 8722 E Sprague, though it's changed its name to the Déjà Vu and shows films that would shock A.T. Dishman.

In 1899, Daniel Corbin, who made his millions building railroads from Spokane into the rich ore country of the Coeur d'Alene Mountains, created an irrigation company to develop another area of the Valley. He called the site of his development, **Greenacres**, making many chortle at the grandiose name for the dry, rocky area. Skeptics became believers in 1900, when the first water trickled through a ditch from Liberty Lake to quench the arid land.

By 1905, the Spokane Canal Company requisitioned water from Newman Lake for **Otis Orchards** and 15,000 more acres of Valley property came under cultivation.

The area known today as **Opportunity** was developed in 1905 as another irrigation project. The name "Opportunity" was selected from contest entries devised as a real estate promotion to name the area. The winner received a grand prize of $10. The first brick building in Opportunity was the I.O.O.F. Hall, which still stands on Sprague near the corner of Pines Road. Today the Valley Repertory Theatre holds its performances within its walls.

With people came industries. In 1911, the **Inland Empire Paper Company Mill** was constructed beside the Spokane River in what is now called **Millwood**. It was the only paper mill east of the Cascades until the 1950s. Today, the company still produces paper for the *Spokesman-Review* and other publications at its 3320 N Argonne location. The mill compliments a quaint block-long section of offices, shops and restaurants, including the Rocket Bakery, the Corner Door and the Windowbox gift shop.

Mirabeau Park is located not far from the mill at 13500 E Euclid. It was named by a paper company engineer who had an interest in French History. Count Mirabeau was the organizer of the French National Guard, which charged the Bastille during the French Revolution.

Antoine Plante, another Frenchman, this time descended from French-Canadian stock, played a vitally important part in the early settlement of the Valley. From 1852 until 1864, he operated a strategic ferry named after him.

Plante was three-quarters French Canadian and one quarter Blackfoot Indian, standing over six feet tall and weighing 200 pounds. His ferry used to cross the Spokane River before bridges were built and was one of the only means of crossing. Charging tolls ranging from $4 for passengers to 15¢ per sheep and hog, Plante made a tidy profit. Later, he grew dismayed at the number of new settlers crowding the Valley area and sold his holdings. Today, **Plante's Ferry**, 12308 E Upriver Drive, is a gracious park bordering the river.

The modern-day dams along the Spokane River make it difficult to understand the importance of this ferry site or the need for reliable transportation in crossing the turbulent waters of the river.

For those who traveled by wagon, then car, the main east-west thoroughfare through the Valley was Sprague Avenue. In the 1960s, I-90 was built and became the new main east-west thoroughfare through the Valley. Sprague was originally called **Appleway** because of the number of orchards bordering its path. Today, you can still find a number of businesses with the word Appleway in their name along Sprague Avenue. Further east, in the Coeur d'Alene area, the name Appleway is still used for this early day road.

Another site of historical significance lies near the Washington-Idaho border. A commemorative monument marks **Horse Slaughter Camp**, located at the west end of the highway weigh station.

In 1858, after defeating members of the Spokan, Yakima and Kalispell tribes, Colonel George Wright, who would later have a local college named after him, ordered the destruction of over 700 horses belonging to the Spokan Indian Tribe. Because horses meant transportation, wealth and the means to sustain the Indians' nomadic existence, the act doomed many tribal members to starvation. As late as 1911, the bleached bones of the slaughtered horses could still be seen along the bank of the Spokane River.

4

Eats, Treats and More

The "Elk" — a popular eating place in Browne's Addition

Photo by Ron Swords

Eats, Treats and More

Originally the bastion of "steak and potatoes" eateries, Spokane restaurants now offer something for every taste. You'll find New York-style bagels, chicken-fried steak with cream-style gravy, Northwest cuisine created by master chefs, Mexican recipes handed down for generations, Thai curry sauces, Vietnamese eggrolls and more.

Long-time residents will enjoy trying new cuisines or revisiting neighborhood institutions. Visitors will return with tales of epicurean experiences not commonly found in the past.

A mix of fine and casual dining, ethnic cuisine, coffee stops, bakeries and dessert locations and pizza places follows. Each eatery is listed geographically: downtown, north, south, east and west. A listing of the specific types of restaurants follows at the end of the chapter.

Not only is Spokane blessed with a variety of culinary experiences, it's also an affordable city for diners. Restaurants in this section are rated according to the cost of a dinner for one: $13 and up is "expensive," between $7 and $12 is "moderate" and $6 or under is "inexpensive." The tab does not include beverages or desserts.

Something to keep in mind when you plan an evening out throughout the Lilac City is the influence of the weather. When sun and the summer months approach, many locations offer extended hours as well as outdoor dining. It's always wise to call ahead for the current opening and closing times.

Downtown

Ankeny's, 515 W Sprague (838-6311). Located atop the Ridpath Hotel, this brass and glass restaurant is a popular lunch spot for the business crowd. Monday nights feature live jazz and blues music, while the rest of the week sports Top 40 music played by regional bands. Dine on Northwest cuisine, choosing from fish, beef, pasta or chicken. The house specialty is prime rib. Full bar. Sunday brunch. Open seven days. Reservations recommended for weekends and holidays. Credit cards. Expensive.

Au Croissant, 224 N Howard (624-6152). For 14 years, this family-owned restaurant has served the world's best croissants, bar none, with a crust so buttery and flaky it borders on sinful. One bite and you'll be spoiled for life. If you can look beyond the selection of croissants and breads, the restaurant offers equally delicious breakfast, lunch and dinner items. Lunch includes salads, soups, sandwiches and special entrees, while the dinner menu focuses on Continental and Persian selections. The Persian lentil and pomegranate soup is not to be missed. Don't overlook the French pastry desserts either. Wine and beer. Open for lunch Monday through Saturday, dinners served Tuesday through Saturday. Closed Sundays and Monday nights. Credit cards. Breakfast and lunch are inexpensive to moderate. Dinners are moderate to expensive.

Au Croissant Bakery Inc.,1222 W 2nd (624-1300). Though 95% of Au Croissant's business is wholesale, customers can walk in and buy fresh baguettes, breads, over a dozen different types of fruit filled croissants, meat-filled croissants, muffins and danish-type pastries. Special orders are taken on items you may have eaten at a local restaurant, but don't see in their display case. Open Monday through Friday 7 a.m.-6 p.m., Saturday 8 a.m.-3 p.m. No credit cards.

Azteca, 200 W Spokane Falls Blvd. (456-0350). Azteca is part of a family-owned chain originating in Seattle. It's a nice place to introduce children to Mexican food and culture. Tortillas are created before your eyes in the entry way, and your waiter will encourage an interest in the Spanish language. Choose from seafood, meat and chicken dishes. Each Christmas season, the restaurant throws its doors open to indigent street people for an off-the-menu dinner. Open seven days a week for lunch and dinner. Reservations recommended for weekend dinners. Credit cards. Inexpensive to moderate.

*Brewhaha Espresso,*12 N Howard (456-4881). Brewhaha's offers extra incentives to sit and sip a cup of espresso. They feature Torrefazione Coffees and Cobblestone Bakery Co. cookies and pastries. Co-owner Mardis Menno's art decorates the walls, while Ray Abrahamson, the other owner, creates "a poem of the day" for his customers' enjoyment. Open Monday through Friday 6:30 a.m.-7:15 p.m.

Cafe Street Music, 117 N Howard (624-7722). Cafe Street Music has only enough room to stand at the counter or slip into one of two outdoor tables. However, this coffee stop makes up for lack of space by its location. Situated in the entryway to Street Music, you can sip an espresso and listen to an eclectic collection of music piped through the store. It's a wonderful spot for an office coffee break or for a pause from shopping. Muffins and cookies offered. Open Monday through Friday 7 a.m.-6 p.m. and Saturday 10 a.m.-6 p.m.

Cannon Street Grill,144 S Cannon (456-8660). This restaurant, called the "best kept secret in Spokane" by its customers, has attracted a strong out-of-town following. Manager/chef, Jerry Schrader, honed his skills serving Margaret Thatcher and the King and Queen of Sweden. The menu features European selections aimed at providing a bistro-style dining experience. Specialties like crispy duck with wild huckleberry sauce draw a crowd. Reservations are strongly recommended for all meals. The menu is small, with only eight entrees and two specials daily, but the attention to detail each dish receives is outstanding. Open for breakfast and lunch Monday through Saturday; dinner Wednesday through Saturday and brunch only on Sunday. Credit cards. Moderate to expensive.

China Best, 223 W Riverside (455-9042). Over 145 menu items drawn from the major provinces of China ensure you'll find something to your liking at China Best. Full bar. Lunch served Monday through Friday. Dinner served seven days a week. Reservations recommended on weekends. Credit cards. Moderate.

C.I. Shenanigan's, 322 N Spokane Falls Court (455-6690). Within a stone's throw of the river, Shenanigan's offers casually elegant waterfront dining beneath a glass atrium or along the umbrella-shaded deck. While you await your choice of Northwest seafood, chicken, prime rib or pasta, you'll enjoy watching pedestrian traffic on the Centennial Trail. During summer months, this peaceful setting is often interrupted by the loud honking of resident geese nesting on the river bank. Full bar. Largest brunch in town served Sunday. Reservations suggested on weekends. Credit cards. Moderate to expensive.

Clinkerdagger, 621 W Mallon (328-5965). Clinkerdagger's has offered consistent dining pleasure since the days of Expo '74. The riverside window seating is most spectacular during the spring run-off. Old English decor makes this a pleasant spot to entertain business acquaintances and visiting guests. The steak soup and burnt cream dessert get rave reviews. Clinkerdagger has the distinction of serving the most prime rib in the entire Restaurants Unlimited chain. Full bar. Open for lunch and dinner Monday through Saturday. Sunday is dinner only. Reservations strongly recommended at all times. Credit cards. Expensive.

The Coyote Cafe, 702 W 3rd (747-8800). The Coyote specializes in Mexican food, but the baby back barbecue ribs and "anytime" sandwiches are great too. Plastic-covered table tops, booth and table seating, and a wall of windows make this a comfortable setting for friends to meet. Even the ceiling is interesting with corner to corner advertisements. Limited bar with specialty drinks. Open seven days. Lunch and dinner menus are the same. Credit cards. Moderate.

Craven's, 111 S Cedar (747-6424). When you step into this small establishment with its aroma of roasting beans and wall display of coffee growing regions around the world, you'll know you're in coffee heaven. The company name was inspired by the owner's grandmother, Mildred Craven from Yorkshire, England. Craven's focuses on the sale of coffee and coffee beans, nothing else. While 95% of their business is wholesale, individual customers are welcome to taste, learn and talk coffee. Whole beans and ground coffee come in a wide range of roasts, blends and variety. Open Monday through Friday 7:30 a.m.-6 p.m. and Saturday 10 a.m.-4 p.m. Closed Sunday.

Cucina! Cucina!, Crescent Court at Wall and Main (838-3388). Part of a restaurant chain originating in Seattle, this popular Italian bistro offers one of the best outdoor dining experiences in Spokane. Located in the downtown Crescent Court, the restaurant seats 90-outdoor diners among planters, old-fashioned street lamps and park benches situated along Wall Street. Indoor diners enjoy an upbeat environment featuring butcher-paper table tops and plenty of color, sounds and enticing smells. The menu features antipasti, soups, pizza, pastas and sandwiches. Customers can eat in or order items to go. During the week, an espresso and pastry bar opens at 7 a.m., offering fresh-baked Italian cinnamon rolls, fruit, yogurt and breakfast pizzas. Open for lunch and dinner, seven days a week. Reservations accepted for lunch, but not dinner. Moderate.

Cyrus O'Leary's, 516 W Main (624-9000). At Cyrus O'Leary's, flagship of the Cyrus Vaughn area restaurants, expect to spend as much time enjoying the wait staff and decor as you do eating. The servers dress in costumes ranging from baseball players to harem dancers. Walls are jam-packed with everything from a barber shop pole to a carrousel horse. Adults and kids both savor watching the toy train chug around the bar ceiling and the mechanical clown flip double loops. The menu offers 120 different items. Full bar. Open seven days. Weekends can get hectic. Reservations are taken only for parties of eight and larger. Credit cards. Moderate.

Cyrus O'Leary's Wholesale Pies, 319 W 2nd (624-5000). Cyrus Vaughn has a ready-made market for his signature pies and cheesecakes through his restaurants, *Cyrus O'Leary's, Just Like Home Buffet, Tomato Brothers* and *Coyote Cafe*. So if you crave popular favorites like Kahlua Cream, Strawberry-Rhubarb or Chocolate Peanut Butter pies, or frozen Turtle cheesecake, this is the place to find them. Though a variety of pies are displayed, it's recommended that you give 24-hour notice to reserve your favorite. Pies are sold whole only and are strictly for take-out. Open Monday through Friday 8:30 a.m.-5 p.m. No credit cards.

Dick's Hamburgers, 10 E 3rd (747-2481). Dick's has been a local institution since 1965. This is as much a people-watching spot as a place to order a quick bite. "Hamburgers by the bagful" pretty well describes the cuisine, though you can order fish, chicken, pizza or french fries. Wait people at the walk-up window memorize your order rather than write it down. Open seven days. Inexpensive.

Domini Sandwiches, 703 W Sprague (747-2324). Domini's has been a downtown landmark for good, big sandwiches for over 30 years. If you're unable to squeeze into the establishment during the busy lunch or after work rush hours, try ordering by fax (747-7422). Popcorn, soft drinks, beer,wine and espresso drinks round out the menu. Closed Sunday. No credit cards. Inexpensive.

Elk, 1931 W Pacific (456-0454). In 1902, Misters Stone and Sutherland opened the Elk Drug Store. The wrap-around soda fountain served malts and cold beverages to many a thirsty customer. After a brief closing, The Elk reopened offering breakfast, lunch and dinner. Now you can order deli sandwiches, homemade soups, great desserts and daily specials "'cooked on a whim." Try one of the vegetarian dishes, an espresso or an old-fashioned malt. The hardwood floors, high ceilings, 1950s furniture and old-fashioned advertising placards dotting the walls fits nicely with the Browne's Addition neighborhood. Beer and wine. Open Monday through Saturday. Sunday brunch only. No credit cards. Inexpensive.

Entrées on Trays (926-4748). Though technically not a traditional restaurant, Entrées on Trays offers all the convenience of some of the area's best dining establishments delivered right to your front door. Entrées delivers items from a number of establishments including Sully's, Niko's, China Best, Longhorn Barbecue, Makena's and the Lame Duck. Delivery service is offered from 5 p.m.-9 p.m., seven days a week. The delivery charge is $1 per entree. Call for a complete restaurant listing, price list and service area.

Espresso Delizioso, 706 N Monroe (326-5958). This combination coffee house cum restaurant serves hearty peasant food from around the world. The smoking area upstairs with its revolving display of local art work attracts students, while law and business professionals from the nearby Courthouse meet downstairs. Breakfast is served 7 a.m.-11 a.m., lunch 11 a.m.-5:30 p.m. and dinner 5:30 p.m.-11:00. p.m. Friday and Saturday there's a limited menu available from 11 p.m. until closing time (2 a.m.). The extensive menu is complimented by daily specials. Check the monthly music calendar for local bands playing blues, jazz, folk, swing and Celtic sounds. Music starts after 9 p.m., depending on when the musicians arrive. Beer and wine. Closed Sunday. No reservations. No credit cards. Inexpensive to moderate.

Europa, 125 S Wall (455-4051). Europa Pizzaria specializes in pizzas, calzones, hot and cold sandwiches, and pasta dishes. It's also well known for its wonderful bread dough. The dough recipe is based on an Yugoslavian family recipe and has a wonderful texture and flavor. The brick walls and wood beam decor create a nicer ambiance than an ordinary "pizza" establishment. For a tasty treat, try the pita roll ups or one of the homemade desserts. Beer and wine. Open seven days a week for lunch and dinner. No reservations required. Credit cards. Moderate.

Fitzbillie's, 1325 W 1st (747-1834). Fitzbillie's was once the largest automobile showroom in the state and the original 1925 mosaic tile floors are still intact. Brightly lit floor-to-ceiling windows are also well preserved. Take a peek at the pictures dotting the wall behind the self-service counter for more history. Freshly baked bagels, soups, sandwiches, bakery goods and salads, and a wide selection of Northwest micro-brewed beers make this a popular lunch spot. Open seven days. No credit cards. Inexpensive.

Frank's Diner, 1516 W 2nd (455-7402). This 1906 Smith and Barney Observation Car owned by Frank Knight was originally a diner in Seattle. When Knight's lease expired, he had it trucked to Spokane and set on a sight previously owned by a monument company. Frank's operates on a first come, first served basis, with booth and counter seating for only 44. Often, on weekends, there are 15-30 minute waits for the mouth-watering breakfasts. It's worth the wait though, especially if you're hungry for large portions of down-home cooking. Cornbeef hash for breakfast, meatloaf sandwiches for lunch and mashed potatoes and turkey for dinner are only a few of the offerings. Open seven days. No reservations. Credit cards. Inexpensive to moderate.

Four Seasons, N 222 Howard (747-2315). The granddaddy of coffee outlets in Spokane has roasted and served coffee since 1976. In 1982, Four Seasons moved from their original Wall Street location to the Howard Street site. The current location sports red-brick walls, hardwood floors and the smell of roasting beans. In the front of the store you can purchase beans by the pound and browse through a variety of coffee makers, cups, kitchen items and a high quality, seasonal selection of gifts. The rear of the store is a full-service espresso bar offering muffins and some desserts. Indoor seating year-round and patio tables in the summer. Open Monday through Friday 7:30 a.m.-7 p.m., Saturday 7:30 a.m.-6 p.m. and Sunday 11 a.m.-5 p.m. Credit cards.

Fugazzi,1 N Post (624-1133). Fugazzi serves breakfast, lunch and dinner. Though it's only been open a short time by Spokane standards, the restaurant has quickly earned a loyal following. A slate-tiled entry, exposed brick walls and cast iron columns add to the classy-yet-casual atmosphere. Pizza, pasta, sandwiches and salads are served cafeteria-style during the busy lunch hour. Dinner is offered Thursday through Saturday and is served at cloth-covered tables. House specialties include Northwest cuisine and delectable desserts baked on the premises. Wine and beer. Closed Sunday. Lunches Monday through Saturday. Reservations recommended for dinner. Credit cards. Expensive.

Great Harvest, 816 W Sprague (624-9370). Since opening in 1980, the Great Harvest Bread Company has developed a loyal following. They mill their own wheat and use only five main ingredients: flour, yeast, water, and salt, plus honey or molasses as sweeteners. Their most popular bread is honey whole wheat, but don't miss the Oregon herb, sunflower molasses or tomato herb. For those who want to eat in-store, soups, salads, sandwiches and espresso drinks are served. No credit cards. Open Monday through Friday 6:30 a.m.-5:30 p.m.

High Nooner, 237 W Riverside (838-5288). The High Nooner is a recent addition to the downtown area. Eat in the open and airy dining space or have your lunch delivered to your office. Hot and cold sandwiches, salads and soups, and espresso make up the menu. Savor the complimentary chocolate chip cookies for dessert. They also have a Northpointe Plaza location (9996 N Newport Highway, 467-2276) for those traveling near the far northern end of town. Delivery service available for free with a $6 minimum order within a two-mile radius. No alcohol. Open for lunch only, Monday through Friday. No credit cards. Inexpensive.

Java Junky's, N 211 Division (458-2326). The decor is eclectic with wooden spool tables, macramé hangers, a collection of chairs from several different furniture periods and hardwood floors. Java Junky's is a full-fledged coffee house made for sipping, talking with friends and people watching. Don't miss house specialties such as a rice latté or soy carob mocha. Open 24-hours a day, it's populated with a mixture of bohemians, college students and graveyard-shift employees. Muffins, baklava, cookies and such also served. No credit cards.

Luigi's, 113 N Bernard (624-5226). Luigi's takes pasta dining a step beyond a filling meal. Lasagna, seafood, fettuccine, gnocchi, eggplant parmesan, rigatoni . . . it's all here and well prepared. The bread, minestrone soup and house salad make a great light meal. At one time, the high-backed wooden booths similar to the ones you'll find at Luigi's were outlawed in Spokane for providing "too much privacy!" Full bar. Open seven days. Small outdoor area in the summer. Reservations highly recommended. Credit cards. Moderate.

Mayfair, W 2nd and S Washington (624-4206). Mayfair has offered gravy, eggs, meat and potatoes since 1945. This is home cooking served in a Naugahyde and linoleum environment. It ain't fancy, but you do get generous servings and stick-to-your-ribs good food. Lounge. Breakfast, lunch and dinners. No credit cards. Inexpensive.

Metro Cafe, 502 W Riverside (747-8250). The Metro Cafe, located on the second floor at the corner of Riverside and Stevens, offers cafeteria-style eating and a great view. Employees from nearby banks and office buildings flock here for lunch, and the atmosphere can be hectic. The hot entrees served during lunch hours go fast, so come early to assure yourself a serving. Open Monday through Friday from 7 a.m. to 5 p.m. Inexpensive.

Milford's Fish House and Oyster Bar, 719 N Monroe (326-7251). Known for a wide selection of fresh seafood, plus chicken and beef, Milford's is an attractive place to entertain out-of-town guests. High-backed wooden booths, intimate tables and walls filled with old photographs make dining casual, yet refined. The kitchen was originally a pool room and the lobby a barber shop. Full bar. Open for dinner only. Closed Monday. Reservations suggested. Credit cards. Expensive.

Ming Wah, 1618 W 3rd (455-9474). Ming Wah serves Cantonese cuisine piping hot and in large portions. There are no pretensions to authentic Oriental decor. You'll find Naugahyde benches and linoleum table tops, though there is an authentic Lion's head mask behind the cash register. Regular customers don't seem to require more ambiance, and you'll usually find several large parties in the private dining areas. Lounge. Open for lunch Monday through Friday, dinners, Monday through Saturday. Closed Sunday. Credit cards. Moderate.

II Moon Cafe, Mars Hotel, 300 W Sprague (747-6277). The inside of this fine-dining establishment is lined with basalt cliffs. Tree trunks and a waterfall add to the decor, and the cocktail lounge resembles a cave. It's not just the unusual surroundings which draw diners back. The food is as excellent as it is eclectic. From tournedo shiitake to calimari, spinach enchiladas to fish tacos, the menu is constantly evolving and unusual. There's a kids' menu, which is also available for those with smaller appetites. Full bar. Open 24-hours a day, seven days a week. Reservations recommended. Moderate to expensive.

Mustard Seed, 245 W Spokane Falls Blvd. Across from the Opera House (747-2689). The Mustard Seed dishes up a contemporary mix of Oriental/Japanese/Polynesian fare in a casually elegant setting. Shrimp, chicken, beef, pork and vegetable dishes are offered family style or in half portions for children and those with smaller appetites. Most popular meals include Bong Bong Chicken or Chicken Osaka. Lounge. Open seven days with an abbreviated menu from 10 p.m. to 1 a.m., Thursday through Saturday. Credit cards. Moderate.

Niko's, 725 W Riverside (624-7444). For over 14 years, this family-owned restaurant has provided consistently good lamb, chicken, beef and vegetarian dishes. Gyros, moussaka, souvlakia and kabasa are a few of the house specialties. The soup and salad bar is popular during lunch. Beer and wine. Open Monday through Friday for lunch and dinner, Saturday for dinner only. Closed Sunday. Credit cards. Moderate.

Olive Garden, 221 N Wall (624-1853). The Olive Garden is located in what used to be a turn-of-the-century fire hall. It offers traditional Italian fare for families. With ample size servings and a children's menu, this national chain restaurant creates a nice dining experience. Be sure to sample the bread sticks and cappellini primavera. Open seven days for lunch and dinner. Reservations for parties of 10 or more. Credit cards. Moderate.

Onion, 302 W Riverside (747-3852). Owner Larry Brown opened this downtown burger and beer eatery in 1974. Though it's still famous for the burgers, the menu has expanded over the years to include a range of hot sandwiches, pastas, Mexican dishes, salads, stir-fry items and vegetarian selections. This is a popular spot for business meals and family dining, with hardwood floors, an antique bar, pressed tin ceiling and wooden booths as well as tables. Helium balloons and a children's menu available. Same menu for lunch and dinner. Open seven days for lunch and dinner. Reservations recommended for parties of six or more. Credit cards. Inexpensive to moderate.

Patsy Clark's Mansion, 2208 W 2nd (838-8300). Just walking through the doorway of this 1897 mansion, created by Kirkland K. Cutter for mining millionaire Patrick "Patsy" Clark, brings back the days of lavishly spent pre-income-tax wealth. If dining among carved-stucco ceilings, an onyx fireplace, Tiffany lamps, 14-foot stained glass windows, Turkish rugs, Louis XIV furniture, an English grandfather clock and cherubs painted on the ceilings by a French artist do not spell opulence, nothing will.

Patsy Clark's restaurant in Browne's Addition

Photo by Ron Swords

Almost destroyed by the wrecking ball during the 1970s, the mansion was saved and redesigned into a restaurant in 1981. This restaurant is synonymous with elegant dining in Spokane and serves lunch and dinner seven days a week, except Saturday, when only dinner is served. Full bar. Reservations strongly recommended. Credit cards. Expensive.

Rancho Chico, 9205 N Division (467-0022) and 128 W 3rd (456-4806). If you're looking for inexpensive, high-quality Mexican food served fast and in heaping portions, Ranch Chico is a best bet. Their prawn dishes are excellent, as is the peanut butter-based chicken *mole*. Beer and wine. Both locations open seven days a week. Inexpensive.

Rice Time Express, 110 N Post (747-2695). Try this simple fare as an alternative to the soup and sandwich meal. For a wholesome and filling lunch or dinner, chose from chicken, vegetables or beef over white rice. When your meal arrives piping hot, fresh and tasty, you'll wonder why you ever ate burgers in the first place. Open Monday through Saturday. Inexpensive.

Ripples on the River, 700 N Division (326-5577). Located in Cavanaugh's River Inn, Ripples restaurant serves breakfast, lunch and dinner. Fresh seafood, beef, poultry and pasta entrees highlight the dinner menu. The terrific view of the river makes this a popular lunch spot with the professional crowd. Summers, you can dine on the patio. Lounge. Reservations recommended for lunch and weekend dinners. Credit cards. Moderate to expensive.

Riverview Thai, 621 W Mallon. At the Flour Mill (325-8370). The Riverview Thai serves authentic dishes at reasonable prices. There are lunch and dinner specials plus a lunch buffet. Don't miss the peanut or green curry sauces. The peanut sauce in particular is so popular you can order an extra side of it for only a $1. At lunch time, try the buffet as a great way to sample a variety of dishes. Located in the historic Flour Mill shopping complex, the restaurant also provides front-row window seating with a view of the Spokane River. Beer and wine. Open seven days. Dinner reservations accepted. Credit cards. Inexpensive.

Rock City Grill, 505 W Riverside (455-4400). This restaurant cum grill serves a variety of pizza and pasta dishes. Try the Thai or smoked chicken pizza cooked over applewood. Pasta sauces include clam, marinara, alfredo, cajun and tequilla-style to name a few. Vinyl tablecloths, booths, tables and tomato-can decorations provide a family-style atmosphere. Children's menu available. Full bar, large wine list and micro-brew beers on tap. Open for lunch and dinner seven days. Reservations recommended for weekend dinners. Credit cards. Moderate.

Rocky Rococo, 520 W Main (747-1000). Rocky's is known for thick topping, deep-dish pizzas, but you can also order thin crust pizza, pizza by the slice, spaghetti, fettucini or graze through a fair-sized salad bar. The deep rich-colored decor, with raised platform seating to break the noise level, is a step up from traditional pizza places. Children under five receive a free spaghetti dinner with any pizza order. Beer and wine. No credit cards. Inexpensive.

Salty's, 510 N Lincoln (327-8888). Every seat in Salty's has a good view of the Spokane Falls splashing over tiered basalt outcroppings (except during the summer when the river dries to a trickle). The decor is modern with an emphasis on Northwest colors and motifs. The menu focuses on seafood, beef and pasta dishes. Enjoy outdoor-deck dining in the spring and summer. Sunday there's a seafood brunch. Kids under six are served free. Full bar. Open seven days a week for lunch and dinner. Expensive.

Shack, 1301 W 3rd (747-2713). The Shack has been a Spokane institution since the 1930s and still serves all the traditional "diner" fare— steaks, seafood, steamed clams, grilled venison with onions. No one leaves hungry. Lounge. Open for breakfast, lunch and dinner Monday through Saturday. Closed Sunday. Credit cards. Inexpensive.

Spaghetti Factory, 152 S Monroe (624-8916). The Spaghetti Factory is always a good bet when you're looking for consistently good meals that won't leave you hungry. An ideal choice for dining out with kids and/or casual, relaxed dining. Both adult and children's menus have expanded over the last few years and now offer lasagna, tortellini, chicken and fettucini dishes. Full bar. Open seven days a week for dinner only. No reservations taken—first come, first serve basis. Credit cards. Inexpensive.

Spokandy, 1412 W 3rd (624-1969). For over 80 years, Spokandy has been crafting homemade candies. They offer something for every sweet tooth, including mouth-watering specialties such as hand-dipped nuts, mint truffles, peppermint bark and peanut brittle. Candy orders can also be mailed to you or your lucky friends. Open Monday through Saturday 9:30 a.m.-5:30 p.m.

Suki Yaki Inn, 119 N Bernard (624-0022). For 44 years customers have slipped off their shoes and entered private tatami rooms to enjoy chicken, beef and fish dishes prepared in the traditional Japanese manner. Sashimi, sushi, tempura, teriyaki and suki yaki are all offered. Yosa Nabe, a Japanese version of French bouillabaisse, is one of their more popular dishes. Full bar. Open Monday through Saturday for dinner only. Reservations recommended on weekends. Credit cards. Moderate.

Sully's, 259 W Spokane Falls Blvd. (456-7410). In spite of an excellent location near the Opera House and Convention Center, this spot has been plagued with a number of ownership changes. Sully's appears to prove the exception. Along with Northern Italian specialties, the menu offers an array of beef and chicken dishes. Open for lunch Monday through Friday and dinner, Monday through Saturday. Sunday openings only for special occasions such as Mother's Day and Bloomsday. Credit cards. Moderate to expensive.

Thai Cafe, 410 W Sprague (838-4783). The oldest Thai restaurant in Spokane serves a wide variety of chicken, meat, prawn and vegetarian dishes. Owner Val Chalard rates his entrees from one to five stars; one star is the mildest, while five stars is the hottest. The black rice pudding topped with ice cream and coconut milk is an excellent choice for dessert. Open for lunch Monday through Friday and dinner, Monday through Saturday. No credit cards. Inexpensive.

Toucan's Restaurant & Bakery, 912 W Sprague (624-4294). Miniature lights strung along red-brick walls, bright fabric tablecloths, and a large and varied menu make this a pleasantly casual spot. This nice neighborhood restaurant in the heart of downtown serves breakfast, lunch, dinner and the world's largest cookies. Closed Sundays. Credit cards. Inexpensive.

Upstairs Downtown, Howard and Main, 2nd Floor Bennett Block (747-9830). Upstairs Downtown is considered by many to be one of the most romantic dinner spots in town. During the lunch hours, professionals fill the tables fast. It serves an international cuisine with lamb, beef, pork, chicken and fish entrees. Reservations recommended for dinner, but not taken for lunch. Monday through Saturday open for lunch. Dinners served only Friday and Saturday. Closed Sunday. Credit cards. Moderate to expensive.

Viewpoint Restaurant, top floor, Farm Credit Building (838-9219). You can't beat this spot for one of the best views of Spokane. Hardwood floors, potted trees in terra cotta urns and floor to ceiling windows with northern views make this a quiet and relaxing place to have lunch. Marriott Corporation operates the cafeteria-style food line and offers several hot entrees, cold sandwiches, soups, salads and Starbucks coffee. The west end of the dining area is smoking, the east for non-smokers. Open 7 a.m. until 3 p.m. Monday through Friday, catered events are held in the late afternoons and evenings. No credit cards. Inexpensive.

Windows of the Seasons, 303 W North River Drive (328-9526). Located in Cavanaugh's Inn at the Park, Windows affords splendid views of Riverfront Park, the river and the downtown skyline. The menu features Pacific Northwest foods, including seafood, poultry and beef entrees. Full bar. Open seven days. Sunday brunch and dinner only. Reservations recommended. Credit cards. Expensive.

North

Arny's, 1229 N Hamilton (487-9588). Arny's is characterized by tile floors, counter seating, 50s music over the loudspeakers, and good, good food. Expect full servings cooked before your eyes. Kids love watching hashbrowns, pancakes, hamburgers and the huge B-52 Bomber house special (a giant bacon burger) sizzling on the grill, while the milkshake machine whirs around the corner. Espresso drinks served also. Order breakfast, lunch and dinners from the same menu. Come early for meal times because the counter fills fast. Open seven days a week. No credit cards. Inexpensive.

Azar's Cafe, 3818 N Nevada (487-0132). The outside of this small cafe belies the good food inside. Middle Eastern dishes such as gyros, falafil, lentil soup, hummus and pita bread are offered alongside generous hamburgers, grilled cheese sandwiches and french fries. The Lebanese family owning this Azar's is related to the family operating the Monroe Street location. (See next entry). No liquor. Open Monday through Saturday for breakfast, lunch and dinner, Sunday for breakfast and early lunch only. No credit cards. Inexpensive.

Azar's Restaurant, 2501 N Monroe (326-7171). Despite the Lebanese textiles, pictures and jewelry, Azar's still retains a Spokane neighborhood feel. There are some Middle Eastern dishes available here which are not served at the Nevada location. Try the sambosa as an appetizer. Other specialties include gyros, kabobs, souvlaki, vegetarian dishes, baklava and a children's menu with American fare. Espresso is also served. Belly dancing is presented the first and third Fridays of the month. Beer and wine. Open for breakfast, lunch and dinner seven days a week. No credit cards. Inexpensive.

Breadbasket, 800 Shadle Center (across from Lamonts); (326-2515). This is a casual dining spot offering a full menu. House favorites include fresh-baked bread and homemade soup served in a mini-loaf. Breadbasket offers prime rib seven days a week and German specialties Thursday through Sunday. Children's menu available. If Shadle Park Mall is hosting an event, there may be a short wait for a table. Reservations only recommended for parties of eight or more. Lounge. Open Monday through Saturday for lunch and dinner, Sunday for brunch and dinner. Credit cards. Moderate.

Bong's Oriental Garden, 3004 N Monroe (327-3770). Bong's offers a combination of Mandarin, Szechuan and Korean dishes. An American menu is also available. *Bul go ki* (a Korean-style beef dish) and *gar bi* (short ribs) are specialties of the house. Buffet offered Monday through Friday. Full bar. Open seven days a week for lunch and dinner. Credit cards. Inexpensive.

Chapter Eleven, 9304 N Division (467-7011); 105 E Mission (326-0466) or 7720 E Sprague (928-1787). The three Chapter Eleven locations in town are all decorated in a 70s barn-board decor. Each offers beef, chicken and seafood dishes. Choose from four "cuts" of the famous prime rib (petite- to maxi-sized servings), then take a trip through the salad bar. Be sure to sample the house dressing. Children's menu available. Full bar. Open Monday through Friday for lunch and seven days a week for dinner. Weekend and holiday reservations recommended. Credit cards. Moderate to expensive.

Chic-a-Ria, 1812 W Francis, 5 Mile Shopping Center (326-2214).Chic-a-Ria offers fine dining for both lunch and dinners, with a nice selection of appetizers, seafood, pork, lamb, chicken, pasta and salads. Their New Orleans Style Grilled Prawns with rosemary creole butter sauce and Galliano chicken stuffed with prosciutto, jarlsberg cheese and fresh sage are especially popular. There's an 'early bird' dinner special every day until 6 p.m. and a children's menu. Lounge.

A to-go menu is also available. Reservations recommended on weekends. Credit cards. Moderate to expensive.

China Dragon, 27 E Queen, across from Northtown Mall (483-5209). Mandarin, Szechuan, Hunan and Cantonese dishes are brought to your table in large, family-style portions. Cooks prepare your order within view, which fascinates young ones. Live piano music nightly in the ornately decorated dining room with carved wood and embroidered silk tapestries. Booth and table seating available. Full bar. Open seven days. Reservations recommended for parties of six or more. Credit cards. Inexpensive to moderate.

Coffee Caper, N 6900 Division (482-3464) or 4519 N Nevada (482-5504). These two outlets serve espresso drinks using Oregon Coffee Roaster beans. The outlet inside the Eagle store also sells hot dogs, German sausages, corn dogs, chili and nachos. The Nevada Street location carries muffins and brownies, but no hot foods. At either location you can order and pick up whole beans. There are a few tables at both locations, though only in the summer at the Nevada spot. The North Division location is open Monday through Friday 9 a.m.-8:00 p.m., Saturday 8:30 a.m.-7:30 p.m. and Sunday 9 a.m.-7:30 p.m. The Nevada location is open Monday through Saturday 6 a.m.-7 p.m. and Sunday 8 a.m.-6 p.m.

Commellini's, 14100 N Dartford Dr. (466-2088). Looking for a romantic setting? Try Commellini's. The restaurant is located in an older home on a 100-acre estate. The bubbling sounds of the Little Spokane River add to the ambiance. Commellini's has served traditional Italian cuisine since 1938. Their full menu offers over 80 selections to choose from. Full lounge. Open for dinner every day except Monday. Reservations recommended on weekends. Credit cards. Moderate to expensive.

DeCaro's, 922 N Division (327-5259). For years DeCaro's was a landmark on Monroe Street. Since this family-owned restaurant moved to its larger Division Street location, more families have been able to enjoy its casual, comfortable atmosphere. It's a very family-orientated environment with an eight-page menu offering veal, chicken, steak and pasta dishes. Children's menu also available. Large groups can be accommodated. Full bar. Open for lunch and dinner Monday through Friday, for dinner only Saturday and Sunday. Reservations recommended on weekends. Credit cards. Inexpensive.

Dewey Chetham & Howe, 3022 N Division (326-7741). With its brass fixtures and forest green decor, Dewey's creates an upscale, yet casual atmosphere attractive to the professional crowd. The restaurant offers soups, salads, sandwiches and special dishes for lunch. The dinner menu, with its selections of chicken, seafood and beef entrees, makes a sure-bet for entertaining guests and finding something for everyone. Children's menu available. Full bar. Open seven days a week. Reservations recommended for weekends, especially in the non-smoking section. Credit cards. Moderate.

Eat-Rite Vegetarian, Corner of Washington and Montgomery (325-1957). Eat-Rite Vegetarian has offered vegan dishes (free of all animal products, including butter, cream, cheese and eggs) for the past five years. Look for them in the basement of the Look-Rite Wedding Chapel. Eat-Rite serves both lunch and dinner with two special daily entrees. Sandwiches and an extensive salad bar are also available. Open 11:30 a.m.-7 p.m. Monday through Friday. Closed Saturday. Open for brunch on Sunday 10 a.m.-5 p.m. No credit cards. Inexpensive.

Five Mile Heights, 6409 N Maple (328-4764). Be prepared. This place is loud, fun and filled with families and sports teams. The little ones jump in orange balls and ride mechanical toys or play video games, while you choose from a wide selection of appetizers, salads, calzones and pizzas. Beer and wine. Open seven days a week. Credit cards. Inexpensive.

Geno's, 1414 N Hamilton (487-9541). For nearly 30 years, Geno's has served neighborhood hospitality along with generous portions of pizza, lasagna, spaghetti, ravioli and steak dishes. Red and white checked tablecloths, flickering candles and dim interior all add to the casually intimate atmosphere. Families are welcomed as old friends, and the wait staff soon begins calling you by name. Beer and wine. First come, first served basis makes for a bit of a wait on weekends. Closed Sunday and Monday. No credit cards. Inexpensive.

Gloria Jean's Gourmet Coffee, 4570 N Division, Northtown Mall (489-0059). Gloria Jean's is a Chicago-based coffee retailer offering beans and espresso drinks to go. While some of the flavored and regular beans are roasted by their parent company, they also carry beans by Longbottom's. They sell pastries as well as teapots, coffee cups, espresso makers and grinders. Open same hours as the Northtown Mall. Credit cards.

Granny's Buffet, 9606 N Newport Highway (467-3440). At Granny's, you're sure to find plenty to fill your platter. There is a different theme daily: Monday is Seniors' Day with more traditional dishes such as meatloaf, macaroni and cheese and pork roast served; Tuesday, Oriental food is served; Wednesday, Italian; Thursday, Mexican; and Friday, Seafood. Saturday is Family Night and carved roast beef and ham are served. Granny's caters to the senior crowd, even offering a special Senior Club card and a free birthday meal.

Meals for children under 12 cost 45¢ per year of age. No alcohol. Open seven days a week. Credit cards. Inexpensive.

Jandyl's Desserts, 1404 W Northwest Blvd. (326-2564). Jandyl's has come a long way from its origins in the owner's basement to becoming the dessert served by Alaska and Horizon Airlines. They've recently expanded their deli case for walk-in customers, though most of their cakes, pies, tortes, cookies and cheesecakes are special ordered. A popular favorite is the chocolate torte (a three-layer devil's food cake). Open Monday through Friday. No credit cards.

Just American Desserts, 6406 N Monroe (328-5889). For those accustomed to driving to the south side of town or out to the valley to pick up one of Just American Dessert's cakes and cheesecakes, this northside store is a welcome addition. They sell both by the slice and whole deserts. If you have a favorite—like chocolate velvet mousse cake or white chocolate-raspberry cheesecake—call a day before to ensure it will be available. They take special orders and prepare seasonal holiday desserts. Open Monday through Saturday 10 a.m.-6 p.m. Credit cards accepted for purchases above $10.00.

Lai Lai, 2931 N Division (326-3462). This cozy little restaurant serves Mandarin, Hunan, Szechuan, Cantonese and American dishes, which are fresh and flavorful. They also offer a senior citizen's menu. Full bar. Open for lunch and dinner seven days a week. Reservations taken. Credit cards. Inexpensive.

Lindaman's Cafe, 6412 N Monroe (324-9252). Lindaman's Cafe used to be Lindaman's Lasagna. The owner charged the name because he now offers a variety of dishes. The cafe still serves about seven different types of lasagna daily, and also offers other types of pasta, salads, rice dishes and desserts. The cafe seats about 30. Patio seating is available during the warmer months. Espresso drinks, beer and wine also served. Closed Sunday. No reservations. Credit Cards. Inexpensive.

Little Italy, 7442 N Division (487-7777). The slogan "life is too short for ordinary pizza" and a menu with 11 Italian specialty pizzas tells you you're in serious pizza country. The owner originally hails from New York, which is the next closest stop to eating pizzas that duplicate the famous "Little Italy" style. There's free delivery within a three to four mile radius of Francis and Division and plenty of coupon specials. Try them once, and you'll be hooked for life. Open seven days a week. Call in advance for quick pick up. No credit cards. Inexpensive.

Lotus Seed, 1212 N Hamilton (483-7554). Owners Amy and Philip Tran offer customers an experience to taste food prepared

Vietnamese style. Choose from pork, chicken, rice, noodle dishes, soups and stews. If you can't decide what to eat from the extensive menu, the friendly help will assist you. The decor is unpretentious and silverware must be requested if you choose not to use chopsticks. Eleven tables fill quickly with students and business people; so come early to find a seat. No liquor, though they do offer coconut juice, French coffee and tea. Closed between lunches and dinners. Reservations only for large parties. Credit cards. Inexpensive.

Mama Mia's, 7706 N Division (482-7162). Mama Mia's is owned by the same family as Rudolpho's in the Valley. This small trattoria offers friendly service, filling food and a neighborhood atmosphere. Chicken cacciatore, eggplant parmigiana, calzones, steaks, gnocci and scallops compliment other pasta dishes. Try the tortellini Rodolfo for a filling meal and don't overlook the yeasty, homemade Italian breadrolls. Beer and wine. Open seven days a week for lunch and dinner. Reservations for parties of six or more. Credit cards. Inexpensive to moderate.

Marrakesh, 2008 W Northwest Blvd. (328-9733). The Marrakesh's draped ceilings, floors covered in oriental rugs, hassock or cushioned-bench seating, create an unique dining experience. There is no silverware, instead you receive a generous towel. Once you've washed the meal begins, starting with soup sipped from the bowl, salad scooped up with bread and then a bastila—a pie of crisp pastry and delicate stuffing.

The set price per meal is $14.50 and includes five courses. Choose from lamb, chicken, rabbit, fish, beef or vegetarian entrees. After your meal is cleared away, it's time for a ritual hand washing. If you don't select a dessert, you'll have perfumed water sprinkled over your hands to protect against evil spirits. A heavily sweetened tea flavored with mint is then offered from a silver ewer to aid digestion. Don't expect to rush your meal. Belly dancing is provided on Friday and Saturday nights. Closed Monday. Open for dinner only Tuesday through Saturday. Reservations recommended on weekends. Credit cards. Expensive.

Milk Bottle, 802 W Garland (328-4540). The Milk Bottle, built in 1932 to resemble a giant milk bottle, was once a dairy outlet. Today, it's a restaurant serving hamburgers, hot dogs, pies, fries and sandwiches. A specialty is the Jumbo Burger, a seven-ounce patty of lean hamburger served up with curly fries. If you've got any room left over, sample any of 16 flavors of ice cream while you listen to a working juke box play 50s music. Counter or table seating is available. Closed Sunday and at 6 p.m. the rest of the week. No credit cards. Inexpensive.

The "Milk Bottle" diner in the Garland
district of north Spokane
Photo by Ron Swords

Onion, 7522 N Division (482-6100). Cousin to the Onion restaurant downtown, this spot offers the same varied menu of burgers, sandwiches, Mexican dishes, appetizers, vegetarian specialties, soups and salads. The decor, with its walls of paned windows, dark, rich colors and brass railings, makes it popular for business lunches and entertaining guests. Sunday Brunch offered. Nonsmoking except in the lounge for those 21 or older. Children's menu. Full bar. Reservations taken for week nights and parties larger than five. Credit cards. Inexpensive to moderate.

Panhandler Pies, 3525 N Division (326-0530). Many will remember this as Pioneer Pies. This new restaurant attracts the same family-type crowd looking for something more than a quick bite to eat. The antiques hanging from the walls and dining areas surrounded by sound barriers make dining here a pleasant experience. The fare includes chicken-fried steak, gravies, sauces, burgers and sandwiches. Panhandler Pies serves breakfast, lunch and dinner with children's menu available. And yes, they still serve a variety of pies. No alcohol. No reservations are accepted with seating on a first come, first served basis. Credit cards. Inexpensive.

Papagayo's, 4111 N Division (483-8346). At Papagayo's, a 40-item salsa bar and a dozen low-fat items round out a traditional Mexican menu. Thick adobe walls and hanging parrots create a fun environment. If you're in doubt of what to order for lunch, try the fajita buffet served during the week. Full bar. Open for lunch Monday through Saturday, dinner seven days a week. No reservations taken. Credit cards. Inexpensive to moderate.

Peking North, 4120 N Division (484-4321). Peking North is one of two restaurants owned by the same family. The other restaurant is the Szechuan Restaurant located at 6508 N Division, only two blocks north of Peking North. Both locations serve Mongolian barbecue for lunch and Mandarin and Szechuan dishes for lunch and dinner. The quick service and generous portions have created a loyal following. Full bar. Open seven days a week for lunch and dinner. Reservations for parties of six or more. Credit cards. Inexpensive.

Pete's Pizza, 821 E Sharp (487-9795) or 2328 W Northwest Blvd. (326-1900). Pete's has been a Spokane institution for over 20 years. Serving sandwiches and pizza as well as "the world's best calzone," the small, homey atmosphere attracts families and the college crowd. Open seven days a week. Beer and wine. Credit cards. Inexpensive.

Pleasant Blends, 9301 N Division (467-3790). This small storefront shop sells Longbottom beans roasted in Hillsboro, Oregon, to both retail and wholesale customers. Espresso drinks and pastry items are also offered. A smattering of tables are available for those who want to sit and sip. Open Monday through Friday 7 a.m.-6:30 p.m. and Saturday 8 a.m.-5 p.m. Credit cards.

Red Robin, 9904 N Newport Highway (467-3382). This chain restaurant offers a step up from fast food with the selection of appetizers, salads, burgers and pasta dishes. Children's menu available. Full bar. Open seven days a week. No reservations. Credit cards. Inexpensive.

SS Beryl, 6404 N Wall (467-5490). Discover a seafood taste treat in this small neighborhood restaurant. Decorated with a nautical theme, SS Beryl prepares salmon, cod, halibut and other assorted fish dishes without a lot of fancy sauces and nouveau additions. Open for lunch and dinner seven days a week. Reservations recommended on weekends. Moderate.

Spaghetti Station, 718 E Francis (484-7117). The northside Spaghetti Station features a larger menu than their valley counterpart. Halibut, steak, and veal dishes are available, in addition to the pasta selections. You can dine in a full-sized English bus as a toy train circles the restaurant overhead. Kids' menu available. Full bar. Open Monday through Saturday for lunch, seven days a week for dinner. Reservations accepted. Credit cards. Inexpensive.

Spokane Coffee Exchange & Eatery, 6302 N Market (468-9133). With its French Provincial Country decor, red-brown tile floors and Windsor chairs, this is a charming and refreshing place for breakfast or lunch. Though they have a drive-thru window, try to take the time to enjoy the delightful interior. Coffee by Four Seasons, huge cinnamon rolls, sandwiches, salads, soups and espresso drinks are among the selections. Open Monday through Friday 6 a.m.-3 p.m. and Saturday 8 a.m.-3 p.m. Credit cards.

Sportsman Cafe, 6410 N Market (467-6388). The Sportsman has long been known for its casual, relaxed atmosphere and good service. The menu ranges from home-style favorites like breaded pork chops to more gourmet fare such as jumbo tiger shrimp or filet mignon. Full service bar. Open for breakfast, lunch and dinner seven days a week. Moderate.

Stadium, 4423 W Wellesley (327-1551). With its location across from Joe Albi Stadium, this spot has long been a favorite stop after sporting events. Pizzas, calzones, sandwiches and a salad bar are available for both lunch and dinner. Every Tuesday night, a family special is available, where you pay for a small pizza and receive a medium or pay for a medium and receive a giant one. Open seven days a week. Beer and wine. Credit cards. Inexpensive.

Starbucks, 12408 N Division, Wandermere Mall (468-9461) or 1802 W Francis, 5 Mile Plaza (328-1581). It seemed to take forever for this Seattle based corporation, nationally synonymous with serious coffee drinking, to cross the Cascades and open a Spokane location. They found a ready and waiting audience. Starbucks is known for consistent flavor, freshness and quality from both their beans and brewed drinks. With seating available for only a dozen at a time, most customers walk in to buy a drink, a pound of beans, a mug or gift item to go. Cookies, muffins, scones and some pastries are also available. Both locations are open Monday through Friday 6 a.m.-9 p.m., Saturday 7 a.m.-9 p.m. and Sunday 7 a.m.-8 p.m. Credit cards.

Swackhammer's, 21 E Lincoln Road (467-5210). You can't miss this restaurant. It's the one with the Cadillac sticking out the roof. With walls crammed full of memorabilia, Swackhammer's sets the mood for a fun lunch or dinner. Kids and adults alike delight in everything from a Harley Davidson motorcycle to baseball mitts and trumpets. Choose burgers, sandwiches, salads, pasta and fish dishes from an extensive menu. Children's menu also available. Full bar. Open seven days a week. Reservations for parties of eight or more. Credit cards. Inexpensive to moderate.

South

Adolfson's at the Glover Mansion, 321 W 8th (838-8824). Adolfson's is located in the mansion of Spokane's founding father, James Glover. Northwest Cuisine is featured here. Try the King Salmon wrapped in phyllo pastry with lemon caper sauce. White linen tablecloths and tapered candles create a romantic atmosphere. Try balcony seating for an extra special dining experience. Be sure to request a tour of the Glover home. Rich in architectural details, it showcases the city's first indoor bathrooms. Reservations recommended for lunch. Valet parking is available for both lunch and dinner. Full bar. Lunch served Tuesday through Friday and dinner, Wednesday through Friday. Credit cards. Expensive.

Alpine Deli, 417 E 3rd (455-5148). This store-cum-deli serves lunch from 10:30 to 4:00 p.m. Bratwurst, knackwurst, weisswurt, kassler rippchen and sauerkraut are a few of the house specialties. Many customers are first generation immigrants, who enjoy the bilingual staff and products from Germany. Also browse through the selection of imported groceries, wines, beer steins, delftware, and meat and cheese items, all available for purchase. Open Monday through Saturday. Inexpensive.

Asian Cafe, 1422 S Lincoln (747-4344). This small restaurant specializes in Laotian and Chinese dishes. Among the menu items are stuffed cucumber soup, roast beef salad with lemon juice and a variety of curries made with homemade blended spices. Open Monday through Saturdays for lunch and dinner. Inexpensive.

Café Roma, 2727 S Mt Vernon (NW corner of Lincoln Heights Shopping Center) (534-5540). This two-time winner of *Epicurean Delight* magazine's People's Choice Award offers gourmet Northern Italian dining at its best. Their Spaghetti a la Carbonara is a favorite. Be sure to sample the Chicken Kebob cooked in saffron. They've received nationwide TV exposure for their mushroom burger (offered only at lunch). Both professionals and those seeking a romantic ambiance enjoy the European decor complimented by two solariums, outdoor-patio seating and a profusion of plants. Beer or wine. Reservations recommended. Credit cards. Moderate.

Chapala, 2820 E 29th (534-7388). Chapala's all Mexican chefs produce authentic south-of-the-border cuisine. Though they've been open only a little over three years, the popularity of this site has enabled them to open two northside locations. Enjoy their famous chips and salsa. Open for lunch and dinner seven days a week. Children's menu available. Beer and wine. Reservations for six or more. Credit cards. Inexpensive.

Cobblestone Inn and Baking Co., 620 S Washington (624-9735). Located in a turn-of-the-century banker's home, Cobblestone Bakery combines the ambiance of leaded-glass windows, revolving art created by local artists and hardwood floors with the pleasures of homebaked breads, pastries, espresso drinks and desserts. Soup, salads, and casseroles are served daily for lunch. Open Monday through Saturday 7 a.m.-6 p.m. and Sunday 9 a.m.-4 p.m. Credit cards.

Coffee at the Mill, 1102 S Perry (534-2015). If you've always wanted to step inside a windmill, here's your opportunity. This small espresso bar and ice cream spot with counter stools and one sit down table is located in a 1930s replica windmill, complete with a hatch to look up into the tower. They use Craven's coffee and serve scones, muffins, bagels and other baked goodies as well as cold drinks and ice cream. Open Monday through Friday 7 a.m.-5 p.m., Saturdays 8 a.m.-4 p.m.

Eviva Espresso, 1301 W 14th (456-3534). Craven's coffee and Rocket Bakery products are served at this small coffee bar fronting a dance studio. During warm weather, outdoor tables expand the seating, but the warmth inside is generated all year-round as neighbors and regulars stop by to pull up a stool and visit. Open Monday through Friday 6:30 a.m.-6 p.m., Saturday and Sunday 8 a.m.-3 p.m.

Gertrude's Black Forest Deli, 1002 S Perry (535-9641). It's hard to tell if the customers at Gertrude's are there for the thick lentil and cream soups and sandwiches, or the neighborhood camaraderie. Everyone is welcomed like an old friend, so slide into a booth or pull up a chair, enjoy the polka music and personal attention. Meat, cheese and other deli items are also for sale. Open Monday through Saturday. Credit cards. Inexpensive.

Great Harvest Bread Co., 2530 E 29th (535-1146). This bright, open and airy restaurant-cum-retail bakery offers baked goods to go or sandwiches, soups and espresso drinks on site. In warm weather, outdoor tables expand the limited seating and make a great place to people watch. Come early for the best selection of cookies, cinnamon rolls and even some of their more popular baked breads, like honey whole wheat. No credit cards. Open Monday through Saturday 6 a.m.-6 p.m. and Sunday 7 a.m.-5 p.m.

Just American Desserts, 2812 E 30th (534-7195). The slogan "baking the way it should be" suits Just American Desserts. They sell cakes and cheesecakes whole or by the slice and take special orders as well. One of the most popular items is chocolate chocolate chip cake. Customers have been known to cry if they arrive at the store and find it sold out. Never fear, if you order ahead of time, they'll save one just for you. Open Monday through Saturday from 10 a.m.-6 p.m Closed Sunday. Credit cards for purchases over $10.00.

Lincoln Heights, 2932 E 27th (535-4755). Lincoln Heights is loud and fun. With video games, a children's play area, TV viewing, kitchen tours and a truck-sized salad bar (in a real truck bed) to distract and tempt, you could almost forget to order your meal. Calzones, pizza, hot and cold sandwiches, soups and salads deserve your attention. Try their pesto pizza or seafood calzone for a change of pace. Open seven days a week. Beer and wine. Credit cards. Inexpensive.

Lindaman's Gourmet-To-Go, 1235 S Grand Blvd. (838-3000). Lindaman's is a popular spot, despite entrees served on paper plates and plastic utensils, long lines snaking through the self-serve restaurant during rush hours and an outside asphalt patio flanking traffic on Grand Boulevard. Even so, this place is packed every day with local politicos and professionals networking over an espresso drink. Patrons are drawn by a menu that changes daily, large portions and an array of desserts created to tempt the strongest willed. Come early or late for a seat—they fill fast. Open for breakfast and lunch seven days a week and for dinner Monday through Saturday. Beer and wine. No reservations. Credit cards. Inexpensive.

Linnie Thai, 1325 S Grand (838-0626). Named for the owner's daughter, Linnie's offers leisurely dining in a nice family setting. Although they're known for their peanut and curry sauces, they also have a wide selection of chicken, beef, pork, seafood and vegetarian dishes. Repeat customers from as far away as Seattle rave about Linnie's chef and his skill in the preparation of authentic Thai food. Open Monday through Friday for lunch and Monday through Saturday for dinner. Closed Sunday. No reservations necessary. Credit cards. Inexpensive.

Luna, 5620 S Perry (448-2383). Whether you fall in love with the French country decor or the exquisite food, visiting Luna's is a must. Chef Abby Yerxa creates masterpieces like Mediterrean-crusted salmon atop a bed of flavored white beans, garnished with red onion relish. Beer and wine. Open Tuesday through Sunday for breakfast, lunch and dinner. Closed Monday. Reservations recommended on weekend nights. Credit cards. Expensive.

McGowen's Cafe, 2525 E 29th (535-5802). Until Starbucks opened next door, McGowen's was one of the few places to enjoy espresso drinks and a bite to eat along the 29th Street corridor. It's a small and intimate spot for sandwiches, soups or salads, especially if the weather allows outside dining. The restaurant is small, with less than half a dozen tables, and the same menu is available all day long. Open seven days a week. No credit cards. Inexpensive.

Park Bench, 1928 S Tekoa (456-8066). This sandwich, soup and dessert spot makes an ideal stop when strolling through Manito park. The vintage 1923 basalt rock building originally housed a peanut vender for the defunct Manito Zoo. It sits at a strategic crossroads in the middle of one of the city's most popular parks. Watch for free-loading squirrels harassing you during the summer and dropping chestnuts in the late fall as you enjoy a cup of coffee and the leisure pace of the setting. Open May through September seven days a week. No credit cards. Inexpensive.

Pepper Dine, 2911 E 57th (448-8111). Pepper Dine's, long known for their prime rib and beef selections, also offers seafood and chicken entrees. The decor is heavy on barn boards and more than a few of the tables slant precariously, yet the regulars seem to take it all in stride. Live music and dancing is presented in the lounge Thursday through Saturday. Full bar. Open seven days a week for lunch and dinner. Closed Sunday only in the summer. Reservations recommended for weekends. Credit cards. Moderate.

Scrapbook, 3023 E 28th (535-0617). Though no longer owned by the same people as the Valley Scrapbook, this restaurant still serves a similar menu. Steak, seafood, burgers, salads and chicken are offered for lunch and dinner, and a special brunch is served on Sundays. This is a nice, comfortable atmosphere for entertaining clients and family. During warmer weather, you can enjoy the tiki lanterns and fountain of the outdoor courtyard. Kids' menu available. Full bar. Open seven days. Reservations on weekends for a nice table. Credit cards. Inexpensive to moderate.

Starbucks, 2525 E 29th (534-8971).Whether you sip your espresso drink at one of the half dozen indoor or outdoor tables, order it to-go or buy beans by the pound, you'll receive the same consistent quality product and service at Starbuck's. Scones, cookies and muffins are also served, which makes this a popular Saturday and Sunday morning spot to sit and talk with friends. Open Monday through Thursday 6 a.m.-9 p.m., Friday 6 a.m.-10 p.m., Saturday and Sunday 7 a.m.-10 p.m. Credit cards.

Take the Cake, 139 S Sherman (455-8658). Take the Cake opened in July 1993. Baker/owner Karen Hansen uses the finest ingredients available to craft pastries and desserts in the traditional European style. Using fresh fruits and cream to create these perishable delicacies, she sells about half in slices and whole items from the shop and half as special orders for customers (including some of the finer restaurants in town.) The lemon chiffon cake and three chocolate mousse are among the most popular items, but other tortes, cakes, tarts, pies and cookies sell rapidly. Open Tuesday through Friday 10 a.m.-5:30 p.m. and 10 a.m.-1 p.m. on Saturday—which affords her time to deliver custom wedding cakes. Also open by appointment off-hours. No credit cards.

Uccello Espresso, 2910 E 29th (533-0765). "Uccello" means "bird" in Italian, a play on the owner's name, Duane Byrd. With its black and green modern European decor, this is a coffee spot with a continental feel. They sell fresh-baked cookies, brownies, muffins and other pastry items as well as sandwiches. Choose from chess, checkers, puzzles or etch-a-sketches to entertain you why you inhale the aroma of air-roasted coffees. Try Herman's Blend, named for the owner's grandfather. Open Monday through Friday 6 a.m.-6 p.m., Saturday 6 a.m.-4 p.m. and Sunday 9 a.m.-4 p.m.

East

Au Croissant, University City Shopping Center (926-0267). At this Au Croissant location, you'll find the same great soups, sandwiches, croissants and breads as in the downtown counterpart. Espresso drinks also available. A nice place to stop while you're shopping. Open same hours as the mall. Inexpensive.

Beverly's, 7th Floor, Coeur d'Alene Resort, Coeur d'Alene, Idaho (800-688-4142). Beverly's is considered by many area residents to be "the" place to dine for special occasions. Overlooking Coeur d' Alene Lake, the restaurant fuses Northwest cuisine with breathtaking views of water, mountains and sky. The award-winning food combined with the marble foyer, copper and glass decor make dining here a truly memorable dining experience. Open seven days a week for lunch and dinner. Reservations strongly recommended for all meals. Credit cards. Expensive.

Cedar's Floating Restaurant, Blackwell Island, Coeur d'Alene, Idaho (208-664-2922). For over 25 years, customers have traveled by boat, car and seaplane to this steak and seafood restaurant. It's located only 1/4 mile off Highway 95, near downtown Coeur d'Alene. It truly does float, and the sound of creaking wood greets diners when the waves sweep across the lake. For great views along the octagonal windows, be sure to request window seating. Prime rib, chicken and pasta specialties round out the menu. Open for dinner only, seven days a week. Reservations recommended in summer months. Credit cards. Expensive.

Coeur d'Alene French Baking Co., 220 E Jackson (487-7687). Coeur d'Alene French Baking Company's three varieties of bread (traditional sourdough, cracked wheat sourdough and sweet French bread) contain no preservatives, oils, sugar, dairy products or cholesterol. The breads come in long loaves, large and small rounds and dinner rolls. Though your best bet is to place an advance order, you can walk in and purchase whatever has not been snatched up by area restaurants, grocery stores and other customers. Open Monday through Friday 8 a.m.-6 p.m. and Saturday 9 a.m.-5 p.m.

Corner Door, 3301 N Argonne (921-9253). Named for the entryway door set in one corner, this is a quiet place to grab a bite and a Longbottom's espresso drink. Corner Door offers deli sandwiches, Belgium waffles, stew, soups and a full ice cream fountain with shakes and the like. You're sure to find something to tempt you. Open Monday through Friday 11 a.m.-2 p.m. and Sunday 11 a.m-4 p.m.

Dewey's East, 12909 E Sprague (928-7688). This is a favorite stop for business lunches and entertaining out of town guests. Dewey's offers sandwiches, soups, chicken, seafood, prime rib and pasta dishes. Children's menu available. Banquet and lounge facilities. Open seven days a week for lunch and dinner. Reservations recommended on weekends. Credit cards. Moderate to expensive.

Espresso Shack, 620 N Sullivan (924-4919). This is a step up from your traditional drive-thru, offering two windows to service your orders and free gummy bears for children. Located in a former bank drive-up location, the Espresso Shack offers more than a weekly flavor special. Serving bagels, muffins, sandwiches and a green tossed salad, it's a convenient place to pick up a bite to eat as well as a treat to drink. For a filling meal, try their breakfast bagel, cream cheese and ham. Open Monday through Friday 5:30 a.m.-8 p.m. and Saturday 7 a.m.-8 p.m. and Sunday 8 a.m.-5p.m.

Hallett's, 14109 E Sprague (926-4076). Tom and Cindy Hallett own this cafe/espresso bar/gift shop, where you can indulge your taste buds while shopping for an unusual gift basket, a pound of Panache coffee beans or a specialty food item. Sandwiches, soups, salads and muffins are available Monday through Saturday. Sit down to dine beneath a window atrium or order your meal to go. Don't forget to indulge in some of the family's homemade chocolate candies while you're there. Imported beers and wines. Credit cards. Open Monday through Friday 8 a.m.-6:30 p.m. and Saturday 9 a.m.-5 p.m.

Jimmy D's, 320 Sherman Ave, Coeur d'Alene, Idaho (208-664-9774). Jimmy D's is a relaxed storefront spot serving mouth-watering cuisine. Exposed brick walls and a long, narrow dining area help create an intimate yet casual atmosphere. Lunch features salads, sandwiches, burgers, pasta dishes and daily specials. They bake their own bread, and the focaccia alone is worth the price of a meal. The dinner menu offers a wide range of fish, pork, beef, chicken, pasta dishes and daily specials. For a taste sensation, be sure to sample the fresh mussels (if they're available). Don't miss the extensive wine menu and dessert tray prepared by the resident pastry chef. Cajun night is the first Wednesday of the month. Open seven days a week. Reservations taken for six or more. Since weekends are particularly busy there might be a wait, but don't worry, Jimmy D's Wine Cellar is across the street. They'll call you when your table is ready. Credit cards. Moderate to expensive.

Harry O's Chicken on the Run, 3rd and Sherman (458-2755) and 420 W Francis (468-4090). Wood-roasted chicken is the basis of the small, but tasty menu available at Harry O's. At the 3rd Avenue location, you can grab a table indoors where you have the color, texture and smells of fresh vegetables and fruits surrounding you, or sit outdoors beneath a striped awning. The Francis Avenue restaurant offers seating for 80 indoors and also has pizzas, smoked ribs and turkey added to the menu. You can also order your quarter, half or whole chicken, side salad, or soup to go. Beer and wine. Open seven days a week. No credit cards. Inexpensive.

Just American Desserts, 10625 E Sprague (927-2253). Over nine years ago, a mother and her two daughters started Just American Desserts, and it's still going strong. You'll find many of their creations, such as Wildberry cheesecake, Tuxedo cake and German Chocolate cheesecakes, served at many of the area's finest restaurants. In their two retail shops (2812 E 30th and 6404 N Monroe), they sell pieces by the slice as well as whole desserts. Special orders also accepted. Open Monday through Saturday 9 a.m.-7 p.m. Credit cards accepted for orders over $10.

Lame Duck, 8103 E Trent (926-4600). Lame Duck's specialty of the house is prime rib and jumbo prawns which you can order together or separate. The restaurant's name refers to an accident suffered by the first owner, Mallard, who clearly had a sense of humor. This is a very casual atmosphere with a full bar. Open Monday through Friday for breakfast, lunch and dinner, Saturday and Sunday for dinner only. Reservations recommended for Friday and Saturday nights. Credit cards. Inexpensive.

Little German Inn, 25 S Park Road (924-5970). Little German Inn has been in business for over 25 years. Veal, rumpsteak, dumplings and red cabbage are a few of the German specialties served here. They also offer seafood and chicken dishes. Beer and wine. Open for dinner Wednesday through Saturday. Open for breakfast and lunch seven days a week. Credit cards. Moderate.

Longhorn Barbecue, 2315 N Argonne Road (924-9600). A spin-off from the original westside location, this large, roomy restaurant offers the same finger-lickin' good barbecue menu. Expect casual dining, lots of noise and the need to use your napkin often. Beer and wine. Closed Monday. Reservations recommended for parties of six or more. Credit cards. Inexpensive to moderate.

Luigi's, 329 S Dishman-Mica Road (927-4645). The suburban Luigi's offers the same mouth-watering food as the downtown location. Once you eat here, you'll discover why these family-owned restaurants earned the 1994 "Restaurant of the Year" award from the Spokane Business Association. A cup of their specially blended Four Season's coffee is the perfect ending to your meal. Open seven days. Credit cards. Moderate.

MacDonald's Hudson Bay Resort, Bayview, Idaho (208-683-2211). Located on the southern tip of Pend Oreille Lake, this casual and unique restaurant is well worth visiting. The entire restaurant is an outdoor deck with a bird's-eye view of the lake's boat traffic. The menu, posted on a chalkboard, features beef, chicken, seafood and pasta selections. Since the restaurant is open only during warm weather, it's best to call ahead for both hours of operation and directions. Dinners are served Wednesday through Sunday and lunch on Sundays only. Moderate.

Makena's, 11723 E Sprague (924-5011). This family-owned restaurant offers seafood, pasta, steak and salads with a Polynesian twist. Try the house salad with papaya dressing or pineapple sauce on your broiled fish. The light and airy decor and large booths produces a casual dressy setting. Outdoor dining is available in the summer. Full bar. Open Monday through Friday for lunch, Monday through Saturday for dinner. Closed Sunday. Reservations recommended for weekends and for parties of 5 or more. Credit cards. Moderate to expensive.

Mary Lou's Homemade Ice Cream & More, 821 N Evergreen Road (924-1611). As the name implies, Mary Lou's dishes out homemade ice creams, sherberts, yogurts and pies. They do not use preservatives, dyes or artificial ingredients. Nominated one of the top 10 ice cream parlors in the United States in the Warner Book "The

Very Best Ice Cream and Where to Find it." This family-owned and operated enterprise wins repeat customers not only for the taste and quality of their products, but also because it's located in an original 1900s farmhouse with cheerful red and white interior, heart-shaped chairs and tables built specifically to accommodate kids. If you're not in the mood for one of the 30 to 40 ice creams, such as huckleberry, lemon chiffon or river city fudge, try a bowl of fresh soup, a hot or cold sandwich, chimichanga, salad or lasagna. During January and February, the restaurant opens only Saturdays and Sunday 1 a.m.-6 p.m. and sells pizza and ice cream. From March through December the restaurant opens seven days a week and is full service. Call ahead for exact hours as they vary from winter to summer. Espresso drinks also available. No credit cards.

Mustard Seed, 9806 E Sprague (924-3194). This Mustard Seed location is usually not as busy as the downtown spot and makes a nice professional setting for lunch or dinner. Contemporary Oriental dishes are prepared with fresh vegetables, lean meats and light sauces. Limited bar. Open seven days. Credit cards. Moderate.

Niko's, 321 S Dishman/Mica Road (928-9590). This is the original location of a family-owned two-restaurant operation. The other is located in downtown Spokane at 725 W Riverside. On Thursday night, there's belly dancing at 7 and 8 p.m. Reservations recommended Thursday through the weekend. Closed Sunday. Credit cards. Moderate.

Pastry and More, 408 W Haycroft at Highway 95, Coeur d'Alene, Idaho (208-667-3808). Owner Bill Steele, former pastry chef at The Coeur d'Alene Resort, offers a different bread every day. Varieties include early American mission bread made from rough grain and honey, foccacia, sourdough, oat bran nut and honey, Italian sesame and egg and cinnamon bread with and without raisins. He also sells other bakery products; cakes, pastries, etc., as well as sandwiches and espresso drinks to eat on-site or to go. Open Monday through Saturday 6:30 a.m.-5:30 p.m. No credit cards.

Percy's, 414 University City (924-6022). Percy's provides little touches which enhance your dining pleasure. One example is the five types of homemade mini loaves served with every meal. Many business people find the skylights and live plant decor perfect for entertaining guests. A healthy/wholegrain menu is available as well as a "munchkins" menu for little ones. During warmer weather try their special summer soup. Open Monday through Saturday for lunch and dinner, Sunday for brunch, lunch and dinner. Full bar. Reservations recommended on weekends. Inexpensive to moderate.

Rocket Bakery, 3315 N Argonne (927-2340). Baking begins each morning at 3 a.m. six days a week. Many of the mouth-watering pastries are sold out before the end of the day. Stool seating, as well as two curb-side tables, are available for coffee drinkers, though most of the customers run in for cinnamon rolls, cookies, muffins, quick breads such as pumpkin or poppy seed, or loaf breads. Watch out though, their delicious baked goods are addictive. Little wonder this bakery across from the Millwood paper mill plant is so busy. Open Monday 6 a.m.-noon, Tuesday through Thursday 6 a.m.-5 p.m., Friday and Saturday 6 a.m.-8 p.m. and Sunday 6 a.m.-5 p.m. No credit cards.

Savage House, 700 S Dishman Road (924-3876). There's an Airway Heights Savage House location in addition to this one. Both make homemade pizza dough fresh daily and serve hot and cold sandwiches, calzones, salads and nachos. You can play miniature golf here, and there's a children's play area. Patio seating. Beer and wine. Open seven days for lunch and dinner. Credit cards. Inexpensive.

Scrapbook, 12828 E Sprague (928-6601). Don't discount Scrapbook as a nice place to eat because of its proximity to a bowling alley. With a skylit dining area, carpeted floors, deep, restful colors and high booths, the effect is relaxed, yet classy. Prints, murals and posters of sports figures dot the walls, and sports analogies enliven the large and varied menu. Salads, soups, pasta, seafood, chicken, beef and burgers are all offered. There are also a healthy lite section and children's menu. Lounge. Friday and Saturday night a prime rib buffet is the specialty, and Sunday a breakfast buffet is available.

Senor Guillermo's, 7905 E Trent (924-4304). Locals recommend Senor Guillermo's for a family-owned, family-orientated restaurant. The chef uses authentic recipes handed down in the Rincon family for over 55 years for relleno and gallina con mole. The coarsely chopped cabbage salad served in a tangy vinaigrette is a wonderful dish on its own or used as a salsa. Full bar. Open for lunch and dinner seven days a week. Reservations recommended for parties of eight or more. Credit cards. Inexpensive to moderate.

Skyway Cafe, Felt's Field (534-5986). At this tiny airport eatery, the portions are large and arrive hot off the grill. Enjoy watching taxiing small planes and mingling with the "regulars," who sit and talk shop over the formica table tops. The food is simple fare: hamburgers, chicken, meatloaf and sweet, drippy cinnamon rolls. Don't miss the blueberry pancakes or out-of-the-garden fresh rhubarb pie. Open seven days a week for breakfast and lunch. Beer and wine served. Credit cards. Inexpensive.

Spaghetti Station, 11204 E Sprague (922-0317). Families love the Spaghetti Station. Whether you're sitting in the 1934 bus or the trolley car, examining the gas station or dining on the outdoor patio, there's as much to see here as there is to eat. Kids' menu available. Full bar. Open only for dinner seven days a week. They'll try to accommodate you if you specify where you'd like to sit when you make a reservation. Credit cards. Inexpensive to moderate.

Stagecoach Pizza, N Market & E Liberty (487-7840). Sports teams and large groups gather in this casual atmosphere for pizza, sandwiches, soups, salads or popular appetizers like garlic bread, nachos and bread sticks. Beer and wine. Open seven days. Credit cards. Inexpensive.

Thai Kitchen, 12722 E Sprague (926-8161). Whether you stop in for the five different curry sauces or the variety of rice, noodle, vegetarian and meat dishes offered, you're sure to enjoy your dining experience. The staff will assist in making sure your expectations are more than met. They'll even alter spices to suit each customer's taste. No liquor. Open for dinner, Monday through Saturday and lunches Tuesday through Saturday. Credit cards. Inexpensive to moderate.

West

Asian Restaurant, 5306 W Sunset Highway (747-5760). The Asian Restaurant is nestled among the basalt outcroppings hugging Sunset Highway. It's easy to whiz past this small restaurant, but if you do, you'll miss a good dining experience others have savored for over 18 years. The restaurant serves both Chinese and Thai dishes and offers private rooms as well as booths and tables in the main dining area. Reservations are recommended to book a room, especially on weekends. Beer and wine. Open for lunch Tuesday through Friday, dinnersTuesday through Saturday. Closed Sunday and Monday. Credit cards. Inexpensive.

Buckhorn, Airway Heights (244-3991). For over 50 years, customers have stopped at the Buckhorn for prime rib, steak, barbecue ribs and huge hamburgers. You'll find many patrons from nearby Fairchild Air Force Base filling the booths and tables surrounded by a wood decor. Lounge. Open seven days for lunch and dinner and weekends for breakfast. Credit cards. Inexpensive.

DJ's in the Country, Fish Lake (235-6367). DJ's is located three miles off I-90 and the Cheney/Four Lakes exit. Filled with antiques, DJ's also boasts a four-star chef, who formally worked at Top of the

Mark in San Francisco. The dinner menu runs from pasta to lobster. Half the restaurant is the remnant of a World War II barrack, and there's a private dining area where dinner is served on Currier and Ives china. Breakfast brunch is served Sunday only; other days the restaurant serves lunch and dinner only. Closed Monday. Live rhythm and blues is played every Friday and Saturday nights. Full bar. Moderate to expensive.

House of Seoul, 12713 W 14th, Airway Heights (244-3761). This is as close to Seoul, Korea, as you'll come in Spokane. The storefront restaurant, small and unpretentious, tempts customers with a range and variety of Korean dishes. Side dishes and main entrees both prove delicious and unforgettable, ranging from hot and spicy to sweet and soothing. For a non-hot treat try the *kal bi*—lean beef short ribs sliced thin and permeated with a sweet, gingery marmalade before broiling. *Bul go gi*, a popular traditional dish of marinated beef strips stir fried with mushrooms and vegetables, is another menu star. Rice is served with all meals. Since Korean etiquette dictates that it's impolite to ask for payment, you must approach the cash register and offer to pay. Serving lunch and dinner Monday through Saturday. No liquor though they do offer barley tea, served traditional style after your meal unless you ask otherwise. No credit cards. Inexpensive.

Longhorn, 7611 Sunset Highway (838-8372). Since 1946, the Lehnertz brothers have served up their version of Texas-style barbecue to Spokanites. Though the brothers have since retired, younger members of the family carry on the tradition of serving succulent chicken, ham, turkey and sausage barbecued meals. The meat is slow roasted over a wood-fired barbecue pit to create tender morsels smothered in a smooth, mild sauce. Sandwiches, burgers and some salads are also available. The large barn-like restaurant compliments the casual, loud and fun atmosphere. Try the Sunday buffet to sample virtually everything on the regular menu. Full bar. Closed Monday. Reservations for parties of 6 or more. Credit cards. Inexpensive to moderate.

Savage House, 10724 W Airway Heights (244-5501). The Savage House originated in 1969 in Cheney and was named for The Eastern Washington University (EWU) football team, the Savages. Many EWU alumnae still return to order their favorite sandwich: a #17 Savage—special made with salami and several cheeses, a #19—Hot Reuben on Rye sandwich or any of the 23 different hot sandwiches served here. If you can't find a number that suits you, order hand-tossed pizzas, calzones, nachos, salads or subway sandwiches. A giant screen TV room is constantly busy. Beer served. Open seven days for lunch and dinner. Credit cards. Inexpensive.

Restaurant Listings by Category

Romantic

Adolfson's (S)
Café Roma (S)
Cobblestone Bakery (S)
Luna (S)
II Moon Cafe (D)
Park Bench (S)
Patsy Clark's (S)
Spokane Coffee
 Exchange (N)
Upstairs Downtown (D)

Rooms with a View

Ankeny's (D)
Beverly's (E)
Cedar's (E)
C.I. Shenanigan's (D)
Riverview Thai (D)
Viewpoint (D)

Children Expected

Azteca (D)
Cyrus O'Leary's (D)
Lincoln Heights Pizza (S)
Senor Guillermo's (E)
Spaghetti Factory (D)
Spaghetti Station (N, E)

Fine Dining

Adolfson's at the Glover
 Mansion (S)
Ankeny's (D)
Beverly's (E)
Café Roma (S)
Cannon Street Grill (D)
Cedar's Floating (E)
C.I. Shenanigan's (D)
Chic-a-Ria (N)
Clinkerdagger (D)
Commellini's (N)
Jimmy D's (E)

Luigi's (D,E)
Luna (S)
Milford's Fish House
 and Oyster Bar(D)
II Moon Cafe (D)
Patsy Clark's (D)
Salty's (D)
Sully's (D)
Upstairs Downtown (D)
Windows of the
 Seasons (D)

Casual

Arny's (N)
Au Croissant (D, E)
Breadbasket (N)
Buckhorn (W)
Chapter Eleven (N, E)
Coyote Cafe (D)
Cyrus O'Leary's (D)
DJ's in the Country (W)
Dewey Chetham &
 Howe (N)
Dewey's East (E)
Dick's Hamburgers (D)
Domini Sandwiches (D)
Eat-Rite Vegetarian (N)
Elk (D)
Entrées on Trays (D)
Espresso Delizioso (D)
Europa (D)
Fitzbillies (D)
Frank's Diner (D)
Fugazzi (D)
Granny's Buffet (N)
Harry O's Chicken on
 the Run (E)
High Nooner (D, N)
Lame Duck (E)
Lindaman's Cafe (N)
Lindaman's Gourmet-
 To-Go (S)
Longhorn Barbecue
 (E, W)
Makena's (E)
Mayfair (D)

Milk Bottle (N)
McGowen's Cafe (S)
MacDonald's Hudson
 Bay Resort (E)
Metro Cafe (D)
Onion (D, N)
Panhandler Pies (N)
Park Bench (S)
Pepper Dine (S)
Percy's (E)
Red Robin (N)
Ripples on the River (D)
Rock City Grill (D)
Scrapbook (S, E)
Shack (D)
SS Beryl (N)
Skyway Cafe (E)
Sportsman Cafe (N)
Swackhammer's (N)
Viewpoint Restaurant (D)

Ethnic Cuisine

German
Alpine Deli (E)
Gertrude's Black Forest
 Deli (S)
Little German Inn (E)

Italian
Cucina! Cucina! (D)
Decaro's (N)
Geno's (N)
Luigi's (D, E)
Mama Mia's (N)
Olive Garden (D)
Spaghetti Factory (D)
Spaghetti Station (N, E)

Mexican
Azteca (D)
Chapala (N, S)
Papagayo's (N)
Rancho Chico (D)
Senor Guillermo's (E)
Toucan's Restaurant &
 Bakery (D)

Middle Eastern
Azar's Cafe (N)
Azar's Restaurant (N)
Marrakesh (N)
Niko's (D, E)

Oriental
Asian Cafe (S)
Asian Restaurant (W)
Bong's Oriental
  Garden (N)
China Dragon (N)
China Best (D)
House of Seoul (W)
Lai Lai (N)
Linnie Thai (S)
Lotus Seed (N)
Ming Wah (D)
Mustard Seed (D, E)
Peking North (N)
Rice Time Express (D)
Riverview Thai (D)
Suki Yaki Inn (D)
Thai Cafe (D)
Thai Kitchen (E)

Coffee Stops

Brewhaha Espresso (D)
Cafe Street Music (D)
Coffee at the Mill (S)
Coffee Caper (N)
Corner Door (E)
Craven's (D)
Espresso Shack (E)
Evviva Espresso (S)
Four Seasons (D)
Gloria Jean's Gourmet
  Coffee (N)
Hallett's (E)
Java Junky's (D)
Pleasant Blends (N)
Spokane Coffee
  Exchange & Eatery (N)
Starbucks (N, S)
Uccello Espresso (S)

Bakeries & Desserts

Au Croissant Bakery
  Inc. (D)
Cobblestone Inn and
  Bakery (S)
Coeur d'Alene French
  Baking Co. (E)
Cyrus O'Leary's
  Wholesale Pies (D)
Great Harvest (D, S)
Jandyl's Desserts (N)
Just American Desserts
  (N, S, E)
Mary Lou's Homemad
  Ice Cream & More (E)
Pastry and More (E)
Rocket Bakery (E)
Spokandy (D)
Take the Cake (E)

Pizza

Five Mile Heights (N)
Lincoln Heights (S)
Little Italy (N)
Pete's Pizza (N)
Rocky Rococo (D)
Savage House (E, W)
Stadium (N)
Stagecoach Pizza (N)

5

Shopping

Spokane Marketplace
Photo by Patrice Tobler

Shopping

Malls and Centers

The Spokane area is home to a number of shopping malls, each with its own unique character. Except for the downtown skywalk system and the Crescent Court, all offer free parking and are located near major arterials. The primary malls and a sampling of their shops are listed below.

Downtown Spokane's unique skywalk system, a series of glass-sided tunnels criss-crossing above the city's streets, connects 18 square blocks of shops and department stores into an enclosed weather-proof unit.

The Bennett Block, Howard and Main. Built by B.H. Bennett, (son-in-law of town founder Anthony Cannon) after the great fire of 1889, the Bennett Block retains the original charm of red-brick walls and arched entryways. Kids love downtown's only glass elevator, which serves these three levels of 11 stores, restaurants and shops.

Riverpark Square, Lincoln and Main. Forty-seven stores, restaurants and services, including Nordstrom and Eddie Bauer, are located within this section of the Skywalk system.

The Sherwood Mall, Riverside and Stevens. The furthest eastern edge of the skywalk system includes 13 stores, restaurants and specialty shops. The landmark Old National Bank and Paulsen buildings, both on the National Historic Register, are also located here.

Crescent Court, Main and Wall. With five acres beneath one roof, the Crescent Court is the newest shopping venue in downtown Spokane. Opened fall 1994, it boasts 30 retail shops and restaurants on the first two floors, including Cucina! Cucina!, Harvey's and DJ's Sound City. The lower level of the building is an exhibition hall and the third floor a grand ballroom complete with imported Czechoslovakian chandeliers.

Franklin Park Mall, 5628 N Division. Situated just 2.2 miles south of the North Division "Y" and across the street from Franklin Park, this enclosed mall contains 34 stores, restaurants and services. This mall is anchored by Montgomery Ward and Ross Dress for Less. You'll also find specialty stores like Whiz Kids (educational toys and books for children) and Tobacco Square (pipes and gifts).

Flour Mill, 621 W Mallon. Built in 1895, the Flour Mill was a working mill until the 1970s. The power of the Spokane River turned the wheels, which now form a decorative fence to the east of the building. In preparation for Expo '74, the Mill was converted into a series of 22 shops and restaurants. Today, it stands four-stories tall on Mallon Street and seven-stories tall facing the river. Walking past red-brick walls and along the original hewn wood floors as you shop gives you a feel for the history of the building. Keep your eyes open for the marmots, furry animals related to woodchucks, which populate the rocky crags between the mill and the river. Spotting them is a favorite pastime of visitors to the area.

Garland Village, Garland Avenue between Howard and Monroe. Before Spokane began expanding northward after the 1930s, the edge of the city was marked by this collection of stores lining Garland. As the city pushed further north, this small community-within-a-community retained its distinct identity and charm. In 1987, new sidewalks and trees were installed, tying together 48 shops, stores, restaurants and services within a seven-block area. Most eye- catching is the Milk Bottle Restaurant at the corner of Post and Garland, which once was a dairy store and now serves hamburgers. The art deco detailing of the Garland Theatre at the Monroe Street intersection is a prime example of a by-gone architectural style. The Brown Derby and Ferguson's, fronting Garland Avenue, present a classic 1930s diner appearance.

Lincoln Heights Shopping Center, 2900 E 27th. Though only eight stores, restaurants and services are located in this mall, it's a cornerstone for the South side's Regal and 29th Streets corridor. Hastings, McCoy Craft Village and Payless Drug Store are situated here, as is the delightful Second Look Books store, Café Roma and Betty Bone Boutique.

Northtown Mall, Division and Wellesley. Built in the early 1960s, Northtown Mall was renovated in 1993 from a sleepy, one-level outdoor mall into a two-story, enclosed mall with 93 stores, restaurants and services along with major department stores such as Sears, the Bon Marché, Penney's, the Emporium and Mervyn's. Northtown also has a food court, tiled floors, potted trees, a children's play area and covered outdoor parking.

Northpointe Plaza, N Newport Highway. One of the area's newer malls, Northpointe reflects the population growth toward the northern end of the city. Target, Safeway, TJ Maxx and Shopko are some of the larger tenants in the Plaza. Northpointe's 33 stores, restaurants, services and specialty shops attract customers from Canada as well as from the many sub-divisions of new homes, which have sprung up in the area in the last 10 years.

Shadle Center, W Wellesley and Alberta. Spokane's oldest mall is virtually unchanged from its early days as an open-air shopping mecca, though the three-story slide once gracing its parking lot is gone. Historically, it's a walk through a piece of 1960s suburbia. Currently, one-third of its 31 stores are vacant. Still, Lamonts, Newberrys and Ernst anchor its east end, and smaller shops like The Book Nook and The Clock House keep it viable.

University City Mall, Sprague at University. Sixty stores, restaurants and specialty shops include JC Penney's, Lamont's and Newberry's at this indoor mall. For years, it has been a mainstay for Spokane Valley shoppers and visitors arriving in town from Idaho and Montana. The simple and easy layout, plus two levels of parking, appeal to loyal customers.

Wandermere Mall, N Division at Hastings. This is the newest strip-mall in the area, with 12 stores, shops and restaurants, including Starbucks. The major stores are Albertsons and Payless Drug.

Post Falls Factory Outlet, I-90 at Post Falls, Idaho. No mall directory would be complete without a factory-outlet location and Spokane's nearest is only 20 minutes east from downtown and seven miles west of Coeur d'Alene. The Post Falls Mall features over 50 stores and has plans for expansion. Parking is extensive and, for those not interested in shopping, the Greyhound Race Track is right next door.

Antiques

Spokane's major antique and collectible stores and malls are located relatively near each other though in distinct sections of the city and valley. This proximity makes it easy to plan a day's trip of shopping and browsing.

Downtown

Antiquex, 28 W 3rd (624-6826). Shopping for antiques in an historic building adds to the fun, and here you have a 10,000-square-foot brick building packed with goodies. Oak and walnut furniture, lamps, juke boxes and rugs are a few of the larger items for sale. There are also smaller collectibles such as dolls, paintings, toys and Native American artifacts. Open Wednesday through Saturday 10:30 a.m.-5 p.m.

Antique store in downtown Spokane
Photo by Ron Swords

Carnegie Square Antiques, 1403 W 1st (747-1903). While Oriental rugs and fine art are the owner's specialties, you'll also find a nice collection of furniture and furnishings, including sterling silver, Native American artifacts and jewelry. Open Monday through Saturday 10 a.m.-5:30 p.m. or by appointment.

Hot Flash of America, 112 S Cedar (624-5042). Owner Derald Long points out, "If you're interested in something you won't see anywhere else—come here." From a fake snakeskin cape to beeswax bears, this narrow, but long shop, displays an eclectic collection both fun and offbeat. A good representation of '50s memorabilia, African objects and quilts are displayed among clothing, furniture and what-nots. Open Tuesday through Saturday 10 a.m.-5 p.m.

Schade Brewery Antique Mall, 528 E Trent (624-0272). When you walk through the arched entrance of this brick building, you can almost hear the Clydesdale horses straining to pull their beer barrel wagons. Where brewmasters once labored, 21 dealers now offer an assortment of antiques and collectibles. Café Expressions sells espresso inside and parking is abundant, even though you're only minutes from downtown. Open Monday through Saturday 10 a.m.-5 p.m.

Spokane Antique Mall, 12 W Sprague (747-1466). This plain-faced red brick building is located at the cross streets of Sprague and Division. It's hard to imagine from the outside, the collection of antiques and collectibles inside its 25 shops. Throughout two floors are furniture, primitives, pottery, quilts, linens and loads more. Open Monday through Saturday 10 a.m.-5 p.m. and Sunday, noon-5 p.m.

Sprague Avenue

Antique Emporium, 1906 E Sprague (535-8951). Because the layout and arrangement is so conducive to browsing, you'll hardly notice that there are 40 different shops within this one complex. Collectibles sit atop furniture, while glassware is displayed next to radios and clocks. You'll find a little bit of everything including postcards, jewelry, linens and what-nots. Don't miss the southwest corner of the complex. What once was a private residence has been filled with a mix of period furniture for a step-back-in-time experience. An espresso bar is also open during the mall's regular business hours. Open Monday through Saturday 10 a.m.-5 p.m. and Sunday 11 a.m.-4 p.m.

Benny's Olde & Knew Antiques, 2130 E Sprague (535-4368). Toys, advertising items, furniture, clocks, watches, pottery, glass and postcards are a few of the items Benny's dispalys for sale. Open Monday through Saturday 10 a.m.-4:30 p.m.

McLeod's Antiques, 2118 E Sprague (535-6032). When you ask antique dealers where to find quality antiques, as opposed to collectibles, the name McLeod's surfaces time and time again. Located about 30 feet from Benny's, it's well worth a visit if you are seeking "the real thing". Open Tuesday through Saturday 10 a.m.-5 p.m.

Vintage Postcards, 2130 E Sprague (535-4368). At Vintage Postcards, owner's Burr and Lois Pendleton buy and sell fine postcards and collector supplies. They also stock a general line of furniture and collectibles throughout. Open Monday through Saturday 10 a.m.-4:45 p.m.

North

Aunt Bea's Antiques, 822 W Garland (326-7039). Aunt Bea's carries a nice selection of quality wares including dishes and furniture and Victorian items. Open Monday through Saturday 9:30 a.m.-5 p.m. or later by appointment.

Duprie's Antiques, 920 W Cora (327-2449). This sprawling red building, located at the base of the Monroe Street hill, has been a showcase for antiques for over 39 years. The upstairs has nooks and crannies, drawers and cabinets, with something on and in every one of them. Downstairs you'll find furniture pieces as well as stained glass windows, buggy parts, the odd trunk or two, and the list goes on. Open 10 a.m.-4:45 p.m. Closed Wednesdays and Sundays.

Monroe Street Bridge Antique Mall, 604 N Monroe (327-6398). In the early days of Spokane Falls, citizens had to row across the river to reach the north side. Lucky for us, reaching the Monroe Street Mall in the 1990s is a whole lot easier. Over 50 spaces located within this brick building showcase furniture, collectibles, glassware, toys and more. There's parking behind the store, which is accessible from Post Street. Open Monday through Saturday 10 a.m.-5:30 p.m. and Sunday noon-5 p.m.

Partners in Time, 3038 N Monroe (324-6316). Though Partners specializes in hunting and fishing collectibles, it also offers a selection of toys, glassware, jewelry, dolls and furniture. Open Tuesday through Saturday 10 a.m.-5 p.m., Sunday 11 a.m.-4 p.m.

Robin's Nest Second Hand, 11110 N Market (466-0489). In spite of its name, the Robin's Nest deals mostly with antiques and collectibles, rather than second-hand items. Cookie jars, Black Americana, glassware, jewelry and go carts are among their treasures. They're located two miles north of Francis. Open Monday through Thursday 8 a.m.-4 p.m. and Friday and Saturday 10 a.m.-5 p.m.

Hillyard

Named after Railroad magnate, Jim Hill, Hillyard was once a small business and residential community built around the train yards. Today, you'll find over 40 dealers housed in eight unique antique shops. Furniture, pottery, primitives, china, books, quilts, linens and more are displayed throughout the stores, all of which are within walking distance of one another. Plan for a full day.

Aunt Bea's Attic, 5019 N Market (482-7355). Open Monday through Saturday 9:30 a.m.-4:30 p.m. and Sunday 11:30 a.m.-4 p.m.

B&B Junk Company, 5002 N Market (487-1183). Open Monday through Saturday 9 a.m.-7 p.m. and Sunday, noon-5:30 p.m.

Benson's Antiques, 5215 N Market (487-3528). Open Monday through Saturday 11 a.m.-5 p.m. Closed Sunday.

Cloke & Dagger Antiques, 4912 N Market (482-2066). Open every day from 10 a.m.-4:30 p.m., except Thursday and Sunday when they're closed.

"Collector's Showcase" Antique Mall, 5201 N Market (482-7112). Open Monday through Saturday 10 a.m.-5 p.m. and Sunday noon-5 p.m.

Hillyard Variety Consignment Store, 5009 N Market (482-3433). Open Monday through Wednesday 10 a.m.-4 p.m., Thursday through Saturday 10 a.m.-4 p.m. and Sunday at owner's discretion.

United Hillyard Antique Mall, 5016 N Market (483-2647). Open Monday through Saturday 10:30 a.m.-5:30 p.m and Sunday 11:30 a.m.-4:30 p.m.

Spokane Valley

Irv's Antiques, 12014 E 1st Ave (928-7341). Irv's specialty is primitive pine and oak furniture. He buys, sells and trades pieces and also sells a few collectibles. Located in the rear of the Opportunity Furniture store. Open Monday through Saturday 10 a.m.-5 p.m.

Spokane Valley Antique Mall, 23 S Pines Rd (928-9648). Twenty-five dealers fill the space in the valley's newest antique mall which opened in August, 1993. Here you'll find dolls, jewelry, linens, vintage fashions, pine and oak furniture, pottery and more. Open Monday through Saturday 10 a.m.-5:30 p.m. and Sunday 11 a.m.-4 p.m.

Apparel

Menswear

Anderson & Emami, 806 W Main (838-1652). Anderson and Emami's offers fine men's wear, from $400 suits to $1500 handmade Oxford suits. Polo by Ralph Lauren, Nautica, Timberland, Hickey Freeman as well as other quality names in dress clothes and sportswear highlight the selection. Mssrs. Anderson and Emami are often on hand to personally assist their customers, though all staff are trained in color coordinating, fitting and wardrobe consultation. The tailor, German trained with over 30 years experience, is recognized as one of the best in the Northwest. Open Monday through Saturday 9:30 a.m.-6 p.m.

Hamer's, 802 Riverside (624-9296), Northtown Mall (489-7220), adjacent to the Manito Shopping Center (747-3114) and University Shopping Center (924-4177). A locally-owned men's store stocking everything for men except pajamas. Suits, sport coats, formal wear, dress slacks and sportswear are moderately priced. Generally open 9 a.m.-9 p.m., but hours vary between locations, so call ahead if in doubt.

Men's Wearhouse, 5005 N Division (483-4411). This store sells men's dress wear, suits, coats, slacks, ties and even shoes for 20-40% off retail list price. They offer designer labels such as Oscar de la Renta, Botany 500 and Halston and carry both traditional styles as well as European cut suits. Open Monday through Friday 10 a.m.-9 p.m., Saturday 9:30 a.m.-6 p.m. and Sunday 11 a.m.-5 p.m.

Women's Wear

Betty Bone Boutique, Lincoln Heights Shopping Center (535-4555). For over 20 years, Betty Bone's has been synonymous in Spokane with high quality, upper-end women's wear. A range of styles, from casual St. John's Knits to the most elegant of formal dresses, as well as accessory pieces are in stock. Open Monday through Saturday 10 a.m.-5 p.m.

Bonnie's Apparel, 1014 N Pines Road (926-8515). Though this shop has been operating for over 35 years, the clothing styles represented at Bonnie's are consistently contemporary and classic. Bonnie's offer women's clothes ranging from junior styles to more mature looks. You'll find unique outfits mingled in with more traditional styles throughout the store. Open Monday through Friday 9 a.m.-7 p.m. and Saturday 9 a.m.-6 p.m.

Casual Corner, 814 W Main (747-0881). Women's professional and casual clothes, moderately priced and geared for color coordinating, are the mainstay at this shop. Open during Riverpark Mall hours Monday-Friday 9:30 a.m.-9 p.m., Saturday 9:30 a.m.-7 p.m. and Sunday 11 a.m.-5 p.m.

Creme de la Creme, at the Flour Mill (326-2940). Here you'll discover contemporary women's clothes with an emphasis on styles not found in department stores. One example is hand-painted sweaters. The clothes are both casual and dressy, with many one-size-fits-all styles and outfits sporting elastic waist bands. Open Monday through Friday 10 a.m.-9 p.m., Saturday 10 a.m.-6 p.m. and Sunday noon - 5 p.m.

Eartharts, 10220 N Nevada (467-8210). If you're looking for a tactile experience as well as one-of-a-kind items, this is a must visit shop. Representing 19 regional fiber artists and four jewelers, Eartharts is building an enthusiastic customer base from larger coastal cities such as Portland and Seattle. Hand-grown and crafted, dyed, tanned, woven and sewn are a few of the methods employed in bringing unique pieces to life. Though it's a challenge to find the shop, located at the intersection of Hawthorne and Nevada behind the Northpointe Mall, it's well worth the hunt. Open Tuesday through Saturday 10 a.m. - 5 p.m.

Image Boutique, 510 W Riverside (747-2757). Look for women's clothing with an emphasis on professional wear at the Image. They stock sizes 4-18, year-round cruise and travel outfits, dressier "special occasion" wear as well as leisure styles. Open Monday through Saturday 10 a.m.-5:30 p.m.

Limited, 710 W Main (456-7217). The Limited focuses on moderately priced designer label clothes for young women. Open Monday through Friday 9:30 a.m.-9 p.m., Saturday 9:30 a.m.-7 p.m. and Sunday 11 a.m.-6 p.m.

Louie Permelia Limited, 814 W Main (838-6558) and 210 Sherman Ave, Coeur d'Alene, Idaho (208-765-0886). Upscale casual wear for women is displayed among antiques and framed prints. Louie Permelia's caters to customers in the 30-45 age bracket, offering vintage floral dresses, linen and cotton fabrics, well-known name brands and unique jewelry pieces. Open Monday through Friday 9:30 a.m.-6 p.m., Saturday 9:30 a.m.-7 p.m. and Sunday 11 a.m.-5 p.m.

Marabella Boutique, 221 N Wall (459-1000) and 210 Sherman Ave., Coeur d'Alene, Idaho (208-664-1001). When looking for nicer women's clothing, shopping here is a must. Quality designer labels in a selection which rivals Nordstrom's Gallery are sold along with gift items. The downtown store offers primarily dress wear and city clothes, while the Coeur d'Alene location handles sportswear. Downtown opens Monday through Saturday 10 a.m.-6 p. m. and Sunday noon-4 p.m. The Coeur d'Alene store opens Monday through Saturday 9 a.m.-9 p.m. and Sunday 11 a.m.-6 p.m.

Sheer Madness, Franklin Park Mall (487-3336) and University Mall (927-0382). Though Sheer Madness specializes in women's lingerie, including swim wear, they also offer some men's items, such as silk robes and boxers. Both stores open during regular mall hours.

Talbot's, 706 W Main (455-4563). Elegant women's wear is sold at Talbot's, both career and casual, with an emphasis on classic lines. Though the store carries its own label, it also sells some Bushwacker, Jones and David Brooks items. Petite sizes are also available. Open Monday through Friday 9:30 a.m.-9 p.m., Saturday 9:30 a.m.-7 p.m. and Sunday 11 a.m.-5 p.m.

Men, Women and Children

Bon Marché, Main & Wall, Downtown (626-6000) and Northtown Mall (482-6800). Contemporary and traditional men's, women's and children's clothing are sold throughout this northwest department store. Different departments appeal to different clientele, such as Maternity, Liz Claiborne (designer label clothes for women), The Cube (young women's fashions), Infants and Toddler wear, Men's suits, and at least 10 more. Both locations are open seven days a week during mall hours.

Eddie Bauer Outlet Store, 215 N Post (838-8615). This location was the first of 40 factory-direct Eddie Bauer Outlet store. This store handles traditional Eddie Bauer outerwear and casual clothing, turtle necks, polo shirts, and khaki and denim pants for men and women at discounted prices, but don't expect to find the same range and styles sold through their traditional retail stores. Open Monday through Friday 9:30 a.m.-9 p.m., Saturday 9:30 a.m.-7 p.m. and Sunday 11 a.m.-5 p.m.

GAP Stores, 814 W Main, Riverpark Square (838-8375) and Northtown Mall (482-7086). Both stores carry cotton, denim and cotton knit casual wear for younger men and women. Because of its larger space, the Northtown store may have styles not available at the downtown location. Expect to find moderately-priced and trendy styles with an emphasis on an androgynous look. Open seven days a week during regular mall hours in both locations.

Harvey's Fine Clothes, Crescent Court at Wall and Main (624-1257). Nicer quality men's and women's clothing is sold at this locally-owned store. Labels from Nautica, London Fog, Robert Scott and similar brands indicate that they cater to a professional cliental. The men's section offers casual styles including swimwear. They also rent, as well as sell, formal men's wear. Open Monday through Saturday 9:30 a.m.-9 p.m. and Sunday 10 a.m.-6 p.m.

Jay Jacobs, 714 W Main, Riverpark Square (747-0844) and Northtown Mall (483-4737). This store appeals to young men and women looking for the latest fashion trend. Both locations are open during regular mall hours.

Lamonts, 802 E 29th, Manito Shopping Center (747-2043) and Wellesley and Alberta, Shadle Center (326-5750). This moderately priced northwest chain store carries name brand clothes for the whole family. Open seven days a week during regular mall hours.

Maurice's, 4750 N Division, Northtown Mall (483-7233). At Maurice's you'll find a good selection of young men and women's contemporary and stylish wear, with an emphasis on their house label, Paris Sport Club. Formal wear, shoes, handbags and outerwear are also available here. Prices are quite reasonable. Open Monday through Saturday 9:30 a.m.-9 p.m. and Sunday 10 a.m.-6 p.m.

Nordstrom, 724 W Main (455-6111). Nordstrom, a family-owned enterprise which began in Seattle and has since spread across the country, is synonymous with outstanding customer service. The stores are designed to make shopping a pleasant experience with soft, ambient lighting and parquet or carpeted floors. Sales clerks are trained to be attentive and helpful. Periodically they will have a pianist playing for their customers enjoyment.

Customers shop Nordstrom for the outstanding service and high quality men's, women's and children's clothing, accessories and shoes. The company also sells fine gifts near the skywalk entrance on the third floor. On the lower level is the "Rack," where clearance items are sold at substantially reduced prices. Another nice feature is the Café Express, serving hot and cold drinks and a variety of sandwiches, soups, and salads. During warmer weather, an outdoor espresso bar fronts Main Avenue — it's also a great people-watching vantage point. Open Monday through Friday 9:30 a.m.-9 p.m., Saturday 9:30 a.m.-7 p.m. and Sunday 11 a.m.-6 p.m.

Pacific Trail Outlet Store, 13524 Sprague (922-4860). This is an outlet store for Pacific Trail; add the London Fog label, and you have an excellent selection for off-price outerwear. Though most of the merchandise is comprised of coats, bib overalls, parkas and shells, etc., Pacific Trail Outlet also carries seasonal casual, sportswear. Prices are very reasonable and the selection is large. You'll find men's, women's and children's sizes. Open Monday through Saturday 10 a.m.-5 p.m.

Pendleton, Crescent Court at Wall and Main (624-1257). Pendleton sells men's and women's classic casual and professional wear. Seventy-five percent of their clothes carry the famous Pendleton label, while Lanz and David Brooks are represented among the other styles on hand. They also have a wide selection of Native American and traditional blankets, stadium blankets and knit throws. Open Monday through Saturday 10 a.m.-6 p.m.

Ross Dress for Less, 5504 N Division (487-4545). Men's, women's and children's clothes for up to 70% off retail price are available at this national chain store. Ross's handles retailers' surplus, off-season clothes and some irregulars, with the discount marked on each item's ticket. Sizes from infants, to Women's 24 and men's extra-large make this a great place for family discount shopping. Open Monday through Saturday 9:30 a.m.-9 p.m. and Sunday 11 a.m.-6 p.m.

TJ Maxx, Northpointe Plaza (467-0603). Hunting through the racks at TJ Maxx can save you 50-80% on name brands for the whole family. This is part of the national chain of TJ Maxx stores. Though most of their clothes are overstock from major retailers, you do need to keep your eye open for irregulars or imperfections. Open Monday through Saturday 9:30 a.m.-9:00 p.m. and Sunday 11 a.m.-7 p.m.

Children's and Maternity Wear

Cotton Fields, 10623 E Sprague (928-2034). If you're looking for a great deal on kid's cotton basics, head for this store. Nearly hidden by the McDonald's restaurant on Sprague, it's easy to pass this store without realizing the shopping opportunities that lie behind the wrapping-paper covered windows. This is a factory outlet for the Cotton Fields brand, sold at regional retail stores such as Nordstrom and the Bon Marché. Sizes start at 12-month infant and run up to 14 girls'. The racks and tables are filled with leggings, T-shirts, turtle necks and "sweats" in pastel colors or bright and bold patterns. Every August they hold a month-long sale—a boon to back-to-school shoppers. Open Monday through Saturday 10 a.m.-5 p.m.

Dill Pickle, 212 N Howard (624-5530). For over 50 years, the Dill Pickle has been supplying mothers-to-be with maternity clothes for every occasion. You can choose from fun T-shirts, dressier professional wear, and a large selection of lingerie and nursing tops. Owner Martha Cummings is often on hand to assist with your needs. Open Monday through Thursday 9:30 a.m.-5:30 p.m., Friday 9:30 a.m.-6 p.m. and Saturday 9:30-5 p.m.

Especially For You, Coeur d'Alene Plaza on Sherman Avenue, Coeur d'Alene, Idaho (208-667-1375). When price is of no concern, this is the place to shop for children's clothes. High quality, trendy, fanciful and traditional designer clothes for kids are sold in sizes preemie to 6x. Open Monday through Saturday 9:30 a.m.-9 p.m. and Sunday 10:30 a.m.-6 p.m.

Mums & Sprouts, 12623 E Sprague (924-4817). You'll find maternity fashions, including lingerie, as well as infants' and children's clothes at this shop. Petite through plus sizes for "mums" in both career and casual styles are available. Open Monday through Friday 10 a.m.-6:30 p.m. and Saturday 10 a.m.-5 p.m.

Specialty Wear

Empire Dance Shop, 214 S Post (747-7808). Since 1951, this shop has outfitted dancers in a four-state and two-province area. They have largest selection of dancewear in the region. If you're looking for ballet, jazz, tap, aerobics, gymnastics or ice skating apparel, this is the place to visit. There's also a large selection of dance footwear. And if they don't have what you're looking for in stock, they'll be glad to order it for you. Open Monday through Friday 10 a.m.-5:30 p.m. and Saturday 10 a.m.-5 p.m.

Indiana Harness & Saddlery Co., 3030 E Sprague (535-3400). For over 67 years, Indiana Harness has attracted folks who live, work or simply enjoy horses. Western-style suits and shirts, dusters, sportcoats, breeches and hunt coats, custom chaps, hats and gloves—you name it in the equestrian line, and they sell it for the entire family. Open Monday through Saturday 9 a.m.-6 p.m.

Olsen Brothers Clothing, 1325 N Division (328-4617). You can't miss this store on Division. It's the one with the giant yellow horse on the roof. Since 1919, family-owned Olsen Brothers has been selling western wear, including boots and hats, to men, women and children. They also stock leather wear for motorcyclists. Open Monday through Friday 10 a.m.-6 p.m., Saturday 10 a.m.-5 p.m.

Spokane Uniform House, 526 W Main (838-3172). Like the name implies, if it's a uniform, you'll probably find it here, including outfits for the Spokane area private schools. They also stock a nice selection of white shoes. Open Monday through Friday 9 a.m.-6 p.m. and Saturday 10 a.m.-5 p.m.

Traders & Trappers, 214 N Howard (838-5820). This store sells functional, heavy-duty clothes suitable for safaris and hunting expeditions. They stock items for both men and women with an emphasis on cotton and wool basics. They also carry a large selection of hats. Open Monday through Saturday 8:30 a.m.-4 p.m. during the summer; winter hours vary, so call ahead.

Zanie's, 2718 N Division (326-8400). This is the only store in town devoted solely to rock-and-roll clothing. Tie-dyed shirts and novelty T-shirts are interspersed throughout the store with items such as lava lamps, pewter pieces, crystals and black-light posters. The Dead Rock Café sells espresso drinks within the store. Open Monday through Saturday 10 a.m.-6 p.m.

Consignment

Country Kids Koalaty Clothing, 18 S Union (922-8262). You may have trouble finding this store sandwiched on a side street just off two very busy streets, but it's well worth the hunt. It can be found two blocks west of Pines Road and south of Sprague Avenue. As owner Carolea Peterson describes her selection, "We sell Bon Marché quality at K-Mart prices," and she's right. It's hard to tell which 30-40% of the stock is new and which is reused. Carolea buys pieces outright for either in-store trade or cash and has a very high standard for her selections. The front room contains newborn to size 7, while a backroom is geared for older children with sizes 8 through 12. Items are purchased by appointment only. Open Tuesday through Saturday 10 a.m.-5p.m.

The Dwarf Cottage, 9437 Newport Highway (467-9513). This establishment began in a garage on Wall Street over 13 years ago. As the demand for quality children's clothes, furniture and accessories grew, so did the Dwarf Cottage. Its third and current site near the North Division "Y" intersection offers both new and used children's items up to size 18. Consignments accepted by appointment. Open Monday through Saturday 10 a.m.-5 p.m.

The Elegant Peasant, 911 1/2 W Garland (325-9857). This seven-plus-year-old shop specializes in bridal and formal wear for men and women. They also stock a full line of men, and women's casual and dress clothing, including accessory pieces. Consignments are accepted Monday and Tuesday without an appointment. Open Monday through Saturday 10 a.m.-5:30 p.m.

Funky Groovy Threads, 2415 N Monroe (325-6332). If you're looking for an "original" mini skirt from the days of Lyndon Johnson or a double-breasted pin striped suit, aka Cary Grant, this is the place. Both men's and women's vintage clothes are sold with an emphasis on the 1940s through 1960s. The store buys clothes outright and recommends making an appointment if you have items to sell. Open Monday through Thursday 11 a.m.-6 p.m. and Friday and Saturday and noon-6 p.m.

Reruns for Kids, 321 S Dishman/Mica Rd (921-1109). When you walk into this brightly lit, well laid out store, you'll be hard pressed to guess they offer used as well as new clothes. Selling new clothes from size 0 to 14 and used clothes from preemie to 6x, Reruns focuses on upscale, name-brand labels. Even their resale policy is unusual. Items may be brought in daily without appointment; by 10 the next morning you'll be notified of acceptance and will be immediately given in-store credit. You may use your credit for any merchandise, clothes or equipment, new or used. Open Monday through Saturday 10 a.m.-5 p.m.

A New Attitude, 9423 N Newport Highway (466-8278). The store motto is "Resale is Recycling," A New Attitude sells recycled women's clothing including maternity wear. Consignments are accepted without an appointment during business hours daily, except Saturday. Open Tuesday through Thursday 11 a.m.-7 p.m. and Friday and Saturday 10 a.m.-5 p.m.

The Reclothery, 613 S Washington (624-9741). The Reclothery offers a little something for everyone, with a focus on natural fibers. Children's clothing from size 4 through 12, women's clothing to size 18 and men's clothing to size 46 are stocked. Accessories, including mint condition shoes, are also for sale. Consignments are accepted by appointment only and clothes must be less than two years old. Open Monday through Saturday 10 a.m.-5 p.m. with extended hours on Monday and Wednesday until 6 p.m.

Sherry's Second Choice, 721 N Hastings (466-4015). Located in the Fairwood Shopping Center, Sherry's specializes in women's clothing from small to plus sizes, including cocktail and dressier wear. Consignments are accepted by appointment. Open Monday through Friday 10 a.m.-5 p.m. and Saturday from 10 a.m.-3 p.m.

Snob Shop, N 9 Washington (747-6434). Spokane's first women's consignment clothing store still retains its high standards. Consignments must not be older than two years and will be accepted by appointment only. Open Monday through Friday 10 a.m.-4:30 p.m. and Saturday 11 a.m.-3 p.m.

Treasure Trunk, 5515 N Alberta (325-0536). Even if you don't get caught up in the women's, juniors' and small children's clothing inside, it's fun to catch the changing window displays at the Treasure Trunk. Consignments are accepted Wednesday through Saturday from 10 a.m.-2 p.m. without an appointment. Open Tuesday through Saturday 10 a.m.-5 p.m.

The Tree House, 122 N Argonne (924-3605). Designer Labels are preferred on the clothing accepted by the Tree House. Specializing in women's clothing, they accept consignments without an appointment, though they do recommend coming in early in the day. Open Monday through Friday 9:30 a.m.-6 p.m. and Saturday 9:30 a.m.-5:30 p.m.

Arts and Crafts Supplies

Arts Supplies

Ratels Art Supplies, 811 W Garland (327-4437). Good prices are available on a well-rounded supply of fine art and graphic supplies at Ratels. They also offer custom framing. Open Monday through Friday 8:30 a.m.-5:30 p.m. and Saturday 9 a.m.-5 p.m.

Spokane Art Supply, 1303 N Monroe (327-6628). For over 40 years, Spokane Art has been synonymous with quality art supplies for artists throughout the region. Both fine art and graphic items are sold, and a special area of the store is devoted to children's art supplies. From hand-marbled paper to drafting tables, custom frames to modelling clay, you'll find it here. They also offer art classes for adults and children. The extensive reader board contains local artists' business cards and flyers publicizing area art events. Open Monday through Friday 8:30 a.m.-5:30 p.m and Saturday 9 a.m.-5 p.m.

Crafts Supplies

B&B Hobbies, 907 E Francis (487-2122). B&B's sells discounted hobby and craft supplies. Books, ribbons, dried flowers, radio, controlled vehicles and models are all available. Open Monday through Saturday 10 a.m.-6 p.m. and Sunday, noon-5 p.m.

Columbia Cycle - Craft & Hobby, 1808 N Monroe (327-1465). Some people may not think to shop for craft supplies and hobby kits in a bicycle shop, but you do here. For model train, car and plane enthusiasts, there's a wide selection downstairs. For crafters, the upstairs is well stocked with supplies for a variety of projects. They have a full range of supplies for dollmakers, miniature house enthusiasts and beadmakers, as well as tole painters, leather workers and candle makers. Open Monday through Friday 9 a.m.-6 p.m., Saturday 9 a.m.-5 p.m. and Sunday noon-5 p.m.

Homestead Crafts, 1301 N Pines Rd. (928-1986). Homestead focuses on selling decorative painting supplies. Classes are also scheduled. Open Monday through Friday 9 a.m. - 6 p.m. and Saturday 10 a.m. - 5 p.m. Give a call, and if they're open for a class in the evening, you're welcome to stop by to shop.

McCoy's Craft Village, 2727 S Mt. Vernon/Lincoln Heights (534-3422), 13124 E Sprague (928-2814) and 6416 N Division (483-9182). Silk flowers, picture frames, art supplies, ribbons, dried flowers—you name it, and you can probably find it at McCoy's. They also offer classes in a variety of crafts. Each location is open different hours; call ahead for exact information.

Northwest Fabrics & Crafts, 9616 E Sprague (926-4989) and 102 E Francis (489-3366). What once was predominantly a fabric store has branched out to include a wide selection of craft supplies, including books. They also offer craft classes, but you're mostly on your own when it comes to questions while shopping, as most of their staff is still most familiar with fabrics. Both stores are open Monday through Friday 9:30 a.m.-9 p.m., Saturday 9:30 a.m.-6 p.m. and Sunday 11 a.m.-5 p.m.

Books and Comics

Agathon Books, P.O. Box 8645 (624-5624). Agathon buys and sells quality, rare books and specializes in modern first editions. Authors like Faulkner, London, Hemingway and other 19th- and 20th-century writers form the bulk of their collection, though they do handle some 18th-century books and recent signed releases. Most of Agathon's business is transacted by mail, via their catalogue, though they will make appointments by phone for those in the area.

Auntie's Bookstore and Café, 402 W Main (838-0206). Spokane's largest bookstore stocks over 100,000 new and used titles.

This is a book lover's paradise. Contemporary fiction, poetry, gender studies, mystery, children and travel are but a few of their specialties. Auntie's is full of light and excitement. With an attached restaurant called McGowen's, comfortable chairs, autograph sessions and readings by both well-known and soon-to-be-known authors, there's always something happening here. Even their newsletter is fun to read. Auntie's is more than a bookstore, it's an experience, and yes, there really is an Auntie. Open Monday through Saturday 9 a.m.-9 p.m. and Sunday 11 a.m.-5 p.m.

B. Dalton Bookseller, 702 W Main (455-8259), Northtown Mall (487-1655) and University City (928-3770). Owned by Barnes and Noble, this is the largest bookstore chain in the area, and they stock over 25,000 titles. Here you'll find mainstream fiction and non-fiction work by big name authors, as well as a regional section, books for children and gift items for book lovers. Each store caters to a slightly different clientele, and their stock reflects these differences. Look for more travel, tour guides and business books at the downtown location. The Northtown store is the largest store in town and offers padded benches for their customers to sit and browse. Because of space, this is the store where you'll find more author autograph sessions, though all three stores have had in-store author signings. All three stores promote local and regional authors and are happy to steer you to their latest works. The store hours vary between location; so be sure to call for details.

Book Exchange, 1415 N Argonne (928-4073) and 6512 N Division (489-2053). The Book Exchange buys and sells paperbacks, hardbacks, collectible comics and some magazines. They also sell new computer books, auto manuals and remainder books. Both locations are open Monday through Saturday 9 a.m.-9 p.m. and Sunday 10 a.m.-7 p.m.

Booktraders, 907 W Garland (326-7653). For over 12 years owner JoAnn Young has offered one of the best deals on trade-in books in town. Stop in for details and browse through her well-rounded selection of hardback and paperback fiction and non-fiction. There are no new books. Open Monday through Saturday 10 a.m. - 5 p.m.

Children's Corner Bookshop, 814 W Main, Riverpark Skywalk Mall (624-4820). As the name implies, this bookstore specializes in children's books. They offer a good selection of current and classic kids' books and a knowledgeable staff to help you select age- or interest-specific titles for your child. You'll also find books geared to parents and teachers. Full-time teachers or home-schoolers get a 10% discount. Open Monday through Friday 9:30 a.m.-9 p.m., Saturday 9:30 a.m.-6 p.m. and Sunday 11 a.m.-5 p.m.

Clark's Book Store, 318 W Sprague (624-1846). Clark's sells a large selection of used paper and hardback books. This small, multi-roomed store, over eighty years old, has built up a loyal following. They stock all types of fiction and non-fiction, with large selections of western Americana, military history, biographies and children's books. Summers, they're closed Mondays. Otherwise, open Monday through Friday 11 a.m.-5:30 p.m. and Saturday 11 a.m.-4 p.m.

The Comic Book Shop, 9827 E Sprague (926-5186), 1 E Boone (326-7018) and 7312 N Division (483-0250). With over 180,000 back issues in the three stores, the Comic Book Shop is a must stop for collectors. The Valley and Division stores are open Monday through Saturday 11 a.m.-7 p.m. and Sunday 11 a.m.-6 p.m. The Boone store opens Monday through Saturday 10:30 a.m.-7 p.m. and Sunday 11 a.m.-6 p.m.

Dragon Tales, 13910 E Sprague (922-9932). Though they stock other titles, Dragon Tales' specializes in new and used science fiction books, games, jewelry and cards. Open Monday through Friday 10 a.m.-7 p.m., Saturday 10 a.m.-6 p.m. and Sunday noon-4 p.m.

Gusdorf's Books, 10525 E Sprague, University City North (922-2669). It's a treat to scan the floor-to-ceiling stacks of new and used titles in this small store. But Mr. Gusdorf's real forte is searching for out-of-print paper and hardback books for his customers. He has a database of over two million titles, and there's usually a 24-hour turn around time on most searches. Open Monday through Saturday 10 a.m-6 p.m. and Sunday noon-5 p.m. If you need to talk to the senior Gusdorf, stop by or call during the week.

Hastings Book Music and Video, 11324 E Sprague (924-0720), 7304 N Division (483-2865), Lincoln Heights Shopping Center (535-4342) and Shadle at Wellesley and Ash (327-6008). Hastings is the largest provider of discounted books in the region, with four locations and two more super-stores planned for the Spokane area. You can find bestsellers in paper and hardbound editions starting at 30% off list price and overstock and remainder titles at 50-75% off. They also stock a wide selection of magazines. All stores are open seven days a week from 10 a.m.-11 p.m.

Inland Book Store, 123 S Wall (624-9064). Many a bibliophile mourned original owner Dean Gilbert's 1994 retirement, fearing the demise of this 39-year old landmark book store. Fortunately, Gerome Carlson reopened the Inland Book store and continues the tradition of stocking books on art, literature, history, religion and music. Carlson also sells fine editions and leather-bound books. Open Monday through Saturday 11 a.m.-6 p.m.

Merlyn's, 1 N Browne (624-0957). This is a great place to browse, buy, sell and enjoy comic books. They also offer games, software, videos, sci-fi and fantasy books. Open Monday through Saturday 10 a.m.-6 p.m., Friday until 7 p. m. and Sunday noon-5 p.m.

New Dawn Books, 11 S Howard (455-6921). A meditation room is available free to customers who need a break from browsing the selection of books on religious studies, Eastern philosophy, devotion & meditation, yoga and health, astrology, self-help and gender studies. Jewelry, runes and tarot cards, incense and music are also stocked. Guided meditation time is on Friday evening and Saturday afternoon. Call ahead for exact hours. Open Monday through Friday 10:30 a.m.-5:30 p.m. and Saturday 11 a.m.-4 p.m.

Northwest Map & Travel Book Center, 525 W Sprague (455-6981). If you're in the market for maps or guidebooks, don't miss this gem of a specialty store. Teachers, pilots, tourists and boaters, to name just a few of their clients, appreciate the range and selection of topographical, city, state, nautical, aeronautical and foreign maps available here. You can also order custom-made maps. Another bonus is the broad selection of guide books covering all corners of the globe. Open Monday through Friday 9 a.m.-6 p.m. and Saturday 10 a.m.-4 p.m.

The Open Door, 1604 N Monroe (328-8283). This store calls itself "an alternative bookstore." Not surprisingly, you'll find a wealth of New Age music and self-help tapes. They also carry metaphysical literature, Native American and Eastern/Oriental books, tapes and videos, as well as crystals, jewelry, incense, candles, aromatherapy oils and Native American items. Open Monday through Friday 10 a.m.-6 p.m., Saturday 10 a.m.-5 p.m. and Sunday noon-5 p..m.

Ponderosa Books, 1310 N Mullan (922-5457). Almost all Ponderosa's books are used, though they do have a few new children's books at reasonable prices. The shelves are stocked with a good selection of romance titles, sci-fi, mystery and children's books, and a cross-section of other categories and non-fiction works. They sell both hardback and paperback and will special order new books. Open Monday through Wednesday 11 a.m.-6:30 p.m., Thursday and Friday 11 a.m.-8 p.m. and Saturday 10 a.m.-5:30 p.m.

2nd Look Books, 2829 E 29th, Lincoln Heights Center (535-6464). Open 362 days a year, 2nd Look Books offers more than 88,000 new and used hardback and paperback books, as well as magazines, jigsaw puzzles, books on tape and even greeting cards. They also stock the full line of Cliffs notes. This used bookstore has the largest variety of categories in town. If you can't find an item, they'll do both in-store and national searches and will special order books for customers. There's an on-site espresso bar. Open Monday through Friday 9 a.m.-9 p.m., Saturday 9 a.m.-8 p.m. and Sunday 11 a.m.-6 p.m.

Suntree Books, 123 S Wall (747-1373). This store is an oasis for the mind and spirit. Owners Bob and Darlene Turner combine metaphysical, self-help, fiction and non-fiction selections with unusual gift items from around the world. The smell of incense and soft music flows over and around the shelves, nooks and crannies of this store. You'll find a wide variety of items besides books, from blank greeting cards to Indonesian masks and Tarot cards. You may special order books too. There is also a limited selection of used books. Open Tuesday through Thursday 12:30 p.m.-6 p.m. and Friday and Saturday 12:30 p.m.-9 p.m. No credit cards.

Waldenbooks, Riverpark Square (838-6359) and Northtown Mall (483-6552). This national chain specializes in bestsellers and new releases. They offer a wide range of categories, from children's to sci-fis, romance and more. If you can't find what you want, they'll happily special order. Audiotapes of bestsellers are also available—and they offer a mailing service. Open during mall hours seven days a week.

Cameras and Photographic Equipment

Huppin's, 419 W Main (747-6486). Huppin's has the distinction of being the oldest camera store in town, opening in 1908. It's still a family-owned operation. This is the place to buy, sell or trade cameras and purchase photographic supplies. They stock video cameras as well as rental and service equipment. A well-trained and knowledgeable staff is available to assist you. Open Monday through Saturday 9 a.m 6 p.m, Fridays until 9 p.m.

Cooking and Kitchen Supplies

Copper Colander, 621 W Mallon, at the Flour Mill (327-3523). At the Copper Colander, you'll find kitchenware, coffee, tea, wine, cookbooks and whatever else you might need for your dream kitchen. Open Monday through Friday 10 a.m.-9 p.m., Saturday 10 a.m.-6 p.m. and Sunday noon-5 p.m.

Mrs. Cadiddlehopper's, 818 W Garland (328-9772). This store, owned by a mother-daughter team, was named for a character from the Red Skeleton show. You'll always find some member of the family waiting on you. Though small in size, it stocks housewares, a giant selection of cookie cutters, over 55 culinary herbs and spices, as well as bulk teas and Oregon Coffee Roaster coffee beans. Open Monday through Saturday 9:30 a.m.-5:30 p.m.

The Kitchen Shop, Bennett Block Skywalk Level (455-6735). This specialty store offers everything for the kitchen. Kitchen gadgets, specialty cookware and bakeware, even coffee and espresso machines are offered. Open Monday through Saturday 9:30 a.m.-5:30 p.m.

Lechters, Northtown Mall (484-1048). You're sure to find a good price on some gadget or widget you can't live without at Lechters. They stock a nice selection of frames, glassware and supplies for the bath, utility room and closet, as well as standard cookware, bakeware and kitchen gadgets. Open Monday through Saturday 9:30 a.m.-9 p.m. and Sunday 10 a.m.-6 p.m.

The Pottery Place Plus, 621 W Mallon at the Flour Mill (327-6920). What began as a pottery co-op has evolved into a showcase for 15 local artists who create the work for sale and also man the store. Nine potters, working in both stoneware and porcelain, two woodworkers, an iron worker, several jewelers and a pine needle weaver, all sell their works here. Custom orders can also be arranged. Open Monday through Thursday and Saturday 10 a.m.-6 p.m., Friday 10 a.m.-9 p.m. and Sunday 11 a.m.-5 p.m.

Discount Buying

Eagle Hardware and Garden Center, 6900 Division (487-2326) and 5204 E Sprague (533-0066). Eagle sells materials for the building trade and the individual home owner. The staff is well-trained and helpful. To get around the daunting "warehouse" environment, departments are divided. There's an extensive indoor area as well as an outdoor garden area. One measure of Eagle's extreme popularity with the home improvement crowd is the length of their check out lines, particularly in the garden and lumber sections. Anticipate a wait, especially on weekends. Both locations are open Monday through Friday 7:30 a.m.-9 p.m., Saturday 7:30 a.m.-7 p.m. and Sunday 9 a.m.-7 p.m.

HomeBase Home Improvement Warehouse, 9718 E Sprague (927-6700). Back when it was still called HomeClub, this was the first megastore for building supplies in the area. According to their ads, they stock 30,000 home improvement items. This gives you an idea of the scope of the operation. Aisles can be long and daunting, but the check out lines move quickly. Recent competition has made them more customer-service oriented, but it's still a very much look-on-your- own-for-what-you-might-need kind of operation. They deliver, for a fee. Open Monday through Friday 7 a.m.-9 p.m., Saturday 7 a.m.-8 p.m. and Sunday 8 a.m.-7 p.m.

Office Depot, 1003 E 3rd (536-7600). Located just east of PriceCostco, Office Depot specializes in office products at discount prices. They handle a wide range of paper products, equipment (including computers, printers, phones and faxes), software, general office supplies and furniture. A low-cost, in-store printing shop is handy for copying projects or ordering business cards. Another bonus is the speed in which they handle customers in their check-out lines. Free delivery is offered on orders of $200 or more within the local trading area. You can order from a catalogue at the same discount prices. Open Monday through Friday 8 a.m.-9 p.m., Saturday 9 a.m.-9 p.m. and Sunday 11 a.m.-6 p.m.

PriceCostco, 800 E 3rd (536-7508) and 7619 N Division (466-7429). At 163,000 square feet, Spokane's 3rd Street PriceCostco location is the third largest warehouse in the United States in this national/international chain of wholesale outlets. This translates into aisles and aisles of consumer goods from groceries to tires at near-wholesale prices. The secret to shopping these megastores is to know what you want before you enter, so you don't become overloaded with the variety of goods piled sky-high before you. Seasonal items, such as lawn furniture and back to school supplies, are also offered. The stock changes, so what you see today may not be available next week.

At both locations, landscaped parking areas have improved the visual impact of shopping a store as large as a hanger, though both lots can be challenging, especially on weekends and during the Christmas season. It's all part of the experience, so relax and enjoy the challenge. Membership is required to shop, and the first two hours during the week are devoted to wholesale customers only. Both stores are open Monday through Friday 9 a.m.-8:30 p.m., Saturday 9:30 a.m.-6 p.m. and Sunday 10 a.m.-5 p.m.

Ziegler Building Center, 620 E Holland (467-4958), 4220 N Market (489-8760) and 17002 E Sprague (922-1800). Ziggy's is

Spokane's locally owned alternative to chain, home-building warehouses. Vern Ziegler owns and operates the lumber stores, while his nephew owns and manages the electrical and plumbing stores, all located within the same buildings. Plenty of friendly staff members are on hand to explain the difference between a widget and a what-not. The Northpointe store on East Holland opens an hour earlier on Sundays and stays open 30 minutes later during the week. Otherwise, hours are Monday through Friday 8 a.m.-6:30 p.m., Saturday 8 a.m.-5:30 p.m. and Sunday 9 a.m.-5 p.m. All stores are open the same hours.

Ethnic and Unique Groceries

Cassano Grocery, 314 E Sprague (747-3888). Though the front of Cassano's Sprague store has been updated through the years, a step inside whirls you back in time. With 72 years of experience behind them, Cassano's is the oldest family-owned Italian grocery store in town and still retains its intimate, neighborhood feel. Here you can find prosciutto, olive oils, cheeses, fresh pastas and whatever else you need to create wonderful Italian meals. Open Monday through Saturday 8 a.m.-5 p.m.

Egger Meats, 902 W Rosewood (328-7701), 5613 S Perry (448-5474) and 10629 E Sprague (926-8772). This is a must stop if you're looking for fresh beef, lamb, veal or poultry. Egger's prepares their own sausages, hams and bacon and other specialty items. The stuffed pork chops are a popular choice. All stores are open Monday through Saturday, though their hours vary. The Rosewood store is open 9 a.m.-6 p.m., the Perry store 8 a.m.-7 p.m. and the Sprague location is open 9 a.m.-7 p.m.

La Tiendita, 3150 N Division (325-0407). You'll experience a kaleidoscope of colors, textures and aromas when you walk through La Tiendita's doors. Pottery bowls and containers hold a variety of dried chilis and spices. You can find blue corn meal and bags of corn husks as well as sombrerros, Spanish language audio cassettes, videos and magazines. There's also a small gift selection. The hot, fresh food from the cafe grill is an extra bonus. Open Monday through Saturday 10 a.m.-6:30 p.m and Sunday 10 a.m.-5 p.m.

Lorien Herbs and Natural Foods Inc., 414 E Trent (456-0702). Lorien's was opened in 1977 and has become a cornerstone of health food for local enthusiasts. Their bulk herb, spice and tea section comprises nearly 200 items. Lorien's also offers organically grown bulk grains, nuts, seeds, flours and beans. You'll also find a refrigerated and frozen food section, food preparation equipment and personal care items. Open Monday through Friday 10 a.m.-6 p.m. and Saturday 10 a.m.-5 p.m.

Mauro's Grocery, 3404 E Euclid (483-2862). Until the summer of 1994, Mauro's was the oldest family-owned Italian grocery store in Spokane. Mauro Senior opened the store in 1919, in the heart of an Italian neighborhood. His sons were raised in a tiny, three-room apartment at the back of the market. Thus, when brothers Silvio and Ralph Mauro sold the store, an era ended. But the new owners provide continuing good service and stock Italian specialties. They offer a range of breads, salamis, olives and Italian meats — plus the locally-famous Italian sausage. Open Monday through Saturday 9 a.m.-8 p.m.

Oriental Food Store, 1312 N Division (327-3478). Though it looks small on the outside, a whole world awaits you inside the Oriental Food Store. Every square inch of shelf space is piled ceiling-high with Oriental groceries, gift items, beauty products, clothes, dishes and books. There are also frozen foods, dried spices, Korean magazines and cassettes. Open Monday through Saturday 10 a.m.- 8 p.m.

Oriental B & Y Food Market, 3403 E Sprague (534-5601). With its warehouse-type space, this store caters to bulk purchases of Oriental foods, and many local restaurant owners patronize it. For the individual consumer, there's an assortment of frozen, packaged and canned goods, as well as some kitchenware and gift items. Open Monday through Saturday 9:30 a.m.-6:30 p.m. and Sunday 10 a.m.-5 p.m.

Phuoc T Thanh, 1210 N Hamilton (483-8136). This store is owned by the Tran family, who also operate the Lotus Seed restaurant next door. Phuoc T Thanh offers a wide range of fresh, frozen, canned and dried Oriental food products. Many Thai specialties are stocked along with a selection of cookware, personal care products and gift items. Open seven days a week 9:30 a.m.-7 p.m.

Rockwood Market and Fine Foods, 315 E 18th (747-1166). The Rockwood Market harkens back to the days of old, where store clerks knew your name and the lack of selection was more than made up for by the quality of products. Here you can order specific cuts of meat for holiday celebrations, find specialty items such as Craven's coffee, Buckeye Beans soups and pastas, and Coeur d'Alene breads and rolls. They also stock a good selection of fine wines and cheeses and, for those lucky enough to live nearby, the Market delivers. Open Monday through Saturday 8:30 a.m.-6 p.m.

Sonnenberg's Market and Deli, 1528 E Sprague (535-4932). This is Spokane's oldest meat market, opening in 1891. It's also one of the city's best kept secrets because of its downtown location. While the town has expanded beyond this corner of Sprague Avenue, Sonnenberg's has remained very much a neighborhood store. Along with groceries, they offer a full-service meat, fish and deli counter and will smoke or process your wild game. Keep an eye out for selections not often seen elsewhere such as tripe, brains, tongue and pig's feet. Open Monday through Saturday 7 a.m.-p.m. and Sunday 10 a.m.-6 p.m.

William's Seafood, 10627 Sprague (922-4868) and 6418 N Wall (467-4635). Unlike the many options available to our coastal cousins across the Cascades, buying fresh seafood locally is not a casual affair. But we do have William's, which stocks the freshest and largest selection of seafood in the area. The extensive saltwater and shellfish selection is complemented by a few farm-raised fresh fish choices such as trout and catfish. Both stores are open Monday through Saturday 9 a.m.-6 p.m., though the Sprague location remains open till 6:30 p.m. during the week.

Florists, Flowers and Fauna

Appleway Florist & Greenhouse, 11006 E Sprague (924-5050). You can tell summer has arrived when Appleway's trademark petunia trees begin blooming along Sprague Avenue. At the front of the store, you'll find fresh flowers, gifts, baskets and dried arrangements made to order, but don't stop there. Enter through a rear door, or by winding your way over wooden sidewalks, and you'll find the working half of the greenhouse. In the back are the annuals and perennials. There are garden experts on hand to help you make a selection. Open Monday through Friday 7 a.m.-5:30 p.m. and Saturday 7 a.m.-5 p.m.

Boehm's Chocolates and Flowers, 2nd Floor Riverpark Square, across from Nordstrom (456-8466). This shop is a delight to the senses. Though small, it offers quality chocolates, fresh-cut flowers, potted plants in unusual baskets, ice cream bars and sugarless candies. Open Monday through Friday 9:30 a.m.-9 p.m., Saturday 9:30 a.m.-7 p.m. and Sunday 11 a.m.-5 p.m.

Floral Design, 180 S Howard (838-1219). Jan Hopwood's store offers more than fresh or dried arrangements. Tucked among wrought iron and wood display stands are baskets galore, single-stem silk flowers, topiaries and terra cotta and glazed pots in a variety of sizes. Much is packed into this corner store, and you'll want to explore it more than once. Open Monday through Friday 8 a.m.-5:30 p.m. and Saturday 9 a.m.-2 p.m. Summer hours are shorter so call ahead.

Liberty Park Florist, E 8th & Perry (534-9381). Liberty Park has been in operation for over 64 years. It's worth a visit just to see the greenhouse. Throughout the year, the floral growth beneath its glass-tiered layers changes from poinsettia red to geranium pink. Even in the dead of winter, twinkling lights create a magical ambiance. Liberty Park sells potted plants and cut flowers year-round. They also have seasonal nursery stock.

Naissance, 141 S Cannon (455-5155). This store is situated behind Elk Drug Store in Browne's Addition. You'll find linens, dried bouquets, herbs and food items draped across a white wrought iron bedstead or displayed against a wooden mantel piece. Open Saturday and Sunday 10 a.m.-4 p.m. and Monday noon-4 p.m.

Palouse Prairie, 703 N Monroe (327-0430). This charming shop is compact, yet full of scent and textures provided by herbs, potted plants and dried flowers. From swags to wreaths, owners Diane and Leila Roche know and love plants and willingly share their knowledge with customers. Especially during the cold, grey days of winter, a 10-minute visit to Palouse Prairie is like stepping into a sheltered oasis of calm and serenity. Open Monday through Saturday 10 a.m.-5 p.m and until 7 p.m. on Thursday.

Peters and Sons, 829 W Riverside (624-4151). After 85 years of family ownership, the original Peters family sold this Riverside location. Luckily, the new owners maintain the same quality and customer service. While Peters sells flowers and plants, it also offers a wide assortment of gifts ranging from stuffed animals and balloons to crystal and china. Open Monday through Friday 8 a.m.-5:30 p.m. and Saturday 9 a.m 3 p.m.

Gifts

The Balcony Boutique, 14th and Grand (624-7263). If you enjoy shopping for that perfect gift in an atmosphere of scented perfumes, singing birds and a fountain bubbling in the background, this is your place. Located on the second floor above the 14th and Grand Salon, this intimate store is constantly changing. They specialize in a European Garden theme, offering terra cotta pieces, live topiaries, silk and dried flowers, candlesticks and greeting cards. Nancy Eubank's hand-painted furniture and birdhouses are an additional delight in this sensual boutique. Open Monday through Thursday 9 a.m.- 8 p.m., Friday and Saturday 9 a.m.-7 p.m. and Sunday 8:30 a.m 4:30 p.m.

Boo Radleys, 5 N Post (456-7479). This is where you can find the wild next to the whimsical. Lava lamps and glow-in-the-dark Madonna statues, cards and wind-up toys, and garage-sale art and books, are all represented in this unique store. Irreverent and tongue-in-cheek at the same time, it's worth visiting, if only to catch a wind-up robot crossing the hardwood floors in front of you. Open Monday through Saturday 11 a.m.-6 p.m.

Display House, 170 S Lincoln (747-4149) and 1510 N Argonne (922-0688). When you're looking for seasonal decorations, this is the place to go. From Fourth of July flags to Christmas tree lights and Halloween costumes to plastic Easter eggs, the Display House carries it. The downtown location stocks its second floor with Christmas items all year-round. The Valley location does not stock store fixtures, but does have the extensive decorations and party supplies. Open Monday through Friday 9 a.m.-6 p.m. and Saturday 10 a.m.-5 p.m.

Cougar Shoppe, Farm Credit Building, 601 W 1st Ave (455-5447). This extension of the Pullman Student Bookstore sells Cougar-imprint clothing and souvenirs, regional books, text books for WSU extended learning courses, WSU picture prints, computer-related items and even Cougar Gold Cheese. Open Monday through Friday 11 a.m.-7 p.m. In the summer, it's open 8:30 a.m.-5:30 p.m.

Country at Heart, 616 E 3rd (747-8867). You'll find a full gamut of items, including custom floral pieces, pine furniture, mirrors, Yankee candles, live plants, window planters, dolls, stuffed animals, and even yard and garden items at Country at Heart. Open Monday through Saturday 10 a.m.-5:30 p.m.

Country Cottage, 1224 S Grand (456-7292) This mecca for handicraft enthusiasts boasts a fine selection of country and Victorian gifts. Within the three-room store are areas devoted to specific themes, such as gifts for teachers, items crafted for men or pieces specifically made for children. Everywhere you'll find lace, dolls, dried wreaths, painted items, porcelain pieces and more. Open Monday through Friday 9:30 a.m.-5:30 p.m. and Saturday 10 a.m.-5 p.m.

Four Seasons, 222 N Howard (747-2315). Four Seasons consistently offers some of the most unique seasonal gifts in town. Customers look forward to the next holiday just to see what delightful and different items will be on display. Throughout the year, a large selection of practical and whimsical cups and mugs is located right across from the coffee roaster. Cards, spices, cooking utensils, coffee beans, cookbooks and more are displayed throughout the store. An extra bonus is the espresso bar in the rear, which encourages a leisurely pause. Open Monday through Friday 7:30 a.m.-7 p.m., Saturday 7:30 a.m.-6 p.m. and Sunday 11 a.m.-5 p.m.

Global Folk Art Bazaar, 1401 W 1st (838-0664). This non-profit store is a project of the Peace and Justice League. Its goal is to directly support third-world craftspeople by selling their items without involving middlemen and markups. The store is staffed by volunteers, and the items for sale can include hand-carved wood and stone pieces, stitched linens, toys, baskets and a range of one-of-a-kind pieces. Open Monday through Saturday 10 a.m.-6 p.m.

Gooseberry Country, 12014 E 1st Ave (924-3000). Owner Marilyn Mauer has sold quality antiques and country accessories for over 10 years. Her store was originally a home built in the late 1800s, and each of its six rooms, including the sunporch, is full of pottery, old and new linens, baskets, Yankee candles, antique pine and oak furniture and country collectibles. It's the only location in Spokane to offer new Fiesta ware. Credit cards accepted. Open Monday through Saturday 10 a.m.-5 p.m.

Joel, 165 S Post (624-2354). When looking for fine-quality gifts, whether crafted from terra cotta or silver, Joel is the place. From birdhouses to books, crystal stemware to cards, children's toys to pottery pieces, Joel is at once traditional and cutting-edge. Along with the constantly changing display of gifts, both seasonal and timeless, they handle dinnerware, cooking utensils, indoor and outdoor furniture and fine glassware. Open Monday through Thursday and Saturday 10 a.m.-6 p.m., Friday 10 a.m.-8 p.m. and Sunday noon-5 p.m.

The Kaufer Company, 907 W Boone (326-7070). Christian gifts, books, music, church supplies, robes, communion ware, medals, rosaries — anything with religious applications is either on hand here or the staff knows where to find it. Open Monday through Thursday and Saturday 9:30 a.m.-5:30 p.m. and Friday 9:30 a.m.-8 p.m.

Made in Washington, Riverpark Square, near Nordstrom (838-1517) and Northtown Mall (482-7379). Both stores offer a tantalizing selection of gift items made, caught or grown in Washington. Owner Bob Dewey, of local Import Market fame, has chosen items as diverse as Mt. St. Helens glass pieces, smoked salmon, huckleberry jams and T-shirts with Northwest motifs. You can create your own gift packs and have them mailed. Stores are open during regular mall hours seven days a week.

The Market, 9704 N Newport Hwy, Northpointe Plaza (468-0260). The Market handles a selection of lotions and body/bath products, candles, cards and gift wraps, wreaths and seasonal items, such as garden ornaments and Christmas decorations. Open everyday at 10 a.m. except for Sunday when they open at noon. They close at 6 p.m., except for Thursday when they close at 8 p.m., Friday at 9 p.m. and Sunday at 5 p.m.

Naturium, 4750 N Division, 2nd Level, Northtown Mall (484-7014). This store specializes in earth-related gifts, many with an educational purpose. The layout, look and product line is nature-oriented. Birdhouses, wind chimes, cassettes of nature sounds and soothing music, rocks, model kits of the solar system and dinosaurs are a few of the items for sale. Open Monday through Saturday 9:30 a.m.-9 p.m. and Sunday 10 a.m.-6 p.m.

Simply Northwest, 11808 E Sprague (927-8206). Started over five years ago, Simply Northwest has carved a niche in the corporate gift-giving market. Now individuals, as well as corporate buyers, are able to purchase ready-made gift containers or design their own by simply stopping by the Valley store. Stocking hundreds of different Northwest food and wine products, as well as crafts created by regional artists, insures a quality gift package which is as unique as the area and reflects the gift-giver. Simply Northwest is open Monday through Saturday 9 a.m.-5 p.m. or by appointment. If you're unable to visit the store in person, you can order a beautiful and unusual gift package by phone.

Tobacco World, 621 W Mallon at the Flour Mill (326-4665). This is a gift store for both smokers and non-smokers. Smokers can find a selection of over 500 pipes and 50 pipe tobacco blends, as well as over 7,000 cigars in a walk-in humidor. For non-smokers, there are limited edition sculptures by Rick Cain and carvings by Big Sky Carvers of Montana. Open Monday though Saturday 10 a.m.-6 p.m., with hours extended on Friday to 9 p.m. and Sunday open 11 a.m.-5 p.m.

Wonders of the World, 621 W Mallon, at the Flour Mill (328-6890). This store brings science class to life, with its stock of jewelry, rocks, fossils, sea shells and even fetishes. Unique and beautiful objects are crafted using natural materials, so you'll find finished pieces as well as raw elements. It's a great place for discovering that one-of-a-kind object. Open Monday through Saturday 10 a.m.-6 p.m., Friday until 9 p.m. and Sunday 11 a.m.-5 p.m.

Home Interiors and Exteriors

La Maison Fabrics, 110 S Cedar (456-5624). Quality mill-direct upholstery and drapery fabrics are sold here. They also have some accessory items, such as baskets, pillows and throws, which complement the range of their fabric selections. Open Monday through Friday 10 a.m.-5 p.m. and Saturday 10 a.m.-3 p.m.

Spokane Tile and Design, 1325 W 1st Ave (624-0339). Created by interior designer Julie Wells, who found herself traveling to Seattle everytime she wanted something unique and different, this shop includes a wide and exciting display of tile colors and textures to fit a variety of tastes. You'll find marbles, terra cotta, slate, limestone and glass selections, and hand-painted tiles from France, Italy and Mexico. Also on display, local potter Andrew Baucom's scalloped pottery, plus bas-relief designs crafted by a husband and wife team living in Odessa, Washington. Prices range from mid-level to high-end, and consultation services are available. Open Monday through Friday 10 a.m.-5 p.m. and Saturday 9 a.m.-3 p.m.

Wallflowers, 2820 E 30th (534-5064). If you're searching for that certain "look" but don't know how to achieve it, try Wallflowers. This store offers one-stop shopping for interior design advice, wallpaper selection, carpets and window coverings. The extensive, high-quality selection includes styles and designs hard to find elsewhere. Right next door is Wallflowers Too (536-9725), which houses in-stock wallpaper and supplies. Open Monday through Friday 9 a.m.-5:30 p.m. and Saturday 9 a.m.-5 p.m.

Carpets and Rugs

Richard Kirishian Oriental Rug Co., 220 E 2nd (624-8084). In 1918, three brothers from Armenia, who learned the craft of carpet weaving from their father in the old country, established a rug store where the Bon Marché now stands. By 1920, they expanded quarters, moving to First and Howard and, by the 1940s, each brother established his own operation. Richard Kirishian's father was one of these brothers and his store occupied a well-known spot at 2nd and Wall. In 1994, the store was relocated and expanded and now offers a variety of fine furnishings as well as carpets from around the world. To walk through the store is to experience quality, from the cloisonné bowls to hand carved wood pedestals, bronze sculptures to hand-painted lamps.

For those interested in expanding their appreciation of fine carpets, there are several educational courses offered. Call for scheduled times and topics. The store is open Monday through Friday 7:30 a.m.-6 p.m. and Saturday 9 a.m.-5 p.m.

Kirishian's Floor Center, 3405 E Sprague (535-1590). Expanding the family tradition of Oriental rug sales, Kirishian's (cousins to Richard Kirishian) offers a broad range of floor coverings, including manufactured carpet, vinyl, tile and even hardwoods. They also clean Oriental rugs and do certified rug appraisals. Open Monday through Friday 8:30 a.m.-5:30 p.m. and Saturday 9:30 a.m.-4 p.m.

Pande Cameron, 1319 W 1st (624-6082). Since they first opened their Seattle store over 50 years ago, Pande Cameron's has specialized in Oriental Rugs. This location is their first shop outside of the Seattle/Bellevue area and was opened in 1993.

To walk through this store is to travel the world of rugs, from traditional Pakistani patterns to more contemporary Scandinavian designs. In-home consultation is available. There's a sign-up sheet for classes in rug appreciation and knowledge. Pande Cameron is a family-owned business strongly committed to the quality and integrity of their product and service. Open Monday through Friday 10 a.m.-5 p.m. and Saturday 10 a.m.-4 p.m.

Furniture

Abodio, Northtown Mall (483-1009). If you like fun, contemporary furniture with simple lines and designs, this is the place to shop. They also offer a range of accessory products from dishes to glassware. Open Monday through Saturday 9 a.m.-9 p.m. and Sunday 10 a.m.-6 p.m.

Buffalo Street Interiors, 9411 N Newport Highway (466-6702). Contemporary, yet classic willow- and pine-style furniture are sold in this small and charming shop. They also sell accessories and gifts to complement the western rustic furniture. Open Monday through Friday 10 a.m.-5:30 p.m., Saturday 10 a.m.-5 p.m. and Sunday 1 p.m.-5 p.m.

Dania International, 319 W Riverside (624-7740). Dania offers contemporary office and home furniture. Most of their pieces have a sleek, European-laminated look, though there are some country and traditional designs. Kids love traveling the antiquated elevator between the three floors. Open Monday through Saturday 10 a.m.-6 p.m., except Fridays when they remain open until 7 p.m. and Sunday noon-5 p.m.

Ennis, 8313 N Division (467-6707). A wide selection of Drexel Heritage's traditional, fine furniture including patio pieces, bedding, lamps and carpets is available through Ennis'. Open Monday through Friday 9:30 a.m. - 6 p.m., Saturday 10 a.m.-5 p.m. and Sunday noon-4 p.m.

Expressions, 313 W Riverside (455-9826). You can mix and match fabrics to furniture styles here to create a custom look for your home. Fun and funky accessories are also on hand. Open Monday through Friday 9:30 a.m.-6 p.m., Saturday 9:30-5:30 p.m. and Sunday, noon-4 p.m.

Joel, 165 S Post (624-2354). Whether it's contemporary or classic, as long as it's quality, you can find it at Joel. From futons to children's bedroom sets, patio furniture to a bookshelf unit with its own ladder, Joel packs a lot into its second-floor furniture space. For discounted items, visit the third floor. Open Monday through Thursday 10 a.m.-6 p.m., Friday 10 a.m.-8 p.m., Saturday 10 a.m.-6 p.m. and Sunday noon-5 p.m.

New Directions, 1328 S Southeast Blvd. (535-1313). It doesn't matter if you need one piece or a whole grouping, New Directions offers an ever-changing display of gently-used fine furniture. Items taken on consignment, by appointment. Open Tuesday through Saturday 10 a.m.-5 p.m.

Opportunity Furniture, 12014 E 1st (928-7341). Since 1945, Jerry Mauer has offered some of the lowest prices on furniture in town. At one time, he sold "seconds" under the name Second Time Around, but now it's 100% new household items; no appliances or TVs. "It's so affordable, people don't want to believe it's new," said Irv Scheller, who operates Irv's Antiques in the rear of the building. The small, no-frills setting allows for the savings, which Jerry passes along. Open Monday through Saturday 9 a.m.-5 p.m.

Spear's, 1300 N Argonne Rd. (926-1600). Spear's offers Thomasville furniture in both contemporary and traditional designs. They also sell carpeting. Open Monday through Thursday 9:30 a.m.-6 p.m., Friday 9:30 a.m.-7 p.m., Saturday 9:30 a.m.-6 p.m. and Sunday noon-4 p.m.

Lighting

Luminaria, 154 S Madison (747-9198). If you're looking for mass-produced, run-of-the mill lamps, don't stop here. On the other hand, if you want a vintage fixture, unusual lamp or quality cloth lampshade, this is your place. Not only does Luminaria sell lamps, fixtures and supplies, they do restoration and repair work, design custom-made pieces and offer consultations. Open Tuesday through Friday 10 a.m.-5:30 p.m. and Saturday 10 a.m.-3 p.m.

Windows

Graham Window Coverings, 6520 N Ash (327-3144). Family-owned and operated since the 1920s, Graham's provides custom-made window coverings at a reasonable price. Pleated shades, draperies, window quilts, roller shades, you name it and they can make it. They offer free in home estimates and, at the store, carry a limited supply of misfit pieces that are marked way below value. Open Monday through Friday 9 a.m.-5 p.m.

Exterior Materials

Brown Building Materials, 111 N Erie (535-0112). As hard to find as it is unique, Brown's Building is located beneath the James Keefe Bridge next to the Spokane River. There are new and used doors, windows, lights, scrap metal, railroad timbers, pipe, lumber, hardware — the list goes as far as their six-acre spread. Be sure to dress in your grubbies and leave plenty of time for finding unexpected treasures, as it's a definite browse-and-touch type of place. Open Monday through Friday 8 a.m.-5 p.m. and Saturday 8 a.m.-2 p.m.

Layrite Products, 1225 E Trent (535-1737). While in the past Layrite has worked mostly with contractors and professional builders, they've been expanding their retail sales. Natural stones, retaining wall systems, cinder and patio blocks, pavers, pre-formed concrete planters, tables and benches, and even pellet and wood stoves make this a good stopping place for the do-it-yourself home builder. They also carry pre-mix materials to mortar your project in place. Open Monday through Friday 7 a.m.-5 p.m. and Saturday 8 a.m.-2 p.m.

Jewelers

Dodson's Jewelers, 516 W Riverside (624-4163), Northtown Mall (484-4080) and Coeur d'Alene (208-664-6357). When you've been in the jewelry business since before the Great Spokane Fire of 1889, you know you've established a sound reputation for a quality product and service. In addition to jewelry, Dodson's handles Rolex and Seiko sales, china, crystal, silver and fine gifts. Call ahead for store hours.

Jewelry Design Center, 4407 N Division (487-5905) and 1525 N Pines (921-5654). At the Jewelry Design Center, eight certified goldsmiths craft fine jewelry on location. You can buy stock items from their cases, some one-of-a-kind pieces, have an item custom made, or even remount and redesign an existing creation. They work mainly in gold, and some silver, but their furnaces are not built to handle platinum (though they can order it for you). Both stores are open Monday through Friday 10 a.m.-6 p.m. and Saturday 10 a.m.-4 p.m.

Mandell's, 211 N Wall, Skywalk Level (747-7111), University City (926-6220) and Northpointe Plaza (467-0082). For over 50 years, this family-owned business has sold quality engagement sets, wedding bands, fine diamonds, gemstones and watches with names like Lasalle, Pulsar and Seiko. Watch and jewelry repair are done on the premises. They also handle appraisals and make estate and diamond purchases. The Skywalk and Northpointe stores are open Monday through Saturday 10 a.m.-6 p.m., while the University store is open seven days a week during regular mall hours.

Rings and Things, Riverpark Square (624-8949). Owner Russ Nobbs has gathered together an eclectic combination of fun and fanciful jewelry as well as gifts from around the world. Quartz crystals, charms, T-shirts, individual beads and thousands of earrings are represented. There's even a bead room devoted to do-it-yourself jewelry makers. Open Monday through Friday 9:30 a.m.-9:30 p.m., Saturday 9:30 a.m.-6 p.m. and Sunday 11 a.m.-5 p.m.

Weisfield Jewelers, Northtown Mall (484-6208) and University Center (924-6144). Weisfield's specialty is diamonds. Their educated sales staff sells fine-quality pieces, with prices ranging from $100 to $10,000. Periodically, they do in-store promotions with a jeweler on hand; otherwise they work with a local jeweler to set or repair individual pieces. Open seven days a week at both locations during regular mall hours.

Music

CD's We Bee, P.O. Box 141757, Spokane 99214-1757 (922-7378). It would be difficult to ignore CD's We Bee when describing Spokane area music spots, if, for no other reason, than they're the largest mail order compact disc catalog operation in the Inland Northwest. Their catalogue (one-year subscription, $8) lists over 80,000 titles and includes classical, country, jazz, folk, new age, rock and more. Though they handle calls from folks as far away as Europe and South America, they're still a best-kept, backyard secret. For callers outside the Spokane area, call 800-MOST-CDs.

Four Thousand Holes, 1502 N Monroe (325-1914). If you're looking for variety in new and used CDs, cassettes and record imports, this is a good stop. They also handle memorabilia and T-shirts and will do special orders with no hassle. Open Monday through Saturday noon-7 p.m.

Guitar Gallerie, 421 W Riverside (747-1083). Opening four years ago, the Guitar Gallerie has since established a reputation for quality products and great service. They handle mainly new and some used handbuilt and small production guitars noted for their quality tone. Once you've purchased an instrument, they'll custom fit it to your specific needs and style of play. Though a lot of their business is mail order (1-800-346-9042), you can also stop by the store. Open Tuesday through Friday 11 a.m.-6 p.m. and Saturday 11 a.m.-5 p.m.

Hoffman Music Company, 1430 N Monroe (328-3888) and 12412 E Sprague (922-3363). This has been Spokane's full-service music store since 1913. They offer instruments and sound equipment, rentals, financing and even consignment of musical gear through their Music Connection, 440 W Sharp (328-6691) store.

Music World and the Consignment Center, 1215 N Division (328-2853). This is one-stop shopping for musicians. You can buy new equipment, trade used items, have your equipment repaired and purchase sheet music. Open Monday through Saturday 10 a.m.-7 p.m.

Moon Shadow, 2 N Howard (624-7573). For those who listen to the beat of a different drum, Moon Shadow, formerly Moon Bear, is your kind of store. West African djemes, Native American hoop drums, Australian didjeridu and Irish bodhrans are sold next to rainsticks, sitars, gongs and much more. They have an eclectic selection of tapes and CDs featuring mostly percussion instruments. Open Monday through Saturday 10 a.m.-6 p.m.

Petrucelly's Violins, 1505 N Ash (327-5054). This is a full service shop offering appraisals, repairs, sales and rentals of violins, as well as stringed harps, guitars and banjos. During the winter, the store is open 10:30 a.m.-6 p.m., with shortened summer hours.

The Sound Hole, 828 W Sprague (624-5033). Owners Clair and Arvid Lundin offer guitars, mandolins, recorders, instructional materials, banjos, autoharps and harmonics in their small, yet well-stocked store. They also are an excellent source of information for area musical events and activities. Open Monday through Friday 9:30 a.m.-5:30 p.m. and Saturday 10 a.m.-5 p.m.

Sports Cards and Blues Headquarters, 12832 W Sunset Highway, Airway Heights (244-3812). This is your best bet for finding the largest selection of blues music at good prices in the area. Open Monday through Saturday 11 a.m.-6 p.m.

Street Music, 117 N Howard (624-7722). If you enjoy history or music, or both, this is a must-stop spot. The 1891 building, which currently houses Street Music and Cafe Street Music, was once known as Duffy and Butler's Saloon. The old tin-pressed ceiling is visible, and the exposed brick walls add to the ambience of the interior. Also inside you'll find a niche-market music store specializing in special orders. Owner Jack Lindberg focuses on service and offers a large selection of New Age, folk, jazz, classical, Celtic and ethnic music you won't find everywhere. You can also listen to selections before you purchase, which is a great way to expand your musical horizons. Another bonus is Street Music's collection of over 500 classic and foreign videos available for rent. Open Monday through Saturday 10 a.m.-6 p.m.

Nurseries and Garden Shops

La Tierra, 154 S Madison (747-9198). This small shop, adjacent to Luminaria and operated by the same owners, is located in a building originally built to hold furs, then used as a garage. It's also a gem of a find. Offering fine garden and landscape ornaments, La Tierra also stocks items such as carved-crocodile stepping stones, architectural artifacts from England, antique wrought iron fences and even custom, made picnic tables and benches. Open Tuesday through Friday 10 a.m.-5:30 p.m. and Saturday 10 a.m.-3 p.m.

Lamb's Nursery, 101 E Sharp (328-7956). Mention the word "Spokane" to a gardener outside the Inland Northwest, and they'll ask about Lamb's Nursery. Situated in a quaint yellow house near Gonzaga University, Lamb's block of perennials is a never-ending display of color and texture. Though most of their stock is sold via mail order, walk-in customers are more than welcome. Open Monday through Friday 9 a.m.-5 p.m.

Mel's Nursery and Floral, 8800 N Division (467-5132). It's hard to classify Mel's because of the diversity of the products it sells. Some stop by to shop the large garden and nursery area with trees, shrubs, annuals and perennials, as well as garden ornaments and supplies. Others come to Mel's for the quality furniture, complimented by an indoor cage with live birds softly chirping. Then there's a wide range of gift items, cards and housewares including dishes and cookware. Some even come for the indoor espresso bar. During the grey months of winter, their enclosed greenhouse is a haven of gentle sound and light. The whole place is tasteful, constantly changing and a delight to all your senses. Oh, and yes, they do have a floral area also. Open Monday through Saturday 9 a.m.-8 p.m. and Sunday 9 a.m.-6 p.m.

Northwest Seed and Pet, 2422 E Sprague (534-0694) and 7302 N Division (484-7387). For over 50, years local gardeners have gone to Northwest Seed and Pet when they're serious about their outdoor projects. This is an old-fashioned garden store where weather vanes sit next to bins of bulbs and pots and tools are two rows down from the extensive seed display. Northwest Seed stocks it all, from koi to fertilizer, wind chimes to seed pots, bedding plants to garden ornaments. Another plus is their pet area, which tempts child-sized gardeners to tag along with mom and dad for a look at the fish, puppies, pot-bellied pigs and more. Wednesday is "Lady's Day," offering a 10% discount to all women shoppers. The Division store is open Monday through Friday 9 a.m.-9 p.m. and weekends 9 a.m.-6 p.m. The Sprague store opens Monday through Friday 9 a.m.-7 p.m. and weekends 9 a.m.-6 p.m.

Rockford Water Gardens, 320 S River, Rockford, WA (291-5459). One woman's love of water gardens created this outlet specializing in aquatic plants. The owner loves to share her first-hand experiences with building and creating ponds and has several water garden displays set up. Aquatic plants are for sale here also. Open Friday through Monday 10 a.m.-5 p.m.

Stanek's, 2929 E 27th (535-2939). Stanek's is as much a Spokane institution as lilacs in spring. Since 1913, they've advised countless gardeners on the best plants, trees and shrubs for successful landscaping in the Inland Northwest. Between their knowledgeable staff, nursery selection and special recipe fertilizer, you're bound to acquire a green thumb. Seasonal and year-round gift items are available, and Christmas wouldn't be official without a visit through their selection of theme-decorated trees. Open Monday through Saturday 9 a.m.-5:30 p.m., closed Sunday during the summer, but open on Sundays 11 a.m.-5 p.m. the rest of the year.

Special Services

Pet Care

Granny Scoops Poop Patrol (489-POOP). Granny Scoops' listing in the phone book is directly after a restaurant with a similar name, as a result they periodically receive calls asking, "What's on the menu?" In case you couldn't guess their line of work, their advertising slogan says it all: "We pick up where your dog leaves off." This weekly dog-litter program offers service throughout the city and valley. They even offer a senior discount.

Critter Sitter and House Sitting Service, P.O. Box 20035, Spokane 99204 (455-7776). If you plan to be away from home and your pet needs care, call Critter Sitter. They have over ten years experience caring for furred, feathered, finned and scaled animals, which remain in their own homes. You'll receive twice-daily service including water, food and exercise for your pet while you're away, and they'll look after your house at the same time. While this particular service works only the South Hill, they'll be happy to refer you to critter sitters in other areas.

24-Hour Copy Services

Kinko's. With four Spokane locations; N 1320 Hamilton (484-0601), N 7116 Division (484-2679), 2630 E 29th (535-7233), 15204 E Sprague (922-4929), and one Coeur d'Alene outlet, 119 W Appleway, Coeur d'Alene, Idaho (208-664-2880), Kinko's has you covered for a wide range of business services. Though making copies, self-service or otherwise, is the mainstay of their business, they also handle faxes, create posters and banners, rent computers and typewriters, offer binding services, custom-print orders, sell stationary supplies and more. In addition, they're open 24 hours a day, with reduced rates on rental equipment during the off hours.

Newspapers

Jimmy'Z Newsstand and Espresso Café, 521 W Sprague (838-7613). For the largest selection of newspapers and magazines in town, try Jimmy'Z. They carry publications from all over the world and a small spot to sip espresso and read the news. Open seven days a week, Monday through Friday 7 a.m.-7 p.m. and weekends 8 a.m. - 5 p.m.

New to the Area

The Compass Club (928-6982). This is a non-profit social organization for women new to the Spokane area. The third Tuesday of every month, coffee is served at various members homes throughout the area. This is an opportunity to talk to and visit with other club members. There are special interest groups within the club, such as bridge, quilting, moms 'n' tots, couples' gourmet and a book bunch. They also host several annual events to benefit the Spokane Child Abuse and Neglect Prevention Center.

Newcomers Service of Greater Spokane, P.O. Box 13703, Spokane 99213 (624-1661). This locally-owned service will mail newcomers a free, no-obligation packet full of community information, business brochures and special offers. It's a great way to find out about the community without ever leaving your home.

Foreign Exchange

Seafirst Bank, Spokane and Eastern Branch, 601 W Riverside (353-1448). This bank will sell foreign currency, but it requires a five-day lead time. This service is available to both customers and non-customers. English, French, German, Japanese, Australian and Canadian travelers' checks are available at all times during regular banking hours.

Sporting Goods Stores

General Outfitters

Big Five Sporting Goods, 7501 N Division (467-6970) and 5725 E Sprague (533-9811). This California-based chain offers a large selection of equipment, clothes and footwear for a variety of team and individual sports. From archery to racquet ball, and camping supplies to exercise equipment, you'll find name brands and good prices too. They also sell hunting gear including state licenses. Open Monday through Friday 10 a.m.-9 p.m., Saturday 9 a.m.-9 p.m. and Sunday 10 a.m.-6 p.m.

General Store, 2424 N Division (328-8000). Since 1946, the General Store has been outfitting campers, hunters and fishermen of the Inland Northwest. This is where you'll find your basic supplies at reasonable prices. Among other camping gear, they sell stoves, lanterns, archery supplies, fishing tackle, guns and ammo, backpacks and sleeping bags. Open Monday through Friday 9 a.m.-9 p.m., Saturday 8:30 a.m.-8 p.m. and Sunday 9 a.m.-5:30 p.m.

Kimmel Athletic Supply, 202 E Mission (326-7710). Team sports has long been Kimmel's area of expertise. They sell football, baseball, basketball, track and soccer equipment and also do reconditioning and repairs. They can supply custom graphics and embroidery for team jackets and uniforms. Open Monday through Friday 9 a.m.-7 p.m., Saturday 9 a.m.-6 p.m. and Sunday noon-5 p.m.

Mountain Gear, 2002 N Division (325-9000). Mountain Gear specializes in outdoor sporting equipment and lessons in how to use it. Besides having rental equipment available, they can also make repairs on your equipment. The indoor climbing wall and water pool large enough for kayak and canoeing provide hands-on experience during lessons. They have clothing and a good selection of outdoor literature too. Open Monday through Thursday 9:30 a.m.-8 p.m., Friday 9:30 a.m.-9 p.m., Saturday 9:30 a.m.-6 p.m. and Sunday noon-5 p.m.

Play it Again Sports, 86 E Francis (484-1551) and 14208 E Sprague (924-4031). If you have equipment that is not being used, you can sell it at either of these locations. You may also find a great buy on both used and new gear. There's a selection of hockey, golf, tennis, camping, skiing and even in line skating equipment as well as other sporting gear. Both stores are open Monday through Friday 10 a.m.-7 p.m., Saturday 10 a.m.-6 p.m. and Sunday 11 a.m.-4 p.m.

Recreational Equipment Inc. (REI), 1125 N Monroe (328-9900). Here you'll find both equipment and experts in camping, climbing, biking, backpacking, cross-country skiing, canoeing and kayaking. REI sells clothing, supplies, maps, literature and rentals and has a rock climbing wall. For a minimal one-time only membership fee of $15, you'll also earn dividends towards purchasing power the following year. Open Monday through Friday 9:30 a.m.-9 p.m., Saturday 9:30 a.m.-6 p.m. and Sunday 11 a.m.-5 p.m.

Spokane Olympic Sports, 12505 E Sprague (926-1568). Recognized as the Spokane Valley's full-line sports center, this store offers equipment for most of the major team sports. They also provide baseball and softball batting cages and have a silk screen shop to imprint uniforms. Open Monday through Friday 9 a.m.-7 p.m., Saturday 9 a.m.-6 p.m. and Sunday Noon-5 p.m.

Outdoor Sportsman and Sportswear, 1602 North Division (328-1556). The Outdoor Sportsman offers both an archery and fly-fishing pro shop, as well as rod and reel repair. They cater to the hunting, camping and fishing crowd in search of equipment, clothes and footwear. Check out the large selection of rental videos for sportsmen. Open Monday through Thursday 9 a.m.-6:30 p.m., Friday 9 a.m.-7 p.m., Saturday 9 a.m.-6 p.m. and Sunday 9 a.m.-5 p.m.

Tri State Outfitters, 6275 Sunshine Street, Coeur D'Alene (208-772-0613). This store might be one of your best bets for camping and hiking supplies in North Idaho. They also stock tennis, volleyball and other sports equipment. Open Monday through Saturday 9 a.m.-8 p.m. and Sunday 9 a.m.-6 p.m.

White Elephant Surplus Stores, 1730 N Division (328-3100) and 12614 E Sprague (924-3006). The family-owned White Elephant offers basic equipment for hunters, anglers and campers. You can also find boats, motors and boating supplies. Open Monday through Thursday 9 a.m.-6 p.m., Friday 9 a.m.-9 p.m. and Saturday 9 a.m.-6 p.m.

Bicycles

Al's South Hill Schwinn Cyclery, 3713 S Grand (747-4187). For family biking needs from the smallest tot to the experienced rider, Al's is a good bet. This family-owned business also handles repair work on all brands. Open Monday through Friday 9 a.m.-6 p.m. and Saturday 9 a.m.-5 p.m.

Bikeworks, 930 W 2nd (455-9528) and 14705 E Sprague (922-0226). The owner of Bikeworks is also a member of the City of Spokane's Bike Advisory Board. This is just one facet of his commitment to encouraging biking in the area. Either shop handles a medium to high-end range of bikes, has a repair shop and provides two-year servicing of bikes bought through their stores. Both stores are open Monday through Friday 9 a.m.-6 p.m. and Saturday 9 a.m.-5 p.m. The downtown store, on 2nd, is also open Sunday noon-5 p.m.

Columbia Cycle, 1808 N Monroe (327-1465). For over 40 years, this family-owned business has serviced and supplied bikes to Spokane families. Columbia Cycle offers a wide range of bike styles and sizes to fit all ages of your family. Open Monday through Friday 9 a.m.-6 p.m., Saturday 9 a.m.-5 p.m. and Sunday noon-5 p.m.

Garland Cycle and Supply, 603 W Garland (325-9757). This family-owned and operated store is geared to outfitting the whole family with bikes. They're well-versed in servicing all makes of bicycles. You'll also find exercise equipment and snowboards available here. Open Monday through Saturday 9 a.m.-7 p.m. and Sunday 11 a.m.-5 p.m.

North Division Bicycle Shop, 10503 N Division (467-2453). Don't let the size of this shop fool you. Located in a small-sized former home, the store offers sales, service, information and great follow through. Open Monday through Thursday 9 a.m.-6 p.m., Friday 9 a.m.-8 p.m., Saturday 9 a.m.-6 p.m. and Sunday noon-5 p.m.

Boating Supplies

Big Wave Dave's Whitewater Supply, 2529 N Division (325-1665). Try Big Wave Dave's for all your white water supplies, from accessories to clothing. They also stock a full line of inflatable boats suitable for both whitewater or the back pond. There really is a Big Wave Dave behind the name, and he's married to Big Swim Kim. The store is open Monday through Friday 9:30 a.m.-6 p.m. and Saturday 9:30 a.m.-5 p.m.

Lloyd's Watersports Outlet Warehouse, 1233 N Division (326-0690). One of the largest selection of marine equipment in the area is available at Lloyd's. From down riggers, water skis and buoys to clothing, this water sport and appliance store carries a full line of accessories, equipment and even electronics. Open Monday through Friday 10 a.m.-7 p.m., Saturday 9:30 a.m.-5:30 p.m. and Sunday 11 a.m.-5 p.m.

Fishing

Propp's Rod and Fly Shop, 135 S Sherman (838-3474). This is Spokane's fly-fishing specialty shop. You can purchase custom-built rods, have your rod repaired or bamboo restored. A wide selection of fishing books are available. They offer casting and tying classes as well as guided fly-fishing trips. Open Monday through Friday 9 a.m.-6:30 p.m. and Saturday 9 a.m.-5:30 p.m.

Silver Bow Fly Fishing Adventures, 902 N Monroe (325-1960). This is Spokane's oldest fly-fishing guide service. They schedule fishing trips for parties of one or two in eastern Washington and on the Clark Fork in western Montana. A large selection of U.S.-made flies and fly-tying books are available. They also do custom tying and rod building. Open Monday through Saturday 9:30 a.m.-6:30 p.m.

Billiards

Global Billiard Supply, 2025 N Division (327-8858). Along with the new Brunswick tables, Global also has a selection of antique card and game tables, antique juke boxes, professional cues and dart supplies. With over 20 display tables, they offer a wide variety to fit any budget. They also recover tables. Open Monday through Saturday 9 a.m.-6 p.m.

Golf

National Golf, 114 S Dartmouth (927-GOLF) or 8701 N Division (468-0660). National is touted as Washington's largest golf store. You'll find all the major name brands in clubs, bags, shoes and carts here. The store also offers custom clubs and club repair. Both stores are open Monday through Friday 9 a.m.-7 p.m. and Saturday 9 a.m.-6 p.m. Sunday the Dartmouth store is open from noon-5 p.m. and the Division store 11 a.m.-5 p.m.

Nevada Bob's Discount Golf, 1004 N Atlantic (326-3320). You can find name-brand clothing and shoes, as well as clubs, bags, balls, carts, books, videos and accessories at Nevada Bob's. They also offer custom fitting and regripping. Open Monday through Friday 10 a.m.-5:30 p.m. and Saturday 9 a.m.-5 p.m.

Wide World of Golf, 4921 N Division (489-4653). Wide World has been servicing Spokane for over 18 years with pro-line equipment. With brand names like Tommy Armour, Wilson, Callaway and Cobra, you're sure to find the right equipment for your game. They also offer custom building and fitting of clubs as well as club repair. Open Monday through Saturday 9 a.m.-6 p.m. and Sunday 11 a.m.-5 p.m.

Guns

Brock's Gunsmithing Inc., 2104 N Division (328-9788). Brock's has three gunsmiths on site. They also sell a full line of rifles, shotguns, hand guns and hunters' clothing as well as trap and skeet shooting supplies. You'll find new and used models here. Open Monday through Friday 9 a.m.-6 p.m. and Saturday 9 a.m.-5 p.m.

Ed Karrer Gunatorium, 5323 N Argonne (924-3030). This store is the authorized agent for Savage, Winchester, Remington, Colt and Browning weapons. They handle repair work on all makes and models. Collectors note: their specialty is antiques and restoration work. Open Monday through Saturday 8 a.m.-5 p.m.

Running

The Human Race, 1405 N Argonne (927-7573). One of only 16 stores of its kind in the U.S., the Human Race focuses on running shoes, clothing and accessories. It's also the best place in town to find information and details on area events, tracks, trails and runs appropriate to every type of runner. All store employees are runners themselves and are a helpful resource in terms of "what's happening" in the world of running. Open Monday through Friday 9:30 a.m.-7 p.m. and Saturday 10 a.m.-6 p.m., Sunday noon-4 p.m.

Ski and Snow Sports

LouLou's, 428 E Pacific (624-2422) and 9324 N Division (468-8414). Loulou's is known for quality and selection of skis, clothing, snowboards and rollerblades. They also offer ski repairs and tune ups. You can also find discount sporting goods, rental equipment and water sport supplies including canoes and kayaks at both locations. The Pacific location sports an indoor ski school and is only open from August to April. Both store hours vary, with longer winter hours. Call ahead for specifications.

Spokane Alpine Haus, 12710 E Indiana (927-2505).The Alpine Haus specializes in name-brand new and used downhill and cross-country ski equipment, plus K-2 snowboards. They have a junior ski trade-in program where, for an initial cost of $120, plus $15 adjusting and wax fees, your child will be completely outfitted in a pair of used skis, boots and poles. Two years later, for only $20, plus the $15 adjustment and wax fee, your youngster can be upgraded to other used equipment. Open Monday through Friday 9 a.m.-6 p.m. and Saturday 9 a.m.-4 p.m.

Wintersport Ski Shop, 3220 N Division (328-2030). You'll find ski clothing, accessories, equipment and custom-boot fitting at this shop. They also rent snow and water skis, snowboards and in-line skates. For skiers 14 years and younger, Wintersport offers two programs. One is a flat-fee leasing arrangement, where for $125 you can outfit your youngster in new equipment for the year, and then upgrade for the same amount the following year. The other program offers used equipment for a greatly reduced price with second year upgrades at even greater savings, depending upon on size and availability. Open Monday through Saturday 9 a.m.-6 p.m. and Sunday noon-5 p.m.

Scuba Diving

Atlantis Aquatics, 4023 E Sprague (534-2144). The Atlantis Aquatics staff includes a former Navy Seal and a diver with over 18 years experience as two of their instructors. It also sports one of the largest inventories of scuba diving equipment in the area. They rent equipment and offer private or group instruction. Open Monday through Friday 11 a.m.-6 p.m. and Saturday 10 a.m.-5 p.m.

Scuba Center of Spokane, 3607 N Division (326-4653). This shop sells and rents snorkel and swim equipment including prescription masks. The Scuba Center also offers beginner diving packages, diving vacations and instruction in both scuba diving and snorkeling for groups or in private sessions. Equipment repair is available on the premises. Open Monday through Saturday 10 a.m.-6 p.m.

Toys and Hobbies

Beads

Off the Wall, 1225 N Monroe (324-0615). If you're not hooked on beads, one stop in this shop might change your mind. African trade beads, skunk beads, old copper and brass heishe and even elk and hand-carved deer beads are displayed. There are yoruba medicine totems, walking sticks, beaded belts, African masks and handmade baskets nestled beside singing bowls, prayer wheels, bells and dorjes. They also offer an ongoing meditation study group every Wednesday evening. Open Tuesday through Saturday 10 a.m.-5 p.m.

Dolls

Ann's Doll Shop,13524 Sprague (922-5054). Whether you're looking for a custom-made porcelain doll, a pair of kid leather shoes for a doll you already own, or lessons on crafting your own doll, Ann's is the place to visit. In addition to a wide range of supplies for making and dressing dolls, owner Sue Ann Johnson teaches classes to those interested in the craft of doll making. You're welcome to come in and learn at your own pace anytime the store is open, rather than be tied into a pre-arranged class schedule. Open Monday through Saturday 10 a.m.-4 p.m. and Tuesday and Thursday evenings from 7 p.m.-10 p.m.

Marion's Doll Shoppe, 5978 Highway 291, Suite #7 (468-1779). Marion's is located in the Suncrest area north of the city. It's comfortable, friendly and relaxed here. You can learn to create porcelain dolls during regular business hours, purchase parts and supplies or find a ready-made reproduction doll for sale. Open Tuesday through Saturday 11 a.m.-5 p.m.

Tender Loving Crafts, 5507 N Alberta (327-6097). Tender Loving Crafts came into being as the owner's basement hobby grew. Custom-made porcelain dolls can be selected from a display of samples on hand, or you can learn to make your own during one of the classes offered. A large stock of greenware molds, doll-making tools and accessories, eyes, wigs, shoes, etc, are also for sale. Open Tuesday and Wednesday 10 a.m.-9 p.m., Thursday and Friday 10 a.m.-4 p.m. and alternate Saturdays. Call to verify dates and times.

Glass

Gallery of Glass, 9405 E Sprague (924-8560). Custom-made stained glass pieces and supplies can be found here. Lamps, windows and door panels are on display. Custom pieces can be commissioned and classes are also offered. Open Monday through Friday 10 a.m.-5:30 p.m. and Saturday 10 a.m.-3 p.m.

Ryan House Studio of Stained Glass, 101 E Baldwin (327-4591). At the Ryan House, they specialize in larger pieces of glass for residential and commercial buildings. You can also purchase custom-made windows, stained, beveled or etched. They sell stained glass pieces, which can be cut to size, and glass supplies. Stained glass classes are offered, as is repair and restoration work. Open Monday through Saturday 9 a.m.-6 p.m.

Boats, Planes and Trains

RC Hobbies of Spokane, 12609 E Sprague (927-3011). RC's is the area's largest supplier of pieces and parts for radio-controlled cars, planes, helicopters and boats. They also have a selection of pre-assembled vehicles. Open Monday through Friday 9 a.m.-5:30 p.m. and Saturday 9 a.m.-5 p.m.

Sunset Junction Model Trains, 213 E Sprague (838-2379). This is the spot for train enthusiasts. They're authorized to repair and sell Lionel trains and more. Even if you aren't buying, it's even fun just watching the trains that are set up and running. Open Tuesday through Friday 11 a.m.-5:30 p.m. and Saturday 10 a.m.-5 p.m.

Miniatures

Small Wonders, 3527 E Sprague (535-5011). This "small" shop, no pun intended, is reputed to have the largest selection of miniatures in the entire Northwest. They specialize in a large selection of doll houses, miniature furniture and accessories crafted by nationally-known artists. Open Monday through Saturday 10 a.m.-5:30 p.m. and Sunday 11 a.m.-4:30 p.m.

Stamps

A&L Northside Stamp Shop, 4601 N Nevada (487-8953). For over 15 years, A&L Stamp shop has been a mecca for stamp enthusiasts. Counter to the growing trend of protecting fragile stamps by keeping customers at a distance, A&L is a very hands-on oriented place. Browse to your heart's content, or ask the knowledgeable owners to share their love and enthusiasm for collecting. A kids' club meeting on alternate Saturdays during the school year introduces the younger generation to this interesting hobby. Open Tuesday through Saturday 10 a.m.-5 p.m.

Toys and Games

Anakko Toys, Riverpark Square (456-0982). From TV news anchor to mother to owner of this children's store specializing in educational and fun toys, Anali Torrado Weatherhead has done it all. Anakko is Anali's answer to finding toys which challenge and stimulate a child's play. Open Monday through Friday 9:30 a.m. - 9 p.m., Saturday 9:30 a.m.-6 p.m. and Sunday 11 a.m.-6 p.m.

Toys 'R' Us, 6104 N Division (487-3160). If you've never been into the "world's largest toy-store," be prepared for a toy overload. It's like Santa's world, 365 days a year. They also handle children's clothing, furniture and such, so it's not all toys. If you're looking for the latest TV-advertised item, it'll probably be here. Open Monday through Saturday 9:30 a.m.-9:30 p.m. and Sunday 10 a.m.-7 p.m.

White Elephant, 1730 N Division (328-3100) and 12614 E Sprague (924-3006). Before there was a Toys 'R' Us, Spokane had the White Elephant. Imagine shelves piled sky-high with the latest toy on the market nestled next to the traditional favorites of your childhood. This may be the only place in town where you'll find a Brook Shield's doll, an erector-set, a Barney dinosaur and a souvenir from Expo '74 all in one spot. Adults will enjoy it too, because they also stock the latest and greatest in sporting goods. The prices are very reasonable, but leave your credit cards and checks at home. They take cash sales only. Open Monday through Thursday 9 a.m.-6 p.m., Friday 9 a.m.-9 p.m. and Saturday 9 a.m.-6 p.m.

Uncle's Games Puzzles Etc., 402 W Main (456-4607). For those who cried when the Book and Game Company left the Flour Mill, weep no more. Uncle's is the resurrection of this wonderful store. Chock full of both traditional games, like chess and checkers, and newer games geared for travel in the car, Uncle's sells a wealth of fun.

They also handle a good selection of puzzles, so for inclement weather, or a great gift, be sure and check out this store. Open Monday through Saturday 10 a.m.-9 p.m. and Sunday 11 a.m.-5 p.m.

Whiz Kids, 518 W Riverside (456-6536) and 5628 N Division (483-9153). This is a great spot to find educational children's toys and books. Many home-schoolers and teachers at all levels take advantage of the variety of materials and expertise available at both these locations. The downtown store is open Monday through Saturday 9:30 a.m.-6 p.m. and Sunday noon - 5 p.m., while the Franklin Park Mall store opens Monday through Friday 9:30 a.m.-9 p.m., Saturday 9:30 a.m.-6 p.m. and Sunday 11 a.m.-5 p.m.

6

Entertainment

The Radio Flyer in Riverfront Park

Photo by Ron Swords

Entertainment

Spokane offers a range of entertainment options to suit everyone's tastes. Whether you prefer country, classical music or opera, or comedy, live theatre, ballet or clog dancing, you can find it in the Lilac City.

Live Theatre

Spokane

The Best of Broadway Series brings musical theatre productions performed by national companies to Spokane. Shows in the past have included Cats, Les Miserables and The Secret Garden. Tickets are sold by subscription or may be purchased individually. G&B Select-a-Seat (325-SEAT or 800-325-SEAT) offers tickets and further information on upcoming shows.

Rogue Players, 1603 W Belt (327-9907). This grass-roots organization is proud of its small-theatre heritage and still holds all four to six annual productions at the same West Central Community auditorium where they started. The company likes to introduce a new actor or actress each production. This is truly where those new to the world of theatre can "tread the boards" in dramas, comedies, mysteries or kids' shows. The small size of the theatre contributes an air of intimacy between audience and actors. The Rogue's Season begins in October and ends in March.

Spokane Children's Theatre (534-0737). This theatre troupe produces four musical children's plays each season, and has won a loyal following among the younger set and their parents. Performances are held at The Civic Theatre, 1020 N Howard.

Spokane Civic Theatre, 1020 N Howard (325-2507). Spokane's oldest theatre group began performing in 1947. Since the grand opening of the theatre in its North Howard location in 1967, visitors have enjoyed the dramas, comedies, classical plays and musicals performed by the amateur group. The theatre houses two separate auditoriums, the Main Stage and Studio Theatre, each with its own venue. The Studio Theatre, with its smaller, more intimate setting, hosts an annual Playwrights Forum Festival to showcase new playwright talent.

Spokane Interplayers Ensemble, 174 S Howard (455-PLAY). Spokane's resident professional theatre hosts a full season of classic and contemporary comedies and dramas each year. The foyer also serves as a gallery for artwork.

Valley Rep Theatre, Southwest Corner of Sprague and Pines (927-6878). The Valley Rep is Spokane's newest theatre group, located in one of the Valley's oldest buildings. When you enter this intimate theatre via a rear entrance, you'll find yourself in what once was an Odd Fellows ballroom. Seven shows a year are presented and can include comedies, dramas, musicals or classics. The group also offers two children's plays in early summer and an evening of one-act works showcasing new play writers.

Live Theatre

Outside Spokane

There are several well-known and well-received theatre groups within an hour's drive of Spokane.

The popular *Carousel Players* of the *Coeur d'Alene Summer Theatre*, Boswell Hall Auditorium, North Idaho College (208-667-0254; 800-4CdATIX) has been operating over 26 years. As one of Coeur d'Alene's professional summer stock companies, it specializes in Broadway-style musicals out of the spacious Boswell Auditorium.

The Cutter Theatre, Metaline Falls (446-4108). This restored theatre in Metaline Falls hosts wonderfully well-acted melodramas. The theatre group also combines thespian skills with a train ride during several weekends throughout the spring, summer and fall. This outing includes an afternoon train ride for a minimal fee, complete with a "hold-up" by desperados seeking donations for the theatre. For information about the Lion's Club Metaline to Ione Train Ride, call 442-3397.

The Northwest Summer Playhouse, Coeur d'Alene, Idaho (208-667-1323) is the only actors' equity group in the Inland Northwest. This professional summer stock company produces plays in the charming and intimate Lake City Playhouse at 14th and Garden. Fall and winter, the Playhouse offers community theatre plays produced and acted by local talent. The summer series features professional players.

Panida Theatre, Sandpoint, Idaho (208-265-4742). The Unicorn Theatre players present Broadway musicals every year at this community theatre situated in downtown Sandpoint.

Sixth Street Melodrama, Wallace, Idaho (208-752-8871). The Lux Building, Wallace's oldest wood-frame building, once served as a brothel. Now it houses the delightful Sixth Street Melodrama. The company presents turn-of-the-century melodramas.

Colleges and Universities

Many of the Spokane-area colleges and universities listed below offer excellent theatre at bargain prices. Call the box office for information and schedules.

Eastern Washington University, Cheney (359-6400)
Gonzaga University, Russell Theatre, 502 E Boone (328-4220)
Idaho Repertory Theatre, University of Idaho, Moscow, Idaho (208-885-7212 and 208-885-6465)
Spokane Falls Community College, 3410 W Fort Wright Boulevard (533-3592)
Washington State University's School of Music and Theatre Arts, *R.R. Jones Theatre*, Pullman, WA (335-7236)
Whitworth College, West Hawthorne Drive (466-1000)

Movie Theatres

Though several movies have been filmed in Spokane, the number of movie houses is limited. For a theatre with a difference, try the *Magic Lantern*, 123 S Wall (838-4919). In its three intimate theatres, it boasts the widest, and sometimes only, selection of foreign, cult and classic films in town. Don't worry if your seat starts to shake during a film, it's only a train rumbling by on the elevated tracks located adjacent to the building.

The Garland Theatre, 924 W Garland (327-1050) and *Fox Theatre*, 1005 W Sprague (624-0105), both classic 1930s Art Deco buildings, are also the only theatres in town offering $1 seats for all shows. During the summer months the Garland holds special matinee shows for children, cost is 25¢. *The Imax Theatre* at Riverfront Park (625-6686), a legacy from Expo '74, offers a five-story screen and shows family-oriented films.

Ticket Outlets

G&B Select-A-Seat handles tickets to most of the major local events in Spokane, Pullman, Tri-Cities, Cheney, Coeur d'Alene, State Line, Silver Mountain, Schweitzer and Sandpoint. The main ticket outlet is located at the Opera House (325-7328; 800-325-7328). For a small service charge ($1.25 per ticket with cash or check, or 75¢ with credit card), you can purchase tickets at the following outlets: Rosauers'

Supermarkets, at 2610 E 29th (535-3683), 10920 E Sprague (924-3700), 15510 E Sprague (928-3687) and 9414 N Division (467-6812); Cavanaugh's Inn at the Park, 303 W North River Drive (326-8000); Fairchild Air Force Base, Rec Center (247-5649); the Coliseum, 1101 N Howard (325-7328) and the Met, 901 W Sprague (838-3111). All general admission tickets must be purchased by cash or credit card (no checks). You may also order tickets by phone. Charge for this service is $1.50 per ticket, plus $2 to place the order.

Ticketmaster, which sells tickets for events west of the Cascades, are available at DJ's Sound City at University City and Northtown Mall (489-7859). These outlets accept cash only. To use credit card, call 206-628-0888.

Dance

Conservatory Ballet Theatre (747-1235). Owner Reda Brodie is one of only a dozen Ballanchine-trained dancers teaching today. Her company dances Russian-style dance and incorporates the dynamics of Ballanchine's choreography into each ballet. CBT has a repertoire of about 26 classical and neo-classical works and has staged pieces such as *Romeo and Juliet* and *Sleeping Beauty*. The company has also staged the well-received production, *Dracula*, written, produced and choreographed by Brodie. CBT is committed to using the talents of the local community, and showcases local talent in the two productions the group performs each year.

Theatre Ballet of Spokane (838-5705). The Theatre Ballet offers two local productions a year. The group also performs in schools and smaller area communities. They were the first local arts group to sponsor Ballet and Bubbly, a New Year's Eve event. At this popular affair, a champagne reception precedes the ballet. The audience delights at the performance, which comes from a mixed repertoire of full-length classics and commissioned contemporary pieces. In March, the group hosts the *Theatre Ballet at the Met*, 901 W Sprague, where it showcases local dancers along with professional guest performers.

Spokane Folklore Society (747-2640). The Folklore Society started in 1977. The group promotes community awareness of cultural and folk traditions including music and dance. Throughout the year, they stage dances, festivals, workshops and demonstrations for the public. Some evenings are specifically geared to family dancing classes and offer lessons in such dances as contra, swing and square dancing. These are open for anyone willing to participate. The Society holds backroom old-time country dances from 8 p.m.-10 p.m. every Wednesday and the second and fourth Saturday of each month, September to June. Dances are at the Women's Club Hall, 1428 W 9th, and are open to all. There's a small admission fee.

Tea Dances at the Davenport, The Davenport Hotel, 807 W Sprague (455-8888). Enjoy the Big Band sound of Spokane's Jim Baker every Friday night from January to June. Ballroom swing instruction is offered before the dance, which runs from 6 p.m.-9 p.m. Call ahead for more information.

Music

Spokane offers music for every taste and budget. Whether you prefer Handel accompanied by summer evening's cascading fireworks or toe-tapping country western at a local rodeo, you'll find it here. You can choose from a variety of musical entertainment throughout the year. Celebrities such as Willie Nelson often play at local festivals (one is the Festival at Sandpoint). There's always local talent at the Opera House or under the stars in one of the area parks.

Classics

Allegro, Baroque and Beyond, 906 S Cheney (455-6865). Allegro offers classical and romantic music. The group has performed over 10 seasons, both at the Metropolitan Center for the Performing Arts and in area historic homes. Of special delight is the bi-annual Feast of Lights, celebrating the Epiphany with seasonal music.

Connoisseur Concerts (326-4942). Performers from all over the world come together with local musicians for the annual January Northwest Bach Festival. Concerts are held at the Met, 901 West Sprague, and at various churches throughout the city. In July, Connoisseur Concerts stages its second event of the season, "Mostly Mozart on a Summer's Eve." This is held outdoors at Manito Park's Duncan Gardens. You can relax at linen-covered tables and enjoy coffee and desserts, while listening to the melodies of Mozart. Many visitors picnic on the surrounding lawns. Catered meals are available, or bring your own. This is truly an elegant and unique evening. Tickets for both events are available through G&B Select-A-Seat (325-SEAT).

Spokane String Quartet (327-9315). In 1979, members of the Spokane Symphony Orchestra formed the Quartet-in-Residence at Eastern Washington University, though now they are known by the much simpler name, Spokane String Quartet. The group frequently performs works by well-known composers including original manuscripts from the Moldenhauer archives. The Moldenhauer archives are a research collection complied by the late Spokane resident, Dr. Hans Moldenhauer. It is rated as one of the largest and most important collections of manuscripts, documents and letters in the musical world and includes such gems as original works by Brahms and a previously unknown piece by Mahler. The String Quartet performances are traditionally held on Sunday at 3 p.m. at the Met, 901 West Sprague.

Spokane Symphony, 621 W Mallon (624-1200). The Spokane Symphony has celebrated over 50 years of concert performances. Each season, crowds come to listen to a musical repertoire running the gauntlet from classical to jazz. A series of 10 classical and six pop concerts are held every year at the Opera House. Chamber Orchestra concerts are preformed in the more intimate setting of the Met, 901 W Sprague. But the fun doesn't stop there. For those who like variety, the five-concert Discovery series can take you from Brahms to Bourbon Street. These are also free, outdoor summer concerts including the Labor Day Symphony in Comstock Park. Two family concerts are held each year and offer hands-on activities for children, such as touching and getting to play with different instruments.

Uptown Opera (328-1445). What began as an amateur musical over seven years ago in a local coffee house has grown into Spokane's only professional opera company. Sixteen performances a year (24 beginning in 1996) are held at the Met, 901 W Sprague, and run the gamut from traditional opera to operettas and American musical theatre. Songs are sung in English. The intimate environment of the Met makes these opera performances both fun and entertaining.

Continuous Refrains

Cathedral and the Arts at St. John's Cathedral, 127 E 12th (838-4277). The Cathedral and the Arts Association is a non-profit group sponsoring an annual concert series at St. John's Cathedral. One of the most popular events occurs in October, when the group shows a silent movie accompanied by the Cathedral's organ. Sell-out crowds have sat spell-bound watching Lon Chaney films, among others, while listening to the swell of piped music resonating throughout the Gothic-style cathedral.

Other concerts include the December Advent Lessons and Carols done in the tradition of King's College, Oxford and the Candlelight

Christmas Concert, which plays to sold-out crowds every year. A call to G&B Select-A-Seat (325-SEAT) will procure tickets to these and the Association's other events, which are truly enjoyable experiences.

Festival at Sandpoint, Sandpoint, Idaho (208-265-4554). What began in 1982 as an introduction of symphony music for area audiences has grown into a summer-long event of mostly outdoor concerts. With the moon and mountains as backdrops, a group of entertainers as diverse as Willie Nelson, Lyle Lovett and the Count Basie Orchestra entertain hundreds at each performance. There's also a special children's concert. Many people bring blankets, lawn chairs and baskets of food to enjoy a picnic supper before the "concert under the stars."

The Schweitzer Institute of Music holds a month-long training session for new composers in conjunction with the Festival. The Institute is located on Schweitzer Mountain, just north of Sandpoint. A number of jazz and chamber music concerts showcase the talents of 75 students chosen from around the world to attend the Institute. These concerts are held in the alpine setting of Schweitzer Mountain.

Silver Mountain Concerts (208-783-111). These outdoor, summer concerts are located 60 minutes from Spokane, in Kellogg, Idaho. Visitors travel to the mountain peak via the world's longest gondola ride, a 19-minute ascent of 3,400 feet over forested terrain and the towns of Kellogg and Wardner. The 2,000-seat outdoor amphitheater, surrounded by ponderosa pines and mountain peaks, makes a perfect setting for musical events. Bring your own blankets and picnic basket, or purchase your meal from the cafeteria or Alpenhouse restaurant at the nearby Mountain Haus chalet.

Summer Carillon Concert Series is held at the Cathedral of St. John the Evangelist, 127 E 12th (838-4277). The carillon—a large, intricate musical instrument, looking like a cross between a huge piano and a hand loom and sounding like tolling bells—is the only one in all of Washington, Oregon and Idaho. Each summer, during a month-long celebration of sound, carillonneurs from around the world come to Spokane, ride a tiny elevator, then climb five flights of stone stairs to reach the keyboard high in the vaulted enclosure of St. John's Cathedral. Though its easy to hear the ringing bells across a summer's night, listeners often bring chairs or blankets to the grass lawn across from the Cathedral. The free, hour-long concerts begin each Thursday evening at 6 p.m. throughout the month of August.

Spokane Jazz Orchestra is the oldest in-residence, professional jazz orchestra in the U.S. The orchestra produces and sponsors concerts featuring both local talent and celebrity guests, dances,

"Busker" at Spokane Marketplace
Photo by Patrice Tobler

exhibitions and workshops throughout the year. Tickets for the Met performances, floating jazz cruise and annual festival at Spokane Falls Community College are available through G&B Select-a-Seat (325-SEAT) or Street Music (624-7722).

Jazz and blues music have long held toe-holds in an area more known for its country western roots. *The Inland Empire Blues Society* (325-2562) publishes its own monthly newsletter, *Inside Blues*, and keeps local residents informed of upcoming jazz and blues events. Contemporary blues music is highlighted on local radio station KKZX 98.9 FM every Sunday night from 10 p.m.- midnight, KPBX 91.1 FM on Saturdays 9 p.m.-11 p.m. and at KPND 95.3 FM on Thursday 8 p.m.-midnight.

Zephyr (747-0938). Founder Kendel Feeney describes Zephyr as a gesture or approach to music, rather than a specific event or concert. She is on a personal mission to de-mystify music of the 20th century, and every program is different. Zephyr's concerts pair local musicians with talent from outside the area. The performances are held in the intimate setting of the Met, 901 West Sprague. At least one of the three programs Zephyr offers each season (October through April) highlights the work of a Northwest composer, and many of the concerts invite audience participation.

Lessons

Holy Names Music Center, 3910 W Custer Drive (326-9516). Located in one of the former officer's quarters at historic Fort George Wright, the Holy Names Music center offers private lessons, including choir for adults and children and kindermusik lessons for kids ages two to six years. The Suzuki method is offered for those interested. There are monthly student recitals open to the public at no cost and occasional community performances. For information on both events call the center. Recital hall and meeting rooms are available for rent. If you need a musician for any occasion, the center can help you find one.

Nightlife

Ankeny's, 515 W Sprague (838-6311). Situated above the Ridpath Hotel, this night spot offers one of the best views in town as well as live jazz and top-40s music, Wednesday through Saturday 8:30 p.m.-1 a.m.

The Big Dipper, 171 S Washington (747-8036). This dark and inviting tavern, located in the heart of downtown, is the perfect place to enjoy music every night of the week. Tuesday is reggae night, and Sunday evenings feature local DJs. You might also run across poetry, slams (punk-rock bashing) or acoustic music. Music begins at 10 p.m.

Cannon St. Grill, 144 S Cannon Street (456-8660). If the idea of cool jazz accompanying an exquisite meal appeals to you, consider this bistro in Browne's Addition. The menu is small, but offers an epicurean experience. Musicians play during the dinner hour from 5:30 p.m.-8:30 p.m. every Friday and Saturday night.

Chili D's, 152 S Browne (455-9210). Rumor has it Elvis was sighted here Tuesday nights when 50s and 60s rock-and-roll is featured. Wednesday through Saturday are pure country music played with a foot stompin' beat.

Espresso Delizioso, 706 N Monroe (326-5958). This cafe is a popular gathering place for food and drinks. It also offers nightly live entertainment with mainly folk performers. Come hear the jam sessions, Celtic music, hammer dulcimer or guitar picking. Depending on the performer the music runs between 7:30 p.m.-10 p.m.

Fort Spokane Brewery, 401 W Spokane Falls Blvd. (838-3809), offers live jazz and blues four nights a week, Wednesday, Friday, Saturday and Sunday, served up hot to contrast with the pub's cold microbrews. Families are welcome until the live entertainment begins. After that, only those 21 and over are allowed in. The music usually begins by 9:15 p.m. and can last as late as 1:30 a.m.

Hobart's Jazz Lounge, Cavanaugh's Fourth Avenue, 110 E 4th (838-6101). This club hosts the best jazz in town, with an eclectic menu ranging from fusion to swing. It's open six nights a week. Sorry, no music on Mondays. Hours of performances can vary, so call ahead for specifics.

JJ's, 322 N Spokane Falls Court in the Sheraton Hotel (455-9600). Tuesdays through Saturday, you'll find top-40s music played by a live band at JJ's. The piano bar at Mingle's, located on the main floor, is open the same nights. JJ's music begins at 9 p.m., while Mingle's starts around 11 p.m. Both locations provide music until 1 a.m.

Jimmy D's Wine Cellar, 313 Sherman, Coeur d'Alene, Idaho (208-664-WINE). Enjoy blues, jazz and cabaret music in this lower-level wine bar, which also serves dinner and a wide selection of appetizers. The dimly-lit atmosphere, rough-brick walls and cozy seating arrangements create a romantic, yet casual environment. Music begins at 8 p.m. and runs through midnight or later.

Kelly's, 6152 W Seltice Way at State Line, Idaho (208-773-5002). For tush-pushin', two-steppin' dancing to a country beat, the best place in the area is Kelly's. Friday and Saturday nights features live music, with dance lessons Saturday at 7 p.m.

Mother's Pub, 230 W Riverside (624-9828). This Chicago-style sports bar books original, live entertainment, one of only two bars in town to do so. Thursday night is usually packed for their top-40s dance music. Friday and Saturday are alternative rock nights, and you can catch a variety of great out-of-town bands here. Music begins by 9:30 p.m., with the headliner band coming on around 11 p.m. and playing until 1:15 a.m.

Stockyard's Inn, 3827 E Boone (534-1212). The Stockyard's, a Spokane classic, is literally located next to livestock holding pens. The inn offers Karaoke Monday through Wednesday nights. Thursday through Saturday, you can hear the easy rock 'n' roll sounds from the 60s through 80s, played by Don Larson and the Cynics. The band plays from 9 p.m.-2 a.m.

Sully's, 259 W Spokane Falls Boulevard (456-7410). Cushy sofas, subdued lighting and the soft touch of pianist Dave Christenson make this one great piano bar. The tinkling of the keys occurs every Wednesday through Saturday night from 9 p.m.-midnight.

Swackhammer's, 25 E Lincoln (467-5210) Voted best single's bar in Spokane by *Inlander Magazine*, Swackhammer's offers something for everyone seven nights a week. Most nights, a DJ hosts top-40s music. Wednesday night is country night, complete with line dancing lessons. For those not brave enough to face the dance floor, Monday night offers live Sumo wresting. One weekend a month, the bar hosts a live band. Music begins between 8 p.m. and 9 p.m. and lasts until 1:30 a.m.

Brewpubs and Taverns

The Northwest is gaining nation-wide notoriety for its microbrews and justifiably so. Several microbrews are located in Spokane. The city offers a number of places to quench your thirst. Whether you're looking to try a new ale, or you just want to lean back and enjoy a wide-screen-TV or a game of pool, you can find the perfect spot in the Lilac City.

Birkebeinder Brewery, 35 W Main (458-0854). Spokane's newest microbrewery is fast becoming one of its most popular. Birkebeinder is a non-smoking establishment serving an eclectric menu ranging from buffalo burgers to gorganzola/beer soup. The brewery attracts families as well as singles, the after work crowd and adults looking for a place to gather. The brown and cream decor is upscale, and the selection of microbrews is both varied and extensive. Open seven days a week from 11:30 a.m. During the week they can close as early as 11 p.m., but on weekends they stay open until midnight.

Fast Eddie's, 1 W Spokane Falls Blvd. (456-5162). You've got to admire an establishment advertising "high prices, warm beer and lousy food." Truth be known, Fast Eddie's is very popular with the younger set and boasts 20 imported, domestic and microbrews on tap. The tavern also offers quite a selection of hot sandwiches, burgers and 11 varieties of hot dogs. Open daily.

Finnerty's Red Lion Sports Bar and Barbeque, 126 N Division (624-1934). The name of this long-running establishment says it all. There are 10 TVs beaming sports events constantly and walls plastered with sport memorabilia. The menu features barbecued chicken and ribs. The fry bread with honey is served in generous portions and comes with every dinner. The place can get crowded when the satellite dish picks up Sonics, Mariners and Green Bay Packers games. They're open seven days a week.

Fort Spokane Brewery, 401 W Spokane Falls Blvd. (838-3809). Spokane's oldest brewpub offers good food and even better beer. Sample a pint of the standard ales: Blond Alt, Border Run, Red Alt and

Birkebeinder Brewery
Photo by Patrice Tobler

Bull Dog Stout, or try the season's specialty. The menu offers appetizers, pizzas and hot or cold sandwiches. The decor is nothing to write home about, but then that's not what their customers keep coming back for. Wednesday, Friday, Saturday and Sunday are the times to catch both local and national bands playing rock 'n' roll or rhythm and blues. Children must leave when the music starts. Open seven days a week.

Northern Lights, 1701 S Lawson (244-4909). Though not technically a brewpub, Northern Lights is a local brewery in Airway Heights and as such deserves mention. Brewmeister Mark Irvin, who apprenticed at T.W. Fisher's in Coeur d'Alene, produces three types of unfiltered beer—a creme ale, crystal bitter and a chocolate dunkle, which has developed its own cult following. Keep an eye out for the Northern Lights label, available at area music clubs, taverns and lounges, including the Viking Tavern and Cyrus O'Leary's.

T.W. Fisher's, 204 N 2nd, Coeur d'Alene, Idaho (664-BREW). Be sure to check out the impressive collection of tap beers, beer bottles and sports pennants while you enjoy some of the best microbrewed beer in the area. Daily brewery tours are offered. There are also lunch and beer specials. If you're in town, don't miss the annual Octoberfest.

Viking Tavern, N 1221 (326-2942). It's hard to tell from the outside of this yellow, sheet-metal building, what's inside. With 26 beers on tap and over 90 varieties of bottled beer, the Viking has long held a corner on Spokane's beer market. The atmosphere is friendly and comfortable, complete with pool tables, dart boards, long tables for friends to gather about and a great and varied menu.

Wineries

Spokane is blessed with a number of outstanding wineries within minutes of downtown. There's even one in the heart of the city. Whether you venture forth on your own, or take one of the periodic tours arranged through local charities as a fund raising event, you'll find a wealth of diversity and tastes nearby.

Arbor Crest, 4705 N Fruithill Road (927-9894). A visit to Arbor Crest mansion is a must for history enthusiasts, even those who never taste a single drop of wine. This national historic site, clearly visible against the skyline north of I-90 near the Argonne Exit, is perched on a basalt cliff 450 feet above the Spokane River.

The native stone, white stucco and red-tiled-roof home was constructed in 1924 for the Riblet family, who made their fortune building tramways. It set such a stir for the ultimate in living accommodations that a newsreel and several national magazines highlighted it. Until 1956, the only way to reach the main house was via an electric tramway operating on a 1,600-foot cable spanning the River.

In 1985, Arbor Crest purchased the Riblet mansion for the winery and, today, reaching the mansion is much easier. Arbor Crest offers a tasting room, fully landscaped grounds with lawns, flowers beds, rock gardens and a pool as well as the spectacular view. Private events can be scheduled at the mansion. Open daily noon-5 p.m.

Caterina Winery, 905 N Washington (328-5069). Mike Scott, the winemaker here, learned his craft working with the Livingston Winery. You might recognize his style when you sample the tangy, toasty Chardonnay. Caterina's charming tasting room is located in the historic Broadview Dairy building.

As the story goes, more than five centuries ago Caterina and her husband Luigi began a tradition of crafting fine Italian wines in her native Italy. Today the winery bears her name. Though small, it has adhered to tradition, with some experimentation in the cellars. The tasting room offers six tables as well as gift items. The knowledgeable staff is there to answer questions and help with your selections. Open for both tours and tasting daily during summers, noon-5 p.m., and winters Tuesday through Saturday noon-5 p.m.

Knipprath Cellars, 163 S Lincoln (624-9132). There's much to see and sample in the intimate Knipprath tasting room. Outside, traffic rushes past on Lincoln Street, while inside the Victorian tasting parlour offers sampling of all the selections in stock. You can also tour the production and cellar areas and savor the hand-mixed wines. Don't forget to join Knipprath's mailing list for the latest announcements of wine tasting and release parties. Hours: Friday through Sunday 11 a.m.-6 p.m.

Latah Creek Wine Cellars, 13030 E Indiana (926-0164). Tiled walkways lead you through an arched entrance into Latah Creek's Spanish mission-style winery. Owner/winemaker Mike Conway is justifiably proud of Latah Creek's recognition by *Wine Spectator Magazine* as the number-one producer of quality Merlot in the state. Add to that Latah's Chenin Blanc, Chardonnay, Semillion and limited releases of Cabernet Sauvignon, and you'll know why a visit to this winery and tasting room is a must. Also enjoy the one-of-a kind art gallery on site, featuring northwest artists and gift items.

If you're nearby in May, stop over for the annual Mayfest, featuring strawberry- and herb-flavored Maywine. Call ahead for details. The tasting room is open Monday through Saturday 10 a.m.-5 p.m. and Sunday noon-4 p.m. Winter closing time is 4 p.m. daily.

Mountain Dome Winery, 16315 E Temple Road (928-BRUT). Once you arrive at the geodesic dome home of Dr. Michael Manz, you'll understand where the winery received its name. Dr. Manz works exclusively in crafting sparkling wines. If you wish to arrange a tour of the growing facility and learn more about the secrets of Methode Champenoise, simply call for an appointment. The winery is nestled in the foothills of Mt. Spokane.

Worden's Washington Winery, 7217 W 45th (455-7835). In 1980, Jack Worden began Spokane's first winery, using a log cabin as the tasting room and a garage as the winery. Since then, the garage has disappeared and thousands have discovered Worden's award-winning Chardonnay, Cabernet Merlot, Chenin Blanc and Johannisberg Riesling wines. In addition to the tasting room and gift shop, there's a delightful picnic area shaded by pine trees. Open year-round noon-5 p.m. daily or by appointment.

7

Of Public Interest

Riverfront Park

Photo by Patrice Tobler

Of Public Interest

Art

Art for Free

Spokane is rich in art of all kinds. Some of the earliest "art" produced in the area are Native American rock paintings, which are hundreds of years old. Unfortunately, the meaning behind the art has been obscured by time.

You can find the rock paintings at two different locations near Spokane. One series of petroglyphs (drawings created by using crushed red rock mixed with animal fats or fish oil) can be viewed just north of the Rutter Parkway Bridge over the Little Spokane River. The second set, the *Long Lake Petroglyphs*, are further from town, but well worth a visit and not difficult to find. They're located off Highway 291, about 20 miles west of town. A clearly-marked sign directs you to a lot where you can park. You can view the drawings in several different places, two on rocks near the road and the third on the side of the nearby cliff. Sadly, some have been damaged by vandalism.

If your artistic taste tends to run to more recent works, you're in luck. There are a number of public and private galleries as well as public art located throughout the city. Local, regional, national and international artists are represented. Keep your eye open for the name Harold Balazs, the most prolific and versatile local artist. His work is displayed in many courtyards, walls, vestibules and even in the center of the Spokane River.

A free pamphlet published by the *Spokane Arts Commission* details a walking tour of public art in downtown Spokane. The tour follows the south bank of the Spokane River. The map can be obtained by contacting the Spokane Arts Commission, 808 W Spokane Falls Blvd. (625-6050).

Another free pamphlet, *Spokane Art Sights*, is available at the Arts Commission office or most local galleries. This guide contains a description of area galleries and museums, public art collections and public sculptures as well as a map. You can also find a free bi-monthly guide, the *Spokane Arts Events Calender*, at the *Chase Gallery*, lower level of City Hall, 808 W Spokane Falls Blvd. It too is published by the Arts Commission.

The Arts Commission also hosts a free walking tour of visual arts three Friday nights, one each in February, April and October. Call the Arts Commission (626-6050) for exact dates and times. The Commission also hosts an annual preview event, where you can pick up preview information and upcoming season schedules of over 40 participating arts organizations. This is held during the Spokane Symphony's free Labor Day concert at 6:00 p.m. in Comstock Park, 800 W 29th.

If you like to see art in progress, don't miss the annual *Artfest* held in June at the Cheney Cowles Museum, 2316 W 1st. The museum and the Spokane Art School host this extravaganza, which draws up to 25,000 visitors. Live music, food, arts and crafts booths, demonstrations and children's hands-on workshops, all make for a fun time. For exact dates and times contact, Cheney Cowles Museum (456-3931) or the Spokane Art School (328-0900).

Spokane has many interesting outdoor art pieces, several created by the prolific Harold Balazs. His abstract *Centennial Sculpture* is located smack dab in the middle of the Spokane River, beneath the Stevens and Washington street bridges. The abstract aluminum structure appears to be floating and is never static as the play of light from water and sky shimmers across its surface.

Balazs is responsible for much of the public art throughout the downtown core, including enamel on copper murals, stone sculptures and metal pieces. He is also a mentor to many area artists, including Ken Spiering, who immortalized Balazs in the bronze sculpture, *The Call and the Challenge*. This life-sized piece, situated along the Centennial Trail near the Spokane International Ag Trade Center, was commissioned as part of the Centennial celebration for Sacred Heart Medical Center. Balazs is the workman hefting the wheelbarrow, a rather fitting tribute to the artist who has worked so hard to bring art to the city.

Another Spiering creation, this time sans figures, is the *Childhood Express*, often called The Red Wagon. Created in honor of Washington State's 1989 Centennial, this giant replica of a Radio-Flyer red wagon, complete with ladder and slide, has become a favorite with children of all ages, who crowd to its location in Riverfront Park along Spokane Falls Boulevard.

A little further west, at the corner of Spokane Falls Boulevard and Post, is David Govedare's *The Joy of Running Together*. This corten-steel sculpture celebrates Spokane's Bloomsday Race, the largest timed road running race in the world. It's almost as much a tradition to have your picture taken with these immobile runners as it is to participate in Bloomsday.

Just through the Post Street entrance to City Hall, 808 W Spokane Falls Blvd. is Ken Spiering's three dimensional wood sculpture, *Passage: Immediate and Eternal*. This piece was installed in 1984 and generated plenty of attention due to its realistic characters.

Around the corner from City Hall, at the corner of Lincoln and Spokane Falls Blvd. is a wall-sized mural recreating Japanese artist Hiroshige's *The Wave*. Crafted by local artist Charlie Schmidt, this large scene is sure to attract your attention, particularly during Spokane's hot, August days. During the winter months, when heaps of snow pile up against its lower half, you can easily imagine the cold spray of water rising from the briny sea.

For those who wish to view art in an indoor setting, Spokane is home to a number of galleries. The most current information on changing exhibits is available by checking the *Weekend* section of Friday's *Spokesman-Review* or *The Inland Way* section of the weekly publication, *The Inlander*, available free at over 340 local businesses.

Art Galleries

Art Downtown, 221 N Post (747-4843). Contemporary regional work is the focus at this gallery. Art Downtown is an offshoot of the Spokane Art School and is manned by volunteers, many of them the artists whose works are displayed throughout the gallery. Open Tuesday through Saturday 11 a.m.-5 p.m.

Chase Galley at City Hall, 808 W Spokane Falls Blvd. (625-6050). Local and regional artist work is shown here, with exhibits changing monthly. Open Monday through Friday 8 a.m.-5:30 p.m. and during City Council meetings on Monday night.

Colburn's Gallery, 203 W Riverside (838-8412). Original works by local and northwest artists are exhibited at Colburn's. Monthly shows highlight individual artists. A lower-level cafe is open during gallery hours and serves espresso. Open Monday through Friday 9 a.m.-5:30 p.m. and Saturday 10 a.m.-2 p.m.

Cheney Cowles Museum, 2316 W 1st (456-3931). Cheney Cowles features new exhibits monthly. The museum shows local, regional, national and international art. Shows range from traditional 18th-century Dutch Masters to more contemporary juried art. Admission is $3 for adults and $2 for children and seniors. Wednesday, admission is half price until 5 p.m., then free until closing. Open Tuesday through Saturday 10 a.m.-5 p.m., Wednesday 10 a.m. - 9 p.m. and Sunday 1 a.m.-5 p.m.

Corbin Art Center, 507 W 7th (625-6677). This gallery is located in the historic D.C. Corbin Mansion. It's also affiliated with the Spokane Parks and Recreation Department, which teaches art classes in the former home. Monthly exhibits feature local, regional and national artists as well as students' work. Open Monday through Thursday 9 a.m.-4 p.m.

Douglas Gallery, 121 S Wall (624-4179). This is one of only two galleries in the state selling official Disney artwork, including still-life drawings, one-of-a-kind animation stills and videos. The Douglas also offers limited edition prints by national artists and original pieces by Northwest craftsmen. You can also purchase cast bronze statues and sports memorabilia, such as an autographed Joe Montana football and the shoes John Stockton wore in the Olympic games.

The gallery itself is an aesthetic experience. Originally, it was a meat packing plant. Architect Ken Brooks renovated it with skylights, white-washed brick walls and two floors of intimate, yet airy space. Open Tuesday through Saturday 10 a.m.-6 p.m., and by special appointment.

Down Under Gallery and Custom Framing, 12505 E Sprague (927-9960). At the Down Under, you'll find bronze sculptures, Native American wood carvings, limited edition prints and originals by local artists. Open Monday through Saturday 9 a.m.-5 p.m.

Eugenia Stowe Art Gallery, Y.W.C.A., 829 Broadway (326-1190). Named after long-time art instructor Eugenia Stowe, this gallery features monthly new exhibits of local art and ceramics. It also offers consignment space for Y.W.C.A. ceramic students. Open Wednesday through Friday 10 a.m.-4 p.m. and Saturday by appointment.

Madcat Gallery, 621 W Mallon (327-6870). Limited edition prints and graphics are displayed here, and framing services are also available. Open Monday through Saturday 10 a.m.-6 p.m., Friday open until 9 p.m. and Sunday noon-5 p.m.

Pacific Flyaway Art Gallery, 401 W Riverside (747-0812). Pacific Flyaway Art focuses on wildlife, sports, fishing, florals and landscapes. The gallery offers originals, prints, sculptures and boasts the largest collection of Conservation Stamp prints in the Inland Northwest. Open Monday through Friday 10 a.m.-5:30 p.m. and Saturday 10 a.m.-4 p.m.

Print House Gallery, 409 S Dishman Mica Rd (928-2833). Like its name implies, the Print Houses offers limited edition prints, posters and some sculptures. Open Tuesday through Friday 9:30 a.m.-5:30 p.m. and Saturday 10 a.m.-4:30 p.m.

Spokane Art School Center for the Visual Arts, 920 N Howard, (328-0900). The Spokane Art School offers monthly exhibitions by local and regional artists. Keep an eye out for the School's annual Bird House Auction in March, which highlights local artisans' outdoor and garden creations. In early December, the school sponsors a Yuletide Fest, where artists and craftspeople display their wares for sale. Call for exact dates and times. The gallery is open Tuesday through Saturday 11 a.m.-5:30 p.m.

29th Avenue Artworks, 3128 E 29th (534-7959). This turn-of-the-century home, converted into gallery space, features local and regional artists' works in a variety of mediums. The gallery hosts bi-monthly exhibits for selected artists. They can also frame your artwork. Open Monday through Saturday 10 a.m.-5 p.m.

Walsdorf Gallery, 516 W 1st (838-5847). The Walsdorf is located at the 1st Avenue entrance to the Ridpath Hotel. This gallery exhibits local, Northwest, European and Russian artists. Open Monday through Friday 9 a.m.-5 p.m. and weekends by appointment.

Campus Galleries

The following area colleges have galleries that display student and professional art. Don't overlook them as important exhibitors of national and international art. Gonzaga University, for example, has an outstanding Rodin sculpture collection as well as a premier old masters and contemporary print collection, both of which are periodically displayed.

Ad Gallery, Gonzaga University, 502 E Boone (328-4220)
Eastern Washington University (EWU) Gallery of Art, EWU Art Building, Cheney (359-2493)
EWU Photography Gallery, EWU Art Building, Cheney (359-2493)
EWU Pence Gallery, EWU, Pence Student Union, Cheney (359-2493)
EWU Spokane Gallery, 705 W 1st (458-6401)
The Japanese Cultural Center, Mukogawa Fort Wright Institute, 4000 W Randolph Road (328-2971)
Koehler Art Gallery, Fine Arts Building, Whitworth College (466-1000)
Museum of Art, Washington State University, Pullman (509-335-1910)
Spokane Falls Community College Gallery, 3410 W Fort Wright Blvd., Bldg. 6 (533-3710)

Restaurant and Theater Galleries

For many fledging artists, the first commercial venture is through non-traditional means. This helps keep prices low and, though the quality of art varies, if you're lucky, you might discover the next Toulouse Lautrec or Vincent Van Gogh. The following locations feature monthly exhibitions of local artists' works in a variety of mediums.

Auntie's Bookstore and Cafe, 313 W Riverside (838-3616)
Brewhaha, 12 N Howard (456-4881)
Espresso Delizioso, 706 N Monroe (326-5958)
Metropolitan Performing Arts Center, 901 W Sprague (455-6500)
Spokane Civic Theatre Gallery, 1020 N Howard (325-1413)
Spokane Interplayers Theatre Gallery, 174 S Howard (455-7529)
Toucan's Concepts Gallery, 912 W Sprague (838-4763)

Museums

Broadview Museum, 411 W Cataldo (324-0910). The Broadview museum derives its name from the Broadview Dairy, which began producing milk products in Spokane in 1897. The first floor of this renovated building is still a working dairy. The second floor is filled with scenes depicting dairy and farm life since the turn-of-the-century on. Tours are self-guided, though group visits can be arranged. Be sure to visit the elevated viewing area, where you can watch the workings of a modern-day dairy production line. A gift shop is located downstairs. Admission is free, and there is ample parking in the adjoining lot. Open summers seven days a week 10 a.m.-4 p.m. Winter hours are Tuesday through Saturday 10 a.m.-4 p.m.

Cheney Cowles Museum, 2316 W 1st Avenue (456-3931). Spokane's premier museum is located in the heart of the historic Browne's Addition, where many of Spokane's earliest and wealthiest families built their mansions. Cheney Cowles combines several facets within one museum. The main complex houses an art gallery with revolving exhibits and walk-through dioramas detailing life in the Inland Northwest since before the arrival of white men. To the delight of young and old alike, many displays are interactive. A temporary exhibit room, called the Atrium, allows the museum to present changing displays. Highlighted are many items from the combined Museum of Native American Cultures (MONAC) and Cheney Cowles' American Indian collection.

Next door to the museum proper is the 1898 English Tudor revival mansion known as the *Campbell House*. Built for mining magnate Amasa Campbell, the home features a Louis XV reception room with silk moire walls and gold-leaf gilding, a hand-painted, delft-tiled fireplace in the dining room and oak-paneled library. Admission to the Campbell House is included in the museum fee. Register at the museum's front desk, where you'll be issued an official "calling-card" for the next tour through the house.

A museum shop and espresso bar fill what was once the carriage house. The store features greeting cards, a large selection of books detailing area history, one-of-a-kind jewelry and original artwork by notable regional artists. You can also arrange to rent the work of over 30 of the region's best artists. The museum sponsors a series of free public lectures held on Wednesday night at 7:30 p.m. Information is available at the museum, or call 456-3931. The fee for non-museum members is $3 for adults and $2 for seniors and children. Museum members and children under 6 are free. Wednesday the fee is half price until 5 p.m., then it's free until closing time. Museum and Campbell House hours are Tuesday through Saturday 10 a.m.-5 p.m., except Wednesday nights when it remains open until 9 p.m., and Sunday 1 p.m.-5 p.m.

Fairchild Air Force Base Heritage Museum, Fairchild Air Force Base west of Spokane on Highway 2 (247-2100). The exhibits at this museum focus on the legacy of the Air Force Base's history, past and present. Of special interest is an adjacent railroad car, which holds a B-52 cockpit simulator originally used for pilot training. A fine collection of vintage planes is on display throughout the museum grounds. Admission is free, though you'll need to stop at the base's main gates for a visitor's pass before proceeding to the museum. Open Monday, Wednesday, Friday and Saturday 10 a.m.-2 p.m.

Museum of North Idaho, 115 Northwest Blvd. (208-664-3448). This small museum, located within walking distance of the Coeur d'Alene city docks, offers several interesting exhibits. Some depict the history of Kootenai County and surrounding area, while others display information on the local Native American people. The naval training station once located at Farragut is also shown. In addition, the museum houses a research facility and gift shop. Admission is $1.50 for adults, 50¢ for children ages 6 to 16 and $4 for families. This price includes entry to the Fort Sherman Museum (see below). Open April 1 through October 31, Tuesday through Saturday 11 a.m.-5 p.m. During July and August the museum is also open Sunday 11 a.m.-5 p.m.

Fort Sherman Museum, North Idaho College Campus, Coeur d'Alene, Idaho (208-664-3448). This museum was once a part of a military fort. Under threat of war with the Nez Perce in 1877, General William Tecumseh Sherman of Civil War fame, selected an area bordering Coeur d'Alene Lake for the site of a military fort. In 1898, the last garrison left to fight in the Spanish American War. By 1904, the remains of the fort were auctioned or destroyed, except for the officer's quarters, the little red chapel and the powder magazine. This last structure has become the Fort Sherman Museum. Exhibits inside detail the history of the fort. Admission is $1.50 for adults, 50¢ for children ages 6 to 16 and $4 for families and includes entrance to the Museum of North Idaho (see above). Open May 1 through September 30th, Tuesday through Saturday 1 p.m.-4:45 p.m.

Zoos

Walk in the Wild Zoo, one mile north of I-90 off Pines Road (924-7220). Two hundred animals, representing five continents, live in this natural 240-acre zoo. To introduce young visitors to the animals and their habitats, a petting zoo, educational programs, theme events and even musical concerts are offered throughout the year. For $25, you can even adopt a pet, complete with a special certificate. Admission is $3.75 for adults, $3.25 for senior citizens and children 13-17, and $2.25 for children ages 4 to 12, with younger children admitted free. Open daily 10 a.m.-5 p.m., except Thanksgiving and Christmas.

Cat Tales, 17020 N Newport Highway (238-4126). If you like cats, this is the place for you. At Cat Tales, you'll see tigers, lions, pumas and leopards. Tours are self-guided, with plaques detailing the history and native habitat of the animals. This endangered species conservation park is located only six miles north of Spokane. Admission is $3 for adults and $2 for children 12 and under. Cat Tales is open Wednesday through Saturday 10 a.m.-6 p.m.

Area Colleges and Universities

In 1881, Father Joseph Cataldo bought 320 acres from the Northern Pacific Railroad Company to found a Native American school. By the time the first classes began in 1887, the early town fathers had convinced the Jesuit priest of the need for a school for their own sons. Thus, Gonzaga University was born.

Spokane has come a long way since those early days and is now home to several private and public higher educational institutions. Fourteen public school districts, with over 67,000 students, and more than 40 private elementary and secondary schools provide a strong student base for area colleges and universities.

Eastern Washington University, Cheney (458-6200) and Eastern Washington University, Spokane Center, 705 W 1st (458-6401). The main campus of Eastern Washington University (EWU) is located in the rolling hills and farm country 20 minutes west of Spokane. The school offers undergraduate degrees in over 100 academic majors and graduate programs in 19 fields. A student activities hotline (359-6718) keeps students and non-students informed of the cultural, social and athletic events sponsored by the the University throughout the year.

The EWU Spokane Center in downtown Spokane provides educational and cultural services to the community at large and upper-division and graduate students, many whom work full-time day jobs. The center is housed in the former Farm Credit Bank Building, which explains why bank vaults are sometimes used as classrooms. There's a bookstore and cafeteria in the lower level.

Gonzaga University, 502 E Boone (328-4220). Walking across this green campus beneath towering trees only one-half mile from downtown Spokane, it's easy to become lost in the lure of academia. Gonzaga boasts over 107 years of educational experience and offers 49 undergraduate degrees and 26 graduate degrees. Biology, political science and psychology are the most popular majors.

For students and non-students alike, a tour of the Administration Building, which was erected in 1899 and expanded in 1903, is a walk through history. Be sure to view the Rodin sculpture collection, which is on loan to the University. Several pieces are located in the main foyer of the Administration Building.

Not far from the Administration Building is the ***Crosby Student Center*** (328-4220, ext. 4279). This is where the largest collection of Bing Crosby memorabilia in the country is displayed. The popular singer and movie star entered Gonzaga in 1920 to study pre-law, but left to pursue a show business career. Outside the center is a life-size bronze statue of Bing crafted by Deb Copenhaver. The statue is notable for what's missing from the singer's relaxed right hand. Originally it held a detachable pipe. The pipe repeatedly disappeared in late-night student raids, until it was removed from the statue. Now it's on permanent display—inside the center.

Intercollegiate Center for Nursing Education, 2917 W Ft. George Wright (326-7270). The Intercollegiate Center for Nursing

Education (ICNE) is a consortium nursing school for EWU, WSU and Whitworth College. The Center offers baccalaureate and masters degree programs as well as continuing education courses for nurses.

Mukogawa Fort Wright Institute, Japanese Cultural Center, 4000 W Randolph Rd. (328-2971). Where cavalry officers shouldered carbines and paraded their horses, you'll now find students practicing tea ceremonies and learning English. Mukogawa Fort Wright Institute is a branch campus of Mukogawa's Women's University, located in Spokane's sister city, Nishinomiya, Japan.

Japanese students majoring in English and American Studies attend classes in 14-week sessions. They live in the original barracks built between 1899 and 1906 for the officers of Fort George Wright. A stroll down the brick paths of the campus is an historian's delight. The museum displays a permanent collection of Japanese art, crafts and folk art as well as revolving seasonal exhibits. Many cross-cultural classes, including Ikebana, Shiatsu massage and sumi-e brush painting, are offered to non-students throughout the year.

Spokane Intercollegiate Research and Technology Institute, 501 N Riverpoint Blvd. (456-7091). The Spokane Intercollegiate Research and Technology Institute (SIRTI) is a collaborative project of five institutions: WSU, EWU, Gonzaga, Whitworth and the community colleges of Spokane. The focus of the Institute is to improve the economic vitality of the region. SIRTI contributes instruction and research in high-technology disciplines such as engineering, technology, manufacturing and computer science. Educational programs, applied research projects and community lectures are offered to the community at large in this unique business/education partnership.

Spokane Community College, 2000 N Greene (533-7000). Spokane Community College (SCC) is the largest vocational/technical community college in Washington. It offers degrees and certificate programs in over 90 fields including more than a dozen health- related careers. Culinary students practice their art by operating Orlando's, their own eaterie. This restaurant is open to visitors Tuesday through Friday 11:30 a.m.-1 p.m. during the school year. Students and visitors alike delight in the delicious lunch fare served.

Spokane Falls Community College, 3410 W Ft. George Wright (533-3500). A sister college to SCC, Spokane Falls Community College (SFCC) emphasizes pre-major and liberal arts programs. SFCC ranks among the top three community colleges in the state for the number of students who transfer to four-year universities. The school also offers a number of non-credit classes open to the community through their Institute for Extended Learning (533-3770).

Washington State University at Spokane, 601 E 1st (456-3275). Washington State University (WSU) occupies nearly six floors in the Farm Credit Building. This is a branch "campus" of Washington State University at Pullman. At 102 years old, WSU is the state's oldest land-grant university. The school offers 100 undergraduate, 66 master's and 42 doctoral programs in 70 fields. Spokane-based students have access to graduate and research programs and classes as well as the Washington Higher Education Telecommunications System.

Whitworth College, 300 W Hawthorne (466-1000). Whitworth is a private Christian liberal arts college affiliated with the Presbyterian Church. In addition to the college's 44 undergraduate programs, Whitworth offers graduate degrees in international management, education and nursing. Its 200-acre wooded campus is located in a quiet suburban setting just seven miles north of downtown Spokane. At the center of campus is the recently renovated and expanded $4.9 million Harriet Cheney Cowles Memorial Library.

Parks

The first park in the Spokane area was created in 1891 with land donated by town founders J.J. Browne and Anthony Cannon. Called Coeur d'Alene Park, it was named in honor of the Idaho mining district where so many early Spokane families founded their fortunes. This first public green encompassed 10 acres and included lawn plantings, ornamental shrubbery, a wading pool and fish pond, and even an onion-domed band pavilion.

In later years, both Browne and Cannon would have parks named after them as the city and county park system grew to encompass the 60 common grounds enjoyed by residents and visitors throughout the year.

Today's city and county parks are groomed for a variety of recreational lifestyles and include such attractions as flower gardens, water slides, wilderness areas, play equipment and horse arenas. To describe each space would take a book in itself, thus the following are only a sampling of area delights.

Coeur d'Alene Park in Browne's Addition

Photo by Patrice Tobler

City Parks

Audubon. Located adjacent to Finch Elementary school on Spokane's north side, Audubon combines activity areas with a wealth of trees and greenery. Its 26 acres include a wading pool, play equipment, softball and baseball fields, and tennis courts, most of which are grouped at the north end of the park. This leaves the lower level for walking and picnicking beneath the ponderosa pines. The grounds are bounded by Northwest Blvd., Audubon St., Milton St., and Providence Ave.

Cowley Park. This small gem of a park is located on Division Street, between 6th and 7th avenues, within walking distance of the Sacred Heart Medical Complex. In 1875, the Reverend H.T. Cowley erected the first public school in Spokane at the sight of the spring crossing the area. It still flows through the two-acre park, adding to its quiet beauty and charm. A large sign documenting the Rev. Cowley's contribution to Spokane's history is located at the spot where the spring bubbles to the surface. The water once flowed unimpeded to the Spokane River, cutting a channel through what is now prime downtown real estate. Early town settlers used the channel as a garbage dump and eventually filled in the gully. Today, Nordstrom, Eddie Bauer, Riverpark Square and the Crescent Court are all located on this land. Some play equipment is located at the south end of the park, but it's more a contemplative, restful spot than an activity destination.

Finch Arboretum. Parallel to I-90, Finch Arboretum occupies about 65 acres of rolling hillside along Garden Springs Creek in southwest Spokane. Though some visitors come just to enjoy the 2,000 labeled trees and shrubs bracketing the meandering springs, there are special areas worth noting in the Arboretum. In early spring, Corey Glen, located at the far south end of the park, is ablaze with blooming rhododendrons and azaleas sheltered among native trees and shrubs. The Touch and See Nature Trail, located between Corey Glen and the parking lot, includes 850 feet of sloping trail with signs describing native trees and shrubs, both in braille and print. A rope hand rail helps visitors travel the length of the path. Around mid-May is the best time to visit the fragrant, white flowering crabapple collection, which includes over 70 varieties of crabapples and other ornamental trees.

Another favorite spot for children is the pond and waterfall located near the main parking area. Keep in mind there is only one restroom here, and it's quite a hike from the main parking lot. There are no drinking fountains, nor picnic benches. The entrance for the Arboretum is on "F" Street from Sunset Highway.

Highbridge. If you're looking for a quiet picnic area with a different view of the city, Highbridge is the place. Located beneath a trio of bridges crossing Latah Creek, Highbridge is only minutes from downtown, yet feels a world away. This sight, named for a Union Pacific Trestle removed in 1979, was once a former Native American camping area. Of the park's 200 acres, only 63 have been developed. In the heart of the park is a flat, grassy verge, where a restroom, shelter and picnic area are located. Latah Creek joins the Spokane River nearby, blending the sound of running water with the buzz of traffic overhead. This spot is isolated and recommended for daytime visiting only. Highbridge can be reached via Government Way or Riverside Ave. Head south to the picnic area.

Liberty Park. This 22-acre park has a rich and interesting history. Before the first settlers arrived in Spokane, Native Americans camped beneath the basalt cliffs bordering this land. At the turn of the century, a promenade was constructed, leading from the lower level of the park to atop the adjacent cliffs. Young suitors would squire their ladies along this walled walk. Remnants of the basalt walls are still visible along the skyline as you drive along I-90.

Liberty features a swimming pool, tennis courts, baseball field, play equipment and sheltered picnic area next to a pond. Due to its proximity to the freeway though, it's recommended as a daytime visitors' spot, except when the lighted softball field is in use. Liberty is located between 3rd and 5th avenues off of Pittsburg.

Lincoln Park. This park is a double treat—two parks in one. The lower grounds are adjacent to 17th Street and include a wading pool, sheltered picnic area, play equipment and a softball area. At the west end of the park is a white Georgian-style mansion. This home was built for Levi and May Arkwright Hutton, two early day philanthropists who made their fortunes in the Coeur d'Alene mines. Though the Huttons were well known for their involvement in children's charities, including the Hutton Orphanage, few people know they also donated the land for Lincoln Park.

The other park is the 46 acres of undeveloped area above the basalt cliffs. A road, accessible only by foot or bike from the park, leads to this upper area. Or if you prefer to drive up, look for a poorly-marked turn off on Southeast Boulevard. From this vantage point you get a spectacular view of the city. There's a lovely spring-fed pond up here, too. Migratory fowl are constantly lifting off from the pond, which is partially covered with blooming lily pads in the spring and surrounded by cattails in the fall.

Manito Park. Manito is Spokane's grande dame of parks. The area was originally designed by the Olmstead Brothers, who later crafted New York's Central Park. Today, its 90 acres include secluded green alcoves, tennis courts, playgrounds and softball fields as well as other popular attractions. The Joel E. Ferris Perennial Gardens include 16 island and border beds, which illustrate the variety and range of herbaceous perennials growing in the Northwest. Further south is the Duncan Garden. This formal planting bed for annuals boasts spectacular displays of color from mid-July to early October.

More color and scent too, can be enjoyed by stopping atop Rose Hill. Over 1,500 roses are planted in formal beds to create a memorable sensory experience. At the other end of the aesthetic spectrum is the Japanese Garden. Designed in the "strolling pond" style, the garden invites visitors to stop and contemplate the sound of falling water, the pattern of whirls in a sand bed or the flash of color as a Koi swims beneath an arched bridge. The garden is open April 1 through October 31 and is truly a place of tranquility and beauty.

At the heart of the area is Manito pond. This spring-fed natural lake once stretched the length of the lower level of the park. Where turn-of-the-century park-goers canoed along its breadth, today's visitors stroll its gently sloping shores to feed the resident ducks, swans and migratory geese. In winter, the activity along the pond's shores slows but doesn't stop. While families enjoy sledding the steep hill along Grand Boulevard, many a brave youngster tests the frozen pond for a rousing game of ice hockey or crack-the-whip.

People's Park. You won't find this "park" listed on any official roster of city or county parks, as technically it's a part of Highbridge Park (see above). Located adjacent to the Spokane River, this area is home to the only nude sunbathing in town. People's Park is a natural habitat, full of Syringa bushes and ponderosa pines, scrub brush and basalt rocks. It's located less than five minutes from downtown, and many people come here during summer to dip their feet in the river or take a quick swim. In part because of its remoteness, many a vagrant has been known to make a summer home in its environs. A little caution and common sense is always advised in the area. It's most accessible from Riverside Avenue through Peaceful Valley.

Riverfront Park. Before the World's Fair came to Spokane in 1974, Riverfront Park was buried beneath the steel and timber of multiple railroad lines. Many residents viewed the thundering Spokane River Falls (which enticed original settlers to the area) for the first time only after wrecking crews completed their preparations for Expo '74. Today, this 100-acre park is often called the jewel of the city. There's something for everyone here. With its rolling green hills,

Harold Balazs sculpture at south channel of
Spokane River in Riverfront Park

Photo by Ron Swords

pedestrian bridges crisscrossing the river and wandering pathways meant for strolling, the park contrasts nicely with the nearby downtown business district. Yet, this is very much a people's park, geared for large-scale events.

Each 4th of July, the whole city celebrates Neighbor Day with park-wide activities. Concerts are held throughout the summer months, including the Royal Fireworks Concert at the end of July. Bagpipes fill the park during the Scottish Highland games held the beginning of August, and Native Americans gather near the end of August for their annual Pow-Wow. A schedule of events can be obtained by a local call (625-6685; or outside the 509 area code 800-336-PARK).

Visitors and residents alike enjoy riding on the historic 1909 musical carrousel, hand-carved as a wedding gift by Charles Looff for his daughter. You can still reach for the brass ring, or even rent the carrousel for a private party ($175 per hour). Other park attractions include the five-story Imax Theatre (625-6686), a Gondola Skyride over the churning falls of the river and a tour through the park aboard a train. You can even rent bicycles through Quinn's Wheel Rentals (456-6545). Those wishing to purchase souvenirs should visit the Carrousel Gift Shop (625-6632).

County Parks

Sullivan, 2723 North Sullivan. This small, 10-acre park is adjacent to the Spokane River. Don't let its size fool you. The area offers a Western Dance Center, the Radio-Controlled Car Club Track and access to the Centennial Trail. There's also a sheltered picnic area and several barbecue pits. During the lazy days of summer, you can watch many an inner tube drift past this park. However, the slope to the river is steep and the current swift, so small children and non-swimmers should stay back.

Valley Mission Park. This activity-filled park, located just a hop, skip and jump from the Argonne exit off I-90, offers a little something for everyone. Its 22-acres contain a riding arena, busy most weekends throughout the summer and fall, two picnic shelters within walking distance of a small-tots play area, picnic tables near barbecue pits, a swimming pool and water slide, as well as a basketball court. There's also a popular senior's center, used each week by nearly 2,000 senior citizens for bingo, billiards, dances and other activities.

Entertaining Children

Spokane has always prided itself on being a great place to raise kids. A combination of the four-season climate and the great outdoors creates a natural play environment for youngsters of all ages. Whether it's wading pools in the summer or sledding in the winter, kids can always find something fun to do.

For a monthly preview of events and activities geared toward children, look for the free publication, *Family Magazine*. It's available at all area libraries, grocery stores (near the real estate papers) and at the Spokane Regional Convention and Visitors Bureau, 926 W Sprague (747-3230).

Special Events for Children

While most annual events throughout the area include children, some provide specific activities and attention to the younger crowd. These are listed below.

Each August, *Kidsweek* features a whole week of events for kids of all ages. Many events are free and include a wide range of activities from movies to bike rides, tours to parties. Call the special hotline (625-6909) for more information.

Another kids-only event, in fact the largest of its kind in the world, is the annual *Junior Bloomsday* (325-9044). Each April, 10,000 kids, ages 5 to 12, gather at Joe Albi stadium and await the gun shot signifying the start of their age-specific race. With a course geared to different age divisions and a guaranteed t-shirt for all participants, Junior Bloomsday makes for a great day. Kids can also participate in the traditional Bloomsday run in May.

Other events and places in the area offering children-oriented programs or activities include the following:

Artfest, Cheney Cowles Museum, 2316 W 1st (456-3931). This June event features a variety of hands-on art projects.

Art on the Green, North Idaho College Campus, Coeur d'Alene, Idaho (208-667-9346). Each August brings children's on-going art events and booths run by young entrepreneurs as part of the adult's fair of hand-made arts and crafts. There's a play area too.

Silverwood, Highway 95, Athol, Idaho (208-683-3400). This re-created turn-of-the-century mining town offers live stage shows, old-fashioned movies from the 30s, a steam-driven train trip and more. Carnival rides include a corkscrew roller coaster running at 50 miles per hour with a 70-foot freefall, battle boats, a chillingly wet log flume splash and a pony rides. For adults, there's Lindy's restaurant, featuring mouth-watering baby back ribs. The theme park is open daily at 11 a.m. from Memorial Day to Labor Day and on weekends only the rest of the year. Admission is $17.99 for ages 8-64 and $8.99 for ages 3 to 7 and those over 65 or under 48 inches tall. The fee covers the cost of all rides and entertainment.

Spokane Marketplace (482-2627). This is where young people can market their wares at their own booths the last Sunday of each month. Sunday afternoon from noon-2 p.m., there are special craft projects available just for kids. They'll build, sculpt, glue and enjoy the activity. Call and ask for the most current listing of children's activities and events.

Dining on a Booster Seat

Chuck E. Cheese's Pizza, 100 Shadle Center (327-6623). This restaurant chain was created with children in mind. Forget about waiting placidly at your table for the pizza to arrive. The pizza is almost an after-thought. The name of the game here is "play." Kids are encouraged to ride helicopters, jump in a pool of plastic balls and listen to over-sized animal characters croon Elvis songs. Open seven days a week for lunch and dinner. Beer and wine are served.

Knight's Diner, 2909 N Market (484-0015). Knight's restaurant is a restored railroad car, complete with gleaming brass lanterns and polished woodwork. The fare is simple and served on a long, narrow counter with individual stools that swivel, a treat for kids of all ages. Knight's is open for breakfast and lunch seven days a week.

Skyway Cafe, Felt's Field (534-5986). Kids love to watch the small seater airplanes taxi and land outside this vintage, 1931 art deco airport restaurant (see Chapter 4: Eats, Treats and More, for more details).

Spaghetti Station, 718 E Francis (484-7117) and 11204 E Sprague (922-0317). Both Spaghetti Station restaurants serve up pasta and fun for the whole family (see Chapter 4: Eats, Treats and More, for more details).

Feathers, Fins and Fur

Walk in the Wild Zoo, one mile north of I-90 off Pines Road (924-7221) and *Cat Tales*, 17020 N Newport Highway (238-4126) are both favorites with children. Keep in mind that, due to its size and natural terrain, the zoo can prove challenging to small children on hot, summer days. A stop at the gift shop for ice cream and cool drinks often helps (for more details, see Zoo section in this chapter).

Great places to visit animals and fish for sale include the following:
Northwest Seed and Pet, 2422 E Sprague (534-0694); 7302 N Division (484-7387)
Evergreen Aquarium and Pet, 14319 E Sprague (926-6200)

Fun Centers

Bumpers Fun Centers, Northtown Mall, 4750 N Division (489-4000), Riverfront Park (624-6678) and University City in University Center Shopping Mall (928-8445). All three locations offer video games, miniature golf and simulator rides on a pay-per-ride basis. Northtown Mall has an Enchanted Forest miniature golf course. Its Livingston Cellars Pub serves food, beer and wine in a medieval setting. Riverfront Park features the Imax Theatre and carnival rides. University City does not have miniature golf, but does offer arcade games and simulator rides for smaller children. Tokens can be purchased at all centers, and $5 will buy you an additional five tokens. All locations are open seven days a week.

Wonderland Golf and Games, 10515 N Division (468-4FUN). This indoor and outdoor play center offers over 80 video games, two miniature golf courses, nine batting cages and a pizzaria. Admission is free and tokens can be purchased to play the games. Other activities are pay-as-you-go. Open seven days a week until midnight.

Indoor and Outdoor Activities

Ice Skating

Ice skating is a year-round activity in Spokane. Skates may be rented at any of the rinks listed below.
Eagles Ice-A-Rena, 6321 N Addison (489-9295). This rink is open year around.
Riverfront Park Ice Palace (625-6600). Riverfront is an outdoor arena, open from late October through early March.

Manito Pond, 1900 S Grand. During the coldest months of winter, many take to the outdoors for skating activities at Manito. (No skate rentals here.)

Roller skating

Roller skating rinks and rentals are listed below.
Pattison's North Roller Rink, 11505 N Division, (466-8133). Skates here rent for 50¢.
Roller Valley Skate Center, 9415 E 4th (924-7655). Roller Valley accepts cash only. Family night is Wednesday from 8 p.m.-10 p.m. Kids pay admission, while adults skate free.

Crafts Classes

Parks within the city and county offer an array of children's crafts classes, special events and physical activities throughout the year. A call to the *City Parks and Recreation Department* (625-6200) or the *County Parks Department* (456-4730) can bring a world of fun to your attention.

Public Pools

Sun and water go hand-in-hand at a number of city and county parks. Call the *Spokane Pool Hotline* (625-6960) for the latest information on pool hours. Public pools in the city are listed below.
Comstock, 800 W 29th
Mission, 1300 E Mission
Liberty, 1300 E 4th
Cannon, 1900 W Mission
Hillyard, 5800 N Market
Shadle Park, 2100 W Wellesley. Shadle has two pools, including an indoor one which remains open in the winter.

County Pools

For the latest information on Valley pools and the fees they charge, call the Spokane County Parks Department (456-4730).
The county offers four pools:
Park Road, 906 N Park
Valley Mission, 11123 E Mission
Terrace View, 13525 E 24th
Holberg, 9615 N Wall

Water Slides

There are also two water slides near Spokane:

Splash Down, 11123 E Mission, at Valley Mission Park. This is a 3.5-acre park with slides, a hot spa and a picnic area. Tuesday night is family night, with reduced admission fees. Open seven days a week.

Wild Waters, 2119 Government Way, Coeur d'Alene (208-667-6491). This water park features five long and two drop-off slides, a play area for smaller children and a video arcade. It's open seven days a week, with reduced admission prices after 4 p.m.

Other Activities

If you prefer to enjoy the water from the land side, why not try feeding the ducks? Several area parks host spring-fed ponds or waterways which attract a variety of waterfowl. Riverfront Park is a great place to go. One of its best feeding grounds is along the river bank near the *Carrousel*. Or, try *Cannon Hill Pond*, 1900 S Lincoln, *Liberty Park*, 1300 E 4th, or the grand-daddy of all area ponds, *Manito*, 1900 S Grand. The nearby Park Bench, an open air café, sells special packets of duck food in the summer.

For more outdoor fun, visit *Turnbull National Wildlife Refuge*, (235-47230), located four miles south of Cheney on Badger Lake Road. This is an excellent place to walk and run over miles of groomed trails. Fall is a great time to visit this natural sanctuary as the migrating waterfowl cloak the sky. Another must-stop spot if you have children who enjoy hiking is the *Dishman Hills Natural Area* (926-7949). This 450-acre site is located in the heart of the Spokane Valley and offers a number of well-groomed trails and a picnic shelter. No animals are allowed in the area though, and the only restroom is located where the trail head starts. Maps of the area are available at the Spokane Valley Chamber of Commerce (924-4994).

Rainy Days

Though Spokane is blessed with an average of over 200 days of sunshine per year, there are times when outdoor activities take a back seat to indoor recreation. Imagine a crackling fire and a good book, and you have a perfect way to spend a winter's afternoon.

Radio Stations

Two local radio stations have extensive children's story programs. KAZZ-FM (107.1) is a nationally syndicated format from Minnesota, which specializes in children's programming 24 hours a day. KPBX-FM (91.1), Spokane's public radio station, also airs a children's story program each Friday night at 6:30 p.m. Older kids like the contemporary hits of KZZU-FM (93) and the rock format of KNJY-FM (103.9).

Bookstores

A number of area bookstores offer children's books. High on the list of stores with an excellent selection of children's literature are:

Auntie's Bookstore and Cafe, 402 W Main (838-0206)

B. Dalton Bookseller, 702 W Main (455-8529), Northtown Mall (487-1655) University City (928-3770)

Children's Corner Bookshop, 814 W Main on the Skywalk Level (624-4820)

Hastings Book Music and Video, 11324 E Sprague (924-0720), 7304 N Division (483-2865), Lincoln Heights Shopping Center (535-4342) and Shadle at Wellesley and Ash (327-6008)

Waldenbooks, Riverpark Square (838-6359) and Northtown Mall (483-6552)

Whiz Kids Children's Educational Toys and Books, 518 W Riverside (456-6536) and 5628 N Division (483-9153)

Art

Spokane Art Supply, 1303 N Monroe (327-6628), carries a large quantity of arts and craft supplies for children including clay, how-to books, paints and papers. Once you have art supplies in hand, you may want to try one of the many art classes offered at several area locations. ***Spokane Art School***, 920 N Howard (328-0900), and the ***Corbin Art Center***, 507 W 7th (625-6677), both offer classes for children year around.

Music and Theatre

Children often learn by watching others. What better way to learn about music than enjoying a concert played by their peers? The ***Spokane Youth Symphony*** (326-4422) performs a series of concerts throughout the year which adults and children enjoy. Other musical treats for children include the *Spokane Symphony's Symfunnies* program (326-3136), where humor and music is combined for a great introduction to music. The free Summer Parks Concert Series (747-4926) features the 32-piece Spokane River Band playing music throughout the city parks.

If your child prefers the world of the stage, visit the *Spokane Children's Theatre*, 1020 N Howard (534-0737). The theatre performs four different plays each year just for kids. Performances are at the Spokane Civic Theatre.

For a different, but memorable treat, why not tour a dam? Learn the inside and outside workings of *Upriver Dam* on the Spokane River in an informative, one-hour tour which includes a view of the aquifer, control room and wells. The Spokane Department of Water and Hydroelectric Services sponsors the tours, offered year- round, 8 a.m.-3 p.m. For reservations and additional information, call (625-6641).

8
Sports and More

Cross-country skiing at the large skiing area on Mt. Spokane

Photo by Ron Swords

Sports and More

From the long, hot days of summer, to clear, crisp winter days, Spokane is blessed with dramatic seasons. Sport enthusiasts know and appreciate the variety of activities possible in such a climate. Local skiers and snowmobilers eagerly scan the winter skies for the first dusting of snow across Mt. Spokane, while spring is often heralded by the increase of runners pounding the pavement in advance of Bloomsday's May race.

Thanks to the diverse weather, there's bound to be at least one sport every resident or visitor will enjoy. *The U.S. Forest Service* (353-2574) sells a four-state map detailing trails, campgrounds, parks and outdoor areas that is excellent for year-round use. Both Spokane's City and County Parks Departments offer a multitude of opportunities to learn and engage in sporting activities. The City Department publishes a program guide three times a year to outdoor opportunities ranging from camping trips to cross-country ski expeditions and white water raft trips to hiking the area's trails. The program is mailed to all city residents, or you may pick up a copy at the department office, 808 W Spokane Falls Boulevard, 4th floor.

The City Parks Department also publishes a free Spokane City Park map. It highlights all city parks, trails, conservation lands, parkways, community recreation centers, golf courses, swimming pools and sports complexes. The grid format is very user-friendly. Pick up a copy at the department or by calling (625-6200).

The City and County Parks Departments oversee tennis courts, swimming pools, golf courses as well as the year-round classes at these facilities, which are offered to all ages and abilities.

Call for Information:
Spokane Parks and Recreation (625-6200)
Spokane County Parks Department (456-4730)
Turnbull National Wildlife Refuge, 26010 S Smith Rd., Cheney (235-4723)
U.S. Bureau of Land Management, Spokane District (353-2570)
U.S. Forest Service Public Affairs (353-2574), In Idaho (208-765-7223)
U.S. Geological Survey, 920 W Division
Earth Science Information Center (353-2524)
Map Sales (353-2524)
U.S. National Parks (725-2715)

Idaho State Department of Parks and Recreations (208-667-1511)
Washington Department of Fish and Wildlife Regional Office, 8702 N Division (456-4082)
Northern Idaho Field Office, 11103 E Montgomery Dr. (891-6839)
Washington State Department of Transportation, Pass Report Snow Season (456-2824)
Washington State Parks and Recreation Commission, Summer Only (800-562-0990)
Mount Spokane State Park (456-4169; 238-6845)
Riverside State Park (456-3964)
Off-Road Vehicle Information (456-2499)
National Weather Service, Forecast for Spokane-Coeur d'Alene, Idaho, (624-8905)
Joe Albi Stadium (353-6500)
Memorial Coliseum (625-5100)
Spokane Interstate Fairgrounds (535-1766)

Golf

Spokane's warm spring, hot summer and crisp autumn seasons are perfect for golf. Many visitors flock to the area for golf alone. Courses are green and challenging throughout the golf season, which runs from about mid-March to mid-November. When covered by a blanket of white snow, the courses double as sledding hills and cross-country trails.

The year was 1910 when 50 golf enthusiasts gathered to urge the city park board to buy land for Spokane's first golf course. In 1916, a nine-hole course called "Downriver" was purchased for $9,000. Now there are at least 45 golf courses within a short driving distance of the city and most of the best are open to the public. The fees overall are reasonable.

To get a jump on the season, call the City Parks Department (625-GOLF) and sign up for golf lessons. The Spokane Convention and Visitors Bureau (747-3230; 800-248-3230) offers a Golf Getaway Kit, filled with package deals and special offers from area hotels, restaurants and retailers as well as area golf information.

The following courses are divided into public and private links, with fees listed. Keep in mind that on many public greens, fees are reduced for senior citizens, youngsters and members of the military. Check first for specifics.

Public Courses

The Coeur d'Alene Resort Golf Course, 900 Floating Green, Coeur d'Alene, Idaho (208-667-4653). 18 holes/6,309 yards. Some love it, others think it's an aberration to the game, but, either way, most people want to play Coeur d'Alene at least once. The reason for all the fuss is the floating 14th. Literally floating on Coeur d'Alene Lake, this par-3 green is moved daily from 100 to 175 yards from shore, so no matter how many times you play the course, it's constantly different. Shuffling to and from this green by boat takes some getting use to, but judging from the rave reviews most golfers give this course, it's well worth the expense of playing. Green fees cost $175 for 18 holes, though lower-priced golf packages are available through the Coeur d'Alene Resort Hotel (1-800-826-2390).

The Creek at Qualchan, 301 E Meadowlake Road (448-9317). 18 holes/6,425 yards. This is one of the newest courses in the area, located just north of the Hangman Valley Golf Club. The Creek at Qualchan opened in 1993 at the cost of $6 million and is named after a Native American hung along the banks of the Latah Creek. The course features a 5,800-square-foot clubhouse with restaurant, banquet room and pro shop, as well as 65 sand traps and five ponds. Numerous wildlife can be spotted, since parts of the lay skirt a wildlife habitat. Green fees are $16 for Spokane residents and $21 for non-residents. During December, the fairway is ablaze with 90,000 lights creating animated scenes. Tours by car are available with a minimum charge. (See Chapter 12: Annual Events, for more details).

Downriver Golf Course, 3225 N Columbia Circle (327-5269). 18 holes/6,130 yards. The oldest public links in the city, Downriver hosts a steady stream of golfers who enjoy the challenge of hilly, pine-forested terrain. The course is nestled between homes on one side and Riverside State Park on the other. Winter brings many who enjoy the triple-jump sledding hills located just off the main parking lots. Fees are $13 for residents, $17 for non-residents. Sledding is free.

Esmeralda Golf Course, 3933 E Courtland (487-6291). 18 holes/6,071 yards. Known to locals as "Essie," this course boasts a longer season than most in the area, in part due to steady winds and a southern exposure, both of which keep the course snow free and dry. Its convenient location, near Hillyard in Spokane's east side, and longer season, make Essie a popular venue. Fees are $13 for Spokane residents, $17 for non-residents.

The Fairways at West Terrace, 9810 W Melville Road, Cheney (747-8418). 18 holes/6,355 yards. This course lies on relatively treeless land, but offers many man-made hazards as compensation. The

Fairways co-hosts the annual Lilac City Invitational, with a professional purse of $50,000. For non-golfers, the Fairways offers tennis courts, jogging and hiking trails, plus watersports on nearby lakes. Green fees are $15.

Hangman Valley Golf Club, 2111 E Hangman Valley Road (448-1212). 18 holes/6,1119 yards. This is a challenging course, well-conditioned and tough. Its length, including a number of bunkers and water hazards, requires both strength and skill to complete with any success. Hangman Creek, which gives the course its name, comes into play on four holes and borders five others. Green fees are $12.50 for Spokane County residents and $17 for non-residents.

Indian Canyon Golf Course, W 4304 West Drive (747-5353). 18 holes/6,296 yards. Since opening in 1935, this course's sidehill locale has challenged many a golfer. Annually, it's rated among *Golf Digest's* top 75 public courses in the country. In the winter, the same hills reverberate with the sounds of locals flocking to the slopes with sleds and tubes. Green fees are $16 for Spokane residents and $21 for non-residents.

Liberty Lake Golf Course, 24403 E Sprague, Liberty Lake (255-6233). 18 holes/6,398 yards. Best known for two of the longest par-4s in the Northwest, Liberty Lake provides an easy walk and a good assortment of man-made hazards. Slated improvements include the building of eight new greens. Green fees are $12.50 for Spokane County residents and $17 for non-residents.

Meadow Wood Golf Course, 24501 E Valley Way, Liberty Lake (255-9539). 18 holes/6,811 yards. This $3.1 million Spokane County-owned facility opened in 1988, making it one of the newest fairways in the area. Flat terrains mark the first 16 holes, though grassy mounds, sand and water traps offer some diversity. The whole course contains over 70 traps and 20 acres of ponds, so don't let the initial flat terrain fool you, there's plenty of challenge to be found on this course. Green fees for Spokane County residents are $12.50 and $17 for non-residents.

Painted Hills Golf Club, 4403 S Dishman/Mica Road (928-4653). 9 holes/3,089 yards. The lay of this course is flat and fairly wide-open, with the grass-in roughs longer than the fairways. Separated from the driving range by the meandering Chester Creek, the facility boasts a nice clubhouse with pro shop and restaurant. Green fees are $10 for a nine-hole round.

Sundance Golf Course, off Highway 291, Nine Mile Falls (466-4040) 18 holes/5,960 yards. Getting a tee time at Sundance is usually easier than at some of the more well-known in-city links. The course is fairly flat, meandering through pine forests with trees used for definition and hazards. Annual events include the Sundance Amateur and Two-Man Best-Ball. Green fees cost $13.

Wandermere Golf Course, 13700 N Division (466-8023). 18 holes/6,005 yards. Since its opening in 1931, Wandermere has been owned by the Ross family. The course stretches across a rolling terrain and contains over a dozen sand traps and several water hazards, including the Little Spokane River. Wandermere club roster contains over 700 members, and its men's club is one of the largest in the Northwest. Green fees are $15.

Private Clubs

Manito Golf and Country Club, 4502 Hatch Road (448-5829). 18 holes/6,398 yards. Open to members, guests and reciprocates, this tight, tree-lined fairway is dotted with nearly fifty sand traps. The clubhouse has a full-service restaurant, lounge and health club. Non-members playing with a member are charged $24 per person green fees. Members of reciprocal clubs are charged $60 per person, plus half the charge of a cart.

Spokane Country Club, 2010 W Waikiki Road (466-9813). 18 holes/6,679 yards. This country club is the third oldest in the Northwest and hosted the first U.S. Women's Open in 1946. In 1988, the course was remodeled and now boasts over 50 traps and numerous water hazards. Every four years, the course hosts the Spokane Junior League Golf Clinic and Exhibition, with such PGA stars as Arnold Palmer, Jack Nicklaus and Lee Trevino. The course is open to members, guests and reciprocates. If guests play with a member, the cost is $35 per person and there are some restrictions on tee times. If reciprocal club members play the cost is $75 per person.

Teams and Leagues

Baseball

Spokane Indians, Seafirst Stadium, 602 N Havana (535-2922). The Class-A Spokane Indians have belonged to the Single-A San Diego Padres farm system for over 13 seasons. The Indians play in one of the nicest minor league ballparks in the country. Formerly known as Indian Stadium, the name recently changed to Seafirst Stadium when Seafirst Bank contributed to a $300,000 renovation. Hall-of-Fame player Steve Garvey wore the Indians' uniform in 1970 and was led by Tommy Lasorda that same year.

Hockey

Spokane Chiefs Hockey Club, Coliseum, 720 W Mallon (625-5100). The new Spokane Veteran's Memorial Arena hosts the Spokane Chiefs Hockey Club, a junior hockey team which is a member of the Western Hockey League. In 1991, the Chiefs cinched the Canadian Hockey League Memorial Cup title. The Chiefs' members range in age from 16 to 20 and play against Oregon, Washington and British Columbia teams in a season starting in September and ending in March.

College Competition

For exciting basketball play in Spokane, don't miss the *Gonzaga University Bulldogs*. In 1994, they won the West Coast Conference League title and have also won 27 straight at-home games. Martin Centre (328-4220, ext 4203) has had sell-out crowds at 75% of their home games during the last two years, so call early for your tickets. Players of note who have graduated from Gonzaga include John Stockton, an all-star guard now with the Utah Jazz, and Jeff Brown, who was named both the 1994 Player of the year for the West Coast Conference and an Academic All-American for the same year.

Eastern Washington University quarterback Todd Burnett at a 1993 game
Photo by Ron Swords

Martin Stadium in Pullman is home to the Pac 10 **Washington State University Cougars** (1-800-GO-COUGS). The WSU team has built a loyal following bordering on fanatic. Saturday games are teleconferenced to hundreds of Coug Alumini as far away as Washington D.C. For some, the tailgate parties during home games are the quintessential way to spend a college football afternoon. Since 1900, the Cougs have played their rival competitors, the University of Washington Huskies, in a game now known as the Apple Cup. Every other year the game is held in Pullman, drawing thousands from around the area.

In volleyball, the WSU women's team rated the 9th best attended games in the nation in 1993, even though they rated only 6th place in the Pac 10 conference.

Nearby, Eastern Washington University field teams in 16 intercollegiate sports, nine for men and seven for women. In football, the **Eagles** were rated 20th in the Big Sky Conference league for 1993. Their home games are held in Cheney at Woodward Stadium (359-4339).

For pre-college games, the **Greater Spokane League** (GSL) High School football is played regularly at Joe Albi Stadium (353-6500) and basketball at the Spokane Veteran's Memorial Arena, 720 W Mallon (625-5100).

Race Tracks

Auto Racing

Spokane Raceway Park, 101 N Hayford Road (244-3663). From April through October, auto racing fans crowd this track near Airway Heights to watch the stock- and drag-car racing. It's unusual to have a facility catering to both stock and race car enthusiasts. Highlights during the year are the AHRA World Finals, the second weekend in August, and the Fox Hunt Jet Car Show, the middle of July. During regular weekend races, children under 11 are admitted free. Seniors and military personnel also receive discounted tickets.

Stateline Stadium Speedway, 1025 Beck Road N, Post Falls (208-773-5019). This speedway caters to stock car enthusiasts during the April through October season. Races are run three nights a week with three levels of amateur competition. A recent addition to the race track is a dirt track for mini-sprints and motor bikes.

Greyhound Racing

The Greyhound Park, Post Falls, Idaho, (800-828-4880). This park just east of the state line between Idaho and Washington premiered its 1/4-mile track in 1988. Designed for year-round racing, it offers eight programs each week and 12 races at each program. In 1992, fans went home with over $16.6 million paid out on winning tickets. The grandstand features theatre-style seating for up to 1,500 people, with 14 large-screen monitors, a full-service bar, deli and concessions. At the finish line, you'll find terraced-table seating with waiter service and a color monitor on each table.

Thoroughbred Horse Racing

Playfair Race Track, Altamont and Main (534-0505). Washington's only eastern horse racing site outside of Yakima's Meadows, Playfair offers year-round TV simulcasting as well as seasonal live-horse racing. It's one of the few tracks on the circuit where spectators can stand at the rail and view horses, jockeys and owners up close. Children under 12 are admitted free to the course. Fine dining is available in the Turf Club. Another attraction is the free parking. The season runs July through November.

Annual Exhibitions and Events

Basketball

The Washington State "B" Basketball (625-5100) competition features area high school players, boys and girls teams, vying for the State Championship title. Four days of feet stomping, lung imploding cheering and long seated rivalries set off this March event held each year at the Spokane Coliseum and Spokane Falls Community College gym. For amateur players, *HoopFest*, held each June on downtown Spokane streets, is one of the largest 3-on-3 games of its type in the country.

Biking

The number of on- and off-road events has multiplied in recent years. The *King of the Mountain* in Nelson, B.C. (604-354-1830), is an event composed of three different off-road races. The *Mt. Spokane/Selkirk Challenge* (747-3869), which is part of the WIM-NORBA series, features both cross-country and downhill events. *Trek Washington* (206-441-5100) is a 385-mile, seven-day ride from Seattle to Spokane. The *MS Tri-State Bike Tour* (482-2022) begins in Thompson Falls, Montana, and winds through three states and 150 miles before reaching Spokane. *The Autumn Century Classic* (624-3793), held in September, is biking fun for the whole family.

Golf

Every golf course in the area sponsors a series of tournaments, which means that on most days during the golfing season, you stand a good chance of finding tournament play somewhere. Two of particular note include the *Rosauers-Spokane Open*, held at *Indian Canyon Golf Course* in mid-July. This section event for the Pacific Northwest PGA attracts a number of high-caliber players from around the Pacific Northwest. The *Lilac Open*, part of the Lilac Festivities in May, is hosted by the *Fairways Golf Course*.

Running

World-class runners compete in May in the annual 12-k *Bloomsday Race* (838-1579), the largest timed road event in the United States. Over 60,000 people throng the streets for this event, and that's just the runners, walkers and wheel chair participants. The sidelines are packed with cheering, shouting crowds, volunteers by the hundreds man water stations and work behind the scenes, work schedules are adjusted throughout area business so runners can be part of this truly community event. Runners ages 5 to 12 can participate in the annual *Junior Bloomsday* (325-9044) held every year in April at Joe Albi Stadium.

Triathlon

Several triathlons are held throughout the summer, including the *Coeur d'Alene Triathlon* (208-667-3589) and the *Troika Triathlon* (624-2980). The Troika is the only qualifying race in the Pacific Northwest for Hawaii's Ironman Triathlon.

Volleyball

Spokane Falls Community College (325-0740) hosts the Spokane *Spike & Dig* tournament each year. This six-player outdoor event includes collegian and celebrity play, as well as a food fair, amusement rides and games for the spectators.

Team Play

The Spokane City Parks and Recreation Department actively promotes adult team sports and provides facilities for play. For information on flag football, basketball and volleyball, contact them at 625-6200. *The Spokane Youth Sports Association* (536-1800) handles outdoor team sports, such as soccer, baseball, softball and golf, for youngsters ages 6 through 18. *The Spokane Metro Softball Association* (489-2442) sponsors softball leagues for adult men and women. For county residents, the *Spokane County Parks, Recreation and Fair Department* (456-4730) publishes a *Sports Guide* listing team events for men, women and children.

Interactive Sports

Biking

Cycling has boomeranged in popularity over the last dozen years, now rivaling skiing as one of the most popular outdoor activities in the area. During mild winters, bikers can navigate roadways year-round with only an adjustment in clothing.

The railroads, freeway and Spokane River all impede traffic moving north-south. Because of this, many bicyclists travel east-west, using the Centennial Trail as their route. A free Bicycle Guide Map, detailing trails and routes for bicyclists, is available through the local biking organizations or the *Spokane Regional Transportation Council* (625-6370).

Local organizations of interest to bicyclists include the 20-year old *Spokane Bicycle Club* (624-3793), which schedules nine group rides throughout the year and sponsors the annual *September Autumn Century Ride. The Arrivé Cycling Club* (838-3707) promotes bike racing in the area and regularly uses the upper Lincoln Park circle for their racing venue.

Mountain biking offers its own thrills in an area geographically populated with plenty of hills and trails. Favorite areas for mountain biking include *Mt. Spokane State Park* (456-4169), *Farragut State Park* (208-683-2425), *Bear Creek Meadows near Priest River, 49 Degrees North* (458-9208) and *Schweitzer Resort* (208-263-9555) in Sandpoint. At *Silver Mountain* (800-831-8810) in Kellogg, Idaho, mountain bikers can rent equipment at the base village (208-783-1111) and transport their bikes on the world's longest gondola ride. Once you've reached the top of the mountain there are six developed trails ranging from two to 22 miles, with routes for all skill levels.

The **Washington Idaho Montana (WIM) Tri-State Series** sponsors nine events throughout the year which attract mountain bike enthusiasts. For information on this series and other events, contact the **Inland Empire Mountain Bike Club** (533-5459). The club, in addition to handling annual events like the June Mt. Spokane/Selkirk Challenge and the August IMBE Mountain Bike Festival, promotes off-road bicycling through trail maintenance, racing support, responsible riding and trail etiquette.

Bowling

Whether you're a novice or an experienced bowler, you'll find plenty of open lanes in the Spokane area. There are over a dozen bowling alleys listed in the yellow pages in Spokane alone.

For league or competitive play, call one of the bowling centers located throughout the city or county. There are also three bowling associations in the area. **The Spokane Bowling Association** (535-5146) organizes men's leagues. **The Spokane Women's Bowling Association** (926-9926) sponsors competitive play for women and holds an annual city tournament in February. **The Lilac City Young American Bowling Alliance** (467-8866; 466-3390) organizes teams starting with players as young as 2 and continuing through junior and college divisions.

In June, the Lawn Bowling Association challenges local newspaper and television personalities, more for laughs than serious competition. Spokane's lone lawn bowling green is behind Witter Pool on East Mission. Games are played six days a week during warm weather. Everyone is welcome to come by for a lesson or a game. To join the fun, call the **Spokane Lawn Bowling Association** (483-9370).

Bull Riding

Just 15 miles from the Dishman/Mica Road, in the quiet town of Rockford, you'll find the **Rocking Go Arena** (291-6451). Spring through fall, bull riding practice occurs Wednesday nights at 7 p.m. and Sunday at 4 p.m. For $10 per ride, you'll be matched with a bull or bucking horse geared to your size and experience. Clientele range from bank presidents to old rodeo hands. All enjoy the laid-back atmosphere where the doors don't close until the last person goes home.

Canoeing and Boating

With 76 lakes and four major rivers within a 50-mile radius of the city, there's no dearth of boating opportunities. For a copy of local requirements and state laws governing boating, contact the *Spokane Emergency Services, Marine Enforcement Division*, 1121 W Gardner (456-2204). In Washington, all motor boats and sailcraft over 16 feet must be licensed, as well as motor boats less than 16 feet with 10 horsepower engines. Licensing can be done at any vehicle licensing office in the state. In Idaho, any boat with a motor must be licensed.

The Washington State Parks Department has only one public access boat dock in Spokane County, which is located at Long Lake. All other docks or ramps are privately operated or under supervision of the *Department of Wildlife* (456-4082). The Department of Wildlife ramps close from October through mid-April, except for Newman Lake and Long Lake which are open year-round.

Boating safety courses are offered through the *U.S. Coast Guard*, 5101 N Assembly (353-2127). For recreational boating, it is important to keep in mind the congestion which can occur on some area lakes. Traffic is especially heavy on lakes located near the city, both on long, hot weekends and after 5 p.m. during the week.

If you want to leave the piloting to someone else, try a boat cruise. *Daily Lake Coeur d'Alene Cruises* include excursions to the Coeur d'Alene Resort's Floating Green, cuisine cruises and St. Joe River cruises. The boats all depart from the downtown Coeur d'Alene waterfront (208-765-4000 for schedules). For a sternwheeling riverboat cruise harkening back to the paddleboat days of Huckleberry Finn and Mark Twain, *Templin's Resort* (208-773-1611) in Post Falls, Idaho offers daily, custom, dinner and moonlight cruises on the Spokane River and Coeur d'Alene Lake.

The multitude of rivers in the area enable individuals and families to enjoy the sports of canoeing and kayaking. The *Spokane Canoe and Kayak Club* (534-7788) is very family-oriented and lists about 200 family memberships. One of the annual events is Family Fun Day, held at a local lake and geared toward introducing the sport to new members. *The Washington Waterhawks* (534-9386) is comprised of rafters, kayakers and canoeists. They work toward public education, conservation and clean waterways.

The Northwest Whitewater Association (466-2200) focuses more on heavy whitewater and the more experienced boater. They take advantage of the challenges on the lower, more turbulent part of the Spokane River, as well as several rivers in Central Washington, Idaho and parts of Canada. For up-to-date information on river flows and activity information, call the *NWA Information Line* (299-2777).

Renting a canoe can be arranged through *R.E.I.*, 1125 N Monroe (328-9900); *Templin's Resort Hotel in Post Falls* (208-773-1611) and *North Shore Rentals* at the city dock on Lake Coeur d'Alene (208-664-1175).

Several tour operators specialize in rafting and whitewater expeditions. *ROW* (800-451-6034) hosts several trips on Idaho rivers, including the Snake, Salmon and Clark Fork, while *Northwest Voyageurs* (800-727-9977) combine rafting trips with mountain biking, fishing and horseback riding experiences.

Hiking and Climbing

Not only is Spokane graced with hundreds of well-groomed hiking trails suitable for even the smallest of feet, but the area also has innumerable basalt and granite outcroppings, making for excellent climbing surfaces.

Maps and guides to area trails are available from the *U.S. Forest Service Public Affairs Office*, 400 S Jefferson, Suite 106 (353-2574). *The Spokane Sierra Club* (456-3834) sponsors outings and highlights trails in its monthly publication, *The Nature's Advocate*. Local authors Rich Landers and Ida Rowe Dolphin have published an excellent guide, *100 Hikes in the Inland Northwest* (Mountaineers, Seattle, WA). The local Sierra Club publishes two Spokane trail guides (Sierra Club Spokane Group, Spokane, WA), which are inexpensive and easy to pack around.

For organizations promoting and teaching climbing and hiking skills, try the *Northwest Outdoor School* (838-6968) and the *Mountaineers* (838-4974). Both *Recreational Equipment Inc., (REI)* 1125 N Monroe (328-9900) and *Mountain Gear*, 2002 N Division (325-9000) offer indoor rock-climbing walls for hands-on experience.

The *Dishman Hills Natural Area* (926-7949) contains a number of groomed trails throughout its 450 acres and is located in the heart of the Spokane Valley. The trails are accessible through all but the deepest snowfalls, but spring is an excellent time to enjoy the wildflowers scattered across the pine-tree terrain.

Riverside State Park (456-3964) is only minutes away from downtown Spokane. The park's groomed hiking trails span much of its 7,655 acres, many lapping the Spokane River's shoreline. Picnic

Climbing on Minnehaha rocks — a climber's mecca in Spokane
Photo by Ron Swords

areas, barbeque sites, restrooms and overnight camping facilities allow you to hike for hours or days.

Hobo Cedar Grove (208-765-7223). You'll find this 240-acre grove of western red cedar located in the St. Maries, Idaho, Ranger District. A 1/2 mile loop takes you through a lush carpet of lady fern. The trail begins near Hobo Pass on Forest Road #3357, about 12 miles from Clarkia.

The Spokane area is home to world-class mountain climbers such as John Roskelly, who earned his callouses on local rock outcroppings. A favorite climbing site among beginners and more advanced climbers is *Minnehaha Park*. Located only minutes from downtown and adjacent to the Centennial Trail and Spokane River, this series of boulders provides hours of climbing opportunity. With everything from low-angle friction slabs to overhangs with big holds, you'll have ample opportunity to practice a variety of hold techniques.

Horseback Riding

Last Chance Riding Stable, Indian Canyon Park (624-4646). Last Chance offers group rates, lessons, tractor-pulled hayrides, pony rides and camps. There are over 1,000 acres of trails geared for beginners and advanced riders in the Indian Canyon Area, which is just minutes from downtown Spokane. Open year-round 9 a.m. - dark.

Trail Town Riding Stables, Riverside State Park (456-8249). Located on the north side of the Spokane River, Trail Town is only five minutes from the heart of the city. In spite of this, beginner and experienced riders have over 6,000 acres of scenic trails to enjoy. The stables offer overnight horse camps, dinner rides and truck-drawn hayrides, as well as mounts suitable for both beginners and advanced riders. Open year-round, 9 a.m.-dark.

Busy Bee Ranch and Equestrian Center, 14910 W Craig Rd. (244-5049). Busy Bee is the largest commercial arena in Spokane, providing trailrides and hayrides through Deep Creek Canyon. Reservations are required. This is a great place for a group ride or party. Horse and horsemanship classes are also available.

In Idaho, contact the **Idaho Outfitters and Guides Association** (208-342-1438) for information on trails, hayrides and winter sleigh rides.

Hunting

Regulations, seasons, bag limits and permit procedures are all administered by the **Washington Department of Fish and Wildlife,** Region 1 Office, 8702 N Division, Spokane 99218-1199 (456-4082). Publications with details for hunting everything from elk to upland birds are available at the department or at local sporting goods outlets.

There are over 35 different kinds of hunting and fishing licenses issued by Washington State. Hunters under 18 must have proof they've successfully completed an approved hunter education course before they purchase their first hunting license. **The Inland Northwest Wildlife Council** (534-6550) or the **Washington Department of Fish and Wildlife** (456-4082) can provide you with an annual class schedule.

Seniors 70 or older will find reduced fishing license fees. Both seniors and juveniles can apply for special deer hunts offered by the State. Contact the **Washington Department of Fish and Wildlife** (456-4082) for specifics. There are also special seasons for bow hunters and muzzleloaders.

Special access areas for disabled hunters have recently been established. In Northeast Washington contact the **Inland Northwest Wildlife Council** (534-6550) for information. In Southwest Washington the **Gifford Pinchot National Forest** (427-5645) in the Wind River Ranger District has barrier-free hunting (handicap-accessible areas). An application for a Disabled Hunter Permit or a Blind- or Visually Handicapped- Hunter Permit can be obtained from the Olympia Office, Licensing Section, 600 Capital Way N, Olympia, WA 98501-1091 (206-902-2464).

Jogging and Roadrunning

The minute the snow blows off the roadways, the joggers and runners begin preparing for a variety of events. Competitions as diverse as Climb a Mountain, Across the Valley, Run for the Berries and the Yep Kanum offer varied terrains and challenges.

The largest and most well-known race in the area is *Bloomsday*, held the first Sunday in May. From the first race in 1977 to today's record-breaking crowd of participants from world-class athletes to newborns pushed in prams, Bloomsday is a Spokane community event unlike any other. The day before the race, participants celebrate with "carbo" parties throughout the city. The Monday following is an unofficial casual clothing day at many local business, so participants can sport their official Bloomie T-shirt as a mark of accomplishment.

The Bloomsday Road Runners Club, 4118 Stevens (483-RUNN) helps sponsor and promotes several races in town. Their publication, *Race Rag*, is published seven times a year and includes entry forms for Spokane area footraces. It's available free at many area running stores and athletic clubs.

Several specific runs are mentioned if you ask local runners for their favorite course. For hilly and scenic terrain, none beats the Bloomsday Course. It's marked with signs at nearly every turn, or a map is available through the *Bloomsday Lilac Association* (838-1579). For long, flat distance runners, many enjoy the Centennial Trail with its wide, paved pathways. A free map is available from the *Friends of the Centennial Trail* (624-3430). *Riverside State Park* (456-2729) and the *Dishman Hills Natural Area* (926-7949) both offer a number of dirt-packed trails for runners and hikers and are located within minutes of downtown Spokane.

There are also 15 to 20 high school and college tracks in the area, offering both crushed brick and rubberized surfaces. Tracks of particular note include the following: *North Central High School*, 1600 N Howard; *Mead High School*, 302 W Hastings Road; *Northwood Junior High School*, 13120 N Pittsburg; *Ferris High School*, 3020 E 37th; *University High School*, 10212 E 9th and *Gonzaga Preparatory School*, 1224 E Euclid.

Off-Road Vehicles

At the *Spokane County ORV Park* (244-9244), you can enjoy go-kart races, moto-x track races, sand drags, 4x4 obstacle courses and tractor pulls. Off-road vehicle riders will appreciate the moto-cross track, a 1/8-mile clay oval. There's also an obstacle course, a dual and barrel racing course, restrooms, picnic areas and staging areas for major events. The park is open March through October, Thursday through Sunday. Call the **Spokane County Parks Department** (456-4730) for directions to the park.

Orienteering

For those unfamiliar with the sport, orienteering combines cross-country racing or hiking with compass reading skills. Participants compete against the clock and their own expectations, traveling across terrain chosen for its diversity. The **Eastern Washington Orienteering Club** (838-7078) stages a number of events throughout the area all through the year. Instruction for beginners is included with nearly every event, and the terrains covered can vary from a city park to the more primitive areas of local state parks.

Parasailing

For an exciting and unique experience, there's nothing quite like parasailing 500 feet high over the beauty of Coeur d'Alene Lake. **Coeur d'Alene Parasail** (208-765-4627) operates daily from 8 a.m. to sunset. Rides cost $40 for a single rider and $55 per pair. Their boat is moored at Independence Point City dock, next to the Coeur d'Alene Resort. Flyers take off and land directly from the boat.

Shooting

Spokane was one of the earliest settlements in the west to sponsor organized trap shoots, holding competitive events as early as 1882. Today, the **Spokane Gun Club**, 19615 E Sprague (927-1176) is a trap, skeet and sporting clays facility dedicated to shotgun sports. The Club site in the Spokane Valley hosts league shoots and lessons. Parking is provided for RVs.

The Spokane Rifle Club (327-9632) rifle range is located near Riverside State Park and open to the public Friday and Saturday 9 a.m.-6 p.m. For non-members, the fee is $5 per day per shooter.

Swimming

The Spokane City Parks Department (625-6200) maintains seven city-run pools, which are open to the public during the summer months, and one indoor pool, which is open for public swimming all year (though there is a minimal fee). Check with the Spokane Pool

Hotline (625-6960) for the latest information on pool hours. Locations are listed below:

Comstock (wading pool) 800 W 29th
Mission, 1300 E Mission
Liberty, (wading pool) 1300 E 4th
Cannon, 1900 W Mission
Hillyard, 5800 N Market

Shadle Park, 2100 W Wellesley, has two pools including an indoor one, which remains open in the winter. A small fee is charged during the winter months: 50¢ for children and $1.50 for adults.

For the latest information on county pools and fees, call the ***Spokane County Parks Department*** (456-4730).

Spokane county offers four pools:

Park Road, 906 N Park
Valley Mission, 11123 E Mission
Terrace View, 13525 E 24th
Holberg, 9615 N Wall

The Aquatic Center at Whitworth College, 300 W Hawthorne (466-1000), houses an Olympic-size swimming pool where non-students may swim for a nominal fee. Whitworth also offers adult and children's programs in swimming, water aerobics, scuba diving and water polo throughout the year. Other pools open to the public for a fee include the ***Trailer Inns Recreational Center***, 6021 E 4th (535-1811), the ***YMCA*** at Riverfront Park (838-3577) and the ***YWCA*** at 829 W Broadway (326-1190). The Ys also schedule swimming lessons for adults and children.

Tennis

Spokane residents enjoy tennis and the city's many outdoor facilities. Contact the ***City Parks Department*** (625-6200) or ***County Parks Department*** (456-4730) for the dates when nets will be stretched on the courts and also for tennis lesson information. If you're interested in league or tournament play or just have questions about what's happening, your best bet is the ***Spokane Tennis Association*** (467-8357). The Association organizes a spring and summer league, allows players to connect with others of their skill level, and offers a newsletter and two social functions a year.

Central Park Racquet and Athletic Club, 5900 E 4th (535-3554) offers their tennis court, hand ball courts, exercise machines and swimming pool to non-members for a $8 daily entrance fee and minimum per activity fee.

The list below gives both city and county park locations and indicates the number of courts. The symbol "L" means courts are lighted. No city or county courts may be reserved in advance.

Cannon Playfield, 1900 W Mission: 2
Corbin, 400 W Park Place: 2
Comstock, 800 W 29th: 6
Coeur d'Alene, 2100 W 2nd: 1
Edgecliff, 8th and Park Road: 2
Franklin, 100 W Queen: 3
Friendship, 300 E Gretta: 2
Grant, 1100 E 9th: 2/L
Hamblen, 1900 E 37th: 2
Liberty, 1300 E 4th: 2/L
Linwood, 7500 N Country Homes Boulevard: 1
Manito, 1900 S Grand: 3
Minnehaha, 4000 E Euclid: 3
Mission, 1300 E Mission: 5/L
Peaceful Valley, under Maple Street Bridge: 1
Shadle, 2100 W Wellesley: 8
Sharpley/Harmon, 2800 E Bismark: 2/L
Sontag, W 9808 Charles Road: 1
Underhill, 2900 E Hartson: 1
Underfreeway, 4th and McClellan: 4/L
Valley Mission, 11123 Mission: 1
Whittier, 3400 W 7th, off Sunset Highway: 2

Volkssporting

Volkssporting, "a sport of the people," is one of the fastest growing participation sports in the country. Geared toward all ages and physical fitness levels, it's a great sport for the whole family, including the physically challenged. There are four different categories of events: Volksmarches, organized hikes and walks of 10 kilometers or more; Volksswims, organized swims of varying distances; volksbikes, bicycle rides of 20, 40, or 50 kilometers; and Volksskiis, cross-country skiing events usually 10 to 20 kilometers in length.

Anyone paying the registration fee and completing the entire distance of the course—at their own pace—is a winner and receives a medal, patch or other award. You can also participate for free, but do not receive an award.

The Spokane Valley of the Sun Volkssport Club (926-1295) organizes regular walks for fun and hosts several yearly Volksmarching events. The *Lilac City Volkssport Association* (489-3198) sports the annual Green Bluff Walk every fall as one of their yearly events. This stroll through orchards, hills and valleys is a wonderful introduction to fall and a great way to spend a morning or afternoon.

For walkers who prefer an indoor arena, the *Spokane Youth Sports Activity Center*, 3014 E 55th (448-1620) provides (for a nominal fee) an environment in which to walk complete with adult music with a beat from September through May.

Snow Fun

The first big annual snowfall on Mt. Spokane is eagerly awaited by thousands of winter sports enthusiasts. With five major ski resorts within two hours of downtown Spokane, getting to the slopes is not a problem. The challenge is deciding what to do once you're there. The explosion in popularity of snowboarding, cross-country skiing, snowmobiling, telemarking and other winter sports means there are lots of ways to enjoy the dry, white powder area of the Inland Northwest.

Spokane's annual snowfall average is 51.6 inches, with nearby mountains receiving a good deal more. The five- to six-month season usually begins around Thanksgiving and continues through March.

A Sno-Park pass can be purchased at many retail sporting goods stores selling ski and winter equipment. The pass is also available at the *City Parks Department* (625-6200) and at *Kirk's Lodge* (238-9114) on Mt. Spokane. A season's pass costs $20 and is good at seven different Washington state parks and Farragut State Park in Idaho. You can also purchase day passes for $7, or three-day passes for $10.

Snowmobiling

The U. S. Forest Service Public Affairs Office, 400 S Jefferson, Suite 106 (353-2574) issues a free brochure for snowmobilers showing sanctioned trails in the area. By law, snowmobiles must be registered, even if you ride only on your own property. The $15 registration fee includes a free Sno-Park permit for your vehicle.

Washington State Parks and Spokane County Parks administer a trail-grooming program on Mt. Spokane, as well as throughout Spokane, Pend Oreille and Stevens counties. A call to the *County Parks Department* (456-4730) can provide you with a map to these trails. The *Spokane Winter Knights Snowmobile Club* (483-SNOW) promotes family snowmobiling in the area.

Downhill Skiing

Many of the area ski resorts sell discount passes for those impatient enough to think "snow" in the middle of August. With prices up to 40% off the regular season pass, it's well worth the effort to plan ahead. Call the individual resorts in mid summer for specifics. The ski areas below are listed in order of distance from Spokane, from the closest at 35 miles to the furthermost at 450 miles.

Mount Spokane (238-6281). Less than 35 miles from downtown Spokane and offering the most affordable tickets in the state, it's no wonder Mt. Spokane is popular. The runs are wide and long and great for giant slaloms. Thirty-five major runs span the slopes including the mid-run mogul fields. Many also enjoy the groomed snowmobile trails and cross-country trails of Mt. Spokane State Park, which adjoin the ski hill.

49 Degrees North, Chewelah (935-6649). This resort 55 miles north of Spokane attracts a number of families. Its 700 acres of well-groomed slopes offer a combination of moguls, runs and four double chair lifts. The beginners' slope is excellent, and snowboarders love the area's permanent half-pipe and radical runs. There are seldom lift lines at this resort. During the ski season, a scheduled bus run from several Spokane locations is available. Call 935-6649 for details.

Silver Mountain, Kellogg, Idaho (208-783-1111) Silver Mountain is located only 68 miles from Spokane. A spacious, enclosed carriage carries you three miles to the area's Mountain Haus chalet-style resort. One quad chair lift, two triples, two doubles and one surface tow bring you within easy access of 50 trails, the longest running 2.5 miles. A free ski-check area with complimentary wax is available at the Mountain Haus service area. Mountain Haus also has a cafeteria, restaurant and child-care center.

Schweitzer, Sandpoint, Idaho (800-831-8810). This ski resort is 75 miles from Spokane and 54 miles from Coeur d'Alene. With one high-speed quad chair and five double chair lifts, it's easy to access the 48 trails criss crossing this mountain. As part of a 10-year expansion plan to make Schweitzer a destination stop, the road leading to the resort has recently undergone a face-lift, making it easier to access the area. Check out the Headquarters Day Lodge for services (there are four levels for skiers). The base hosts free movies for kids on Saturday night.

Red Mountain, Rossland, British Columbia, Canada (800-663-0105). This resort is situated 125 miles north of Spokane. One triple chair, two doubles and one T-bar take you up the slopes. Ten percent of trails are geared for novice skiers, 45% for intermediate and 45% for advanced. Try the *Uplander Hotel* (800-667-8741) for a good ski package with hotel accommodations.

The Big Mountain, Whitefish, Montana (800-858-5439). The mountain is 260 miles from Spokane. With a summit elevation of 7,000 feet and vertical drop of 2,300 feet, this mountain is aptly named. Nine double chairs and one high-speed quad whisk you to 61 marked trails, over 50% of them for intermediate skiers. Check for passes for some early- and late-season skiing at great prices.

Big White, Kellowna, British Columbia, Canada (800-765-2772) is located 310 miles north from Spokane. Big White is aptly named. The annual average is 223 inches of snow. Three quad chairs, one triple, one double and one T-bar access the 1,010 acres of skiable terrain. Check with the main office for workshops for children, teenagers and adults. These classes will enhance your enjoyment of recreational racing, skiing on powder and moguls and extreme skiing—all available at Big White.

Mount Bachelor, Bend, Oregon (800-829-2442). At 450 miles from Spokane, this is definitely a long trip, but the dry powder snow is often worth the drive. The average snowfall is 250-300 inches. There are six super-express, three triple and one double chair lift in operation, plus a Nordic Center with 56 kilometers of groomed trails. Overnight ski packages are available at several area resorts including *Inn of the 7th Mountain* (800-452-9846) and *Mount Bachelor Village* (800-452-9846).

Cross-Country Skiing

Nordic skiing is gaining in popularity for a variety of reasons. As a cardiovascular workout, it ranks with running. In addition, the scenery is serene and beautiful. Best, the cost is often half or less of downhill skiing. Most, if not all, the region's ski lodges offer cross-country skiing at little or no cost. Rental skis are available at the resort shops and at many in-town locations.

A catalog of nordic trails in Idaho is available from the *Idaho State Department of Parks and Recreation* (208-667-1511).

Try *Kirk's Lodge at Mount Spokane* (238-6281) for park service maintained trails adjacent to the ski resort. *Schweitzer Mountain Resort* (800-831-8810) offers 8.5 kilometers of groomed trails adjacent to its ski resort. Other options include *Silver Mountain* (208-783-1111) with eight kilometers of free groomed trails, *49 Degrees North* (935-6649) with 15 kilometers of trails, *Lookout Pass Ski Resort* (208-744-1301) and *Farragut State Park* (208-683-2425).

Closer to Spokane, the Centennial Trail, has a wide, groomed under-surface perfect for cross-country skiing, though it can get choppy after extensive use. Many area golf courses allow skiing and offer some of the most accessible and enjoyable trails in the area, especially for beginners. Check first to see if you are welcome.

For events, as well as scheduled day and overnight trips in the area, the *Inland Empire Nordic Club* (624-2824) offers a number of venues. They also sponsor a youth program and racing group within the club. *The Mountaineers* (838-4974) and *City Parks Department* (625-6200) both offer classes in cross-country skiing.

9

Area Services

View from the new Public Library

Photo by Ron Swords

Area Services

Health Care

Health care has come a long way since the Sisters of Providence arrived in Spokane in 1886. At that time, 64-year-old Mother Joseph sat down at a dining room table and drew up plans for the 31-room Sacred Heart Hospital. While superintending the construction of the hospital building, Mother Joseph discovered an improperly laid chimney. The next morning, surprised workers found she had dismantled and reconstructed it herself during the night. Popularly known as "the Builder," Mother Joseph was later recognized by the American Institute of Architects as the first architect of the Northwest.

By 1898, the first School of Nursing in the State of Washington started at Sacred Heart Hospital. In 1908, Sacred Heart moved from its location near where the Convention Center now stands to 8th and Browne, where its expanded medical complex still stands.

Today, over 18,000 health care employees make up more than 11% of Spokane's employment base.

Medical Numbers

Emergencies, medical/fire/police (911)
Deaconess Medical Center, 800 W 5th (458-5800)
Deer Park Hospital, Deer Park (276-5061)
Eastern State Psychiatric Hospital, Medical Lake (299-3121)
Holy Family Hospital, 5633 N Lidgerwood (482-0111)
Sacred Heart Medical, 101 W 8th (455-3131)
Shriners Hospital for Crippled Children, 911 W 5th (455-7844)
Valley Hospital and Medical Center, 12606 E Mission (924-6650)
Veterans Medical Center, 4815 N Assembly (328-4521)

Libraries

The city of Spokane offers a main library downtown and four area branches. A Spokane Public Library card is available free of charge to all residents or property owners in the city. You may check out as many as 40 items on your library card at any one time. A Spokane County Library card is also free and available to residents of unincorporated Spokane County and the cities of Airway, Cheney,

Deer Park, Fairfield, Latah, Medical Lake, Millwood and Waverly. The Spokane County Library District has three branches as well as libraries in Cheney, Deer Park, Medical Lake and Fairchild.

The new downtown library, located at the corner of Main and Lincoln, is well worth visiting. You'll enjoy the stupendous view of the Spokane River Falls from the north-facing second and third floor windows. The Eastern Washington Genealogical collection is housed on the third floor. The second floor contains the Northwest Room, where over 5,500 reference books, maps directories, periodicals, photographs and archival documents pertaining to the history and settlement of the Northwest are located.

Public Libraries

Downtown Library, 906 W Main (626-5300)
East Side Branch Library, 500 S Stone (626-5375)
Hillyard Branch Library, 4005 N Cook (626-5380)
Manito Branch Library, 404 E 30th (626-5385)
Shadle Branch Library, Alberta and Wellesley (626-5390)
Outreach Services (626-5332)

County Libraries

Airway Heights, 1213 S Lundstrom, Airway Heights (244-5510)
Argonne Library, 4322 N Argonne (926-4334)
Cheney Library, 610 1st, Cheney (235-7246)
Deer Park Library, City Hall, Deer Park (276-2985)
Fairfield Library, 303 E Main, Fairfield (283-2512)
Medical Lake Library, 321 E Herb St, Medical Lake (299-4891)
North Spokane Library, 44 E Hawthorne (467-5250)
Otis Orchards Library, 22324 E Wellesley, Otis Orchards (921-1500)
Valley Library, 12004 E Main (926-6283)

Campus Libraries

Cooperative Academic Services, 10 N Post, Suite 210 (458-6412). As one librarian described this joint collection of Washington State University (WSU), Eastern Washington University (EWU) and Spokane Medical Library, "We're the Montgomery Ward of libraries."

Though it houses over 14,000 volumes and 3,500 journals, this library specializes in ordering material for advance research. Community users are welcome, and staff are on hand to help train you in accessing the different computer data bases.

The Foley Center, Gonzaga University, 502 E Boone (328-4220-2831). Holdings include more than 300,000 bound volumes, plus extensive microfilm, audio-visual and other special collections including archival and research. Non-students may purchase a library card for $25 to check out materials or spend up to $100 annually to access on-line databases from off-campus.

Harriet Cheney Cowles Library, Whitworth College Campus (466-3260). This liberal-arts collection of 155,000 volumes is especially strong in the American studies, music, education, Protestant theology and biblical study. Students from other area colleges and universities may access the Whitworth collection by producing student identification. Non-students may purchase a yearly membership card for $10.

JFK Library, Eastern Washington University Campus, Cheney (359-6263). This collection consists of over 480,000 volumes and 3,500 current journal, magazine and newspapers. The library owns a large micro-film collection, containing all copies of the *New York Times* as well as many government documents. Non-students residing in Washington state may acquire a library card by presenting photo identification. Most books may be checked out for a month.

Law Library, Gonzaga University, 601 E Sharp (484-6092). The School of Law Library houses more than 190,000 volumes, or equivalents, related to law. Non-students are welcome to use the library's resources, though most of the material does not circulate outside the library.

Spokane Falls Community College (SFCC), Bldg. 2 (533-3800). Non-students have access to SFCC's 40,000 bound volumes, 762 magazines, 12 electronic databases and the 16,000-video collection by presenting photo identification. Many educational and telecourse videos must be viewed on-sight, but other material can be checked out.

Spokane Community College, SCC Campus, Bdlg. 16 (533-7045). This collection focuses on the vocational subjects taught on campus and includes material in the fields of construction, health sciences and automotive. The library is located near the campus' distinctive clock tower. Non-students may access with photo identification.

Local Publications

Family Magazine, P.O. Box 642 (455-3771). This is a monthly magazine providing information and resources for Inland Northwest families. Each month's issue contains a complete calendar of upcoming events of interest to parents and their children. Complimentary copies are available at libraries, most grocery stores and at the Visitors and Convention Center. Subscriptions also are available at $12 for one year and $21 for two years.

Kids Magazine, P.O. Box 8293 (624-1641). This monthly magazine celebrates childhood. Articles and activities are geared toward parents and their school-age children. Distribution is through the school districts.

Nature's Advocate, P.O. Box 413 (456-3834). The Upper Columbia River Sierra Club produces this monthly newsletter on local environmental issues and events. Subscriptions are available for $10 per year.

The Pacific Northwest Inlander, 539 W Sharp (325-0634). This weekly magazine provides insightful and timely information on the arts and entertainment scene. Local and regional news stories also receive in-depth coverage. Over 350 locations in the Inland Northwest distribute the Inlander for free, though subscriptions are available for $26 yearly and $48 for two years.

Spokane Journal of Business, 112 East 1st Ave., (456-5257). If you're seeking information pertaining to the Spokane and Inland Northwest business community, the *Spokane Journal of Business* is your best bet. This bi-weekly publication focuses on the growth and development of area businesses and trends impacting their viability. Rates are $22 for one year and $49 for three years.

Spokane Woman, 112 East 1st Ave. (456-5257). This quarterly publication features issues and interests of concern to women in general as well as local concerns of the women of Spokane. It is available at area newsstands or via subscription to the *Business Journal* at $22 for one year and $49 for three years.

The Spokesman-Review, 999 W Riverside (459-5000). *The Review* has been a major newspaper in Spokane since 1883, though sometimes under other names. Four generations of the Cowles family have operated this daily publication, which delivers over 123,000 daily and 156,000 Sunday papers to Eastern Washington, Northern Idaho and Western Montana.

The Valley Herald, 9618 E First (924-2440). This weekly publication has been in operation since 1920. They write about issues, events, people and places within Spokane county and in the Valley area in particular. Subscription rates for Spokane County residents are $13.50 for six months or $26 for a full year. For rates for subscribers outside the county, call the *Herald*. The newsletter boasts subscribers as far away as Korea.

Radio and Television Stations

FM Radio Stations

88.7 KAGU College — alternative format with specialty programming
89.5 KEWU Jazz, blues, soul, contemporary, news, sports
90.3 KWRS Alternative rock, jazz, new music format
91.1 KPBX Spokane Public Radio — current affairs, classical, jazz
91.9 KSFC Album-orientated rock
92.9 KZZU Contemporary hits
94.5 KKCH Hot adult contemporary
93.7 KDRK Contemporary country, news
96.1 KKPL Solid gold hits from mid-50s to early 70s
98.1 KISC Favorites of the 60s, 70s, 80s and 90s
98.9 KKZX Classic rock
99.8 KXLY Easy listening, news
101.1 KEYF Oldies from the 50s and 60s
101.9 KTSL Christian contemporary
103.1 KCDA Country of the 50s, 60s, 70s, 80s and today
105.7 KEZE Rock 'n' roll
107.1 KAZZ Children's programming 24 hours
107.9 KMBI Christian music and programs

AM Radio Stations

590 KAQQ Original hits of the 40s, 50s and 60s, CNN Headline News
630 KHDL CNN Headline News, local sports, news and weather
700 KMJY Modern country, news, sports, weather
790 KJRB Syndicated talk show format
920 KXLY Local news, business, agriculture, weather and sports
970 KTRW 24-hour sports radio
1050 KEYF Adult pop contemporary favorites
1230 KSBN International, national, local news
1330 KMBI Christian music and programs
1510 KGA Rush Limbaugh, ABC news, traffic, weather
1550 KSVY Classical music

Television Stations

Cox Cable TV, 1717 E Buckeye, 99207
KAYU TV (Fox/Independent - channel 28) 4600 S Regal, 99223
KHQ TV (NBC - channel 6) 4202 S Regal, 99223
KREM TV (CBS - channel 2) 4103 S Regal, 99223
KSPS (PBS - channel 7) 3911 S Regal, 99223
KXLY (ABC - channel 4) 500 W Boone, 99201

Other Important Area Numbers

Spokane Area Chamber of Commerce, 1020 W Riverside
(624-1393)
Spokane Valley Chamber of Commerce, 10303 Sprague
(924-4994)
Spokane Area Economic Development Council, 221 N Wall
(624-9285)
Spokane Regional Conventions and Visitors Bureau,
926 W Sprague (747-3230; 800-248-3230)
Driver's Licensing (482-3882; 921-2357)
Postal Information (459-0222)
Weather (353-2368)
Department of Wildlife (456-4082)
SnoLine Pass Report (1-976-ROAD)
State Patrol (456-4101)

Government Numbers

City of Spokane

City Hall, 808 W Spokane Falls Boulevard
Emergency, police/fire/medical (911)
Animal Control (534-8133)
City Hall (625-6350)
Historic Preservation (625-6370)
Mayor's Office (625-6250)
Parks and Recreation (625-6200)
Police Department (625-4000)
Youth Department and Commission (625-6440)

Canoeing in the Little Spokane Natural
Area of Riverside State Park

Photo by Ron Swords

County of Spokane

County Clerk, 1116 W Broadway
Emergency; police/fire/medical (911)
Animal Control (458-2532)
Commissioner's Office (456-2265)
Parks Department (456-4730)
Sheriff's Office (456-4739)

Outside Spokane

Airway Heights (244-5578)
Cheney (235-6211)
Deer Park (276-8802)
Medical Lake (299-7712)
Millwood (924-0960)

Recreational Facilities

Joe Albi Stadium (353-6500)
Manito Park (456-4331)
Mount Spokane State Park (456-4169)
Playfair Race Track (534-0505)
Riverfront Park (456-4FUN)
Riverside State Park (456-3964)
Splash Down (924-3079)
Spokane Coliseum (353-6500)
Spokane International Ag-Trade Center (353-6500)
Spokane Interstate Fairgrounds (535-1766)
Spokane Pool Hotline (625-6960)
Spokane Raceway Park (244-3663)
Turnbull Wildlife Refuge (1-235-4723)
U.S. National Parks (725-2715)
Walk in the Wild Zoo (924-7221)
Washington State Parks and Recreation (206-753-2027;
summer only 800-562-0990)

Arts and Cultural Events

Allegro (747-7398)
Cathedral of St. John The Evangelist (838-4277)
The Chase Gallery at City Hall (625-6050)
Cheney Cowles Museum and Campbell House (456-3931)
Connoisseur Concerts (326-4942)
Corbin Art Center (625-6677)
G&B Select-A-Seat (325-SEAT)
Interplayers Ensemble (455-PLAY)
The Met (455-6500)
Spokane Art School (328-0900)
Spokane Civic Theatre (325-1413)
Spokane Convention Center (353-6500)
Spokane Opera House (353-6500)
Spokane Symphony Orchestra (326-3136)
Ticketmaster Northwest (206-628-0888)
Uptown Opera Company (325-SEAT)

10

Neighboring Communities

Cycling on the Centennial Trail in the Spokane Valley

Photo by Ron Swords

Neighboring Communities

W ithin 30 minutes of downtown Spokane are a number of communities in Washington and Idaho, each with its own unique attractions and personalities. Many of these smaller areas are dedicated to specific livelihoods such as farming, timber or mining. If you take the time to stop and visit, you'll most likely find a coffee shop or restaurant where the locals gather to share news, a handful of shops geared toward supplying necessities and a town hall, which often shares space with other community service organizations.

East of Spokane are expanding suburban neighborhoods dotting the Valley plain all the way to the Washington/Idaho border. Ponderosa pines bracket the I-90 freeway until you reach Coeur d'Alene. From here, the freeway climbs into the Coeur d'Alene Mountains, where the largest silver mining district in the world is located.

Small communities started in the heyday of the 1880s gold and silver rush remain today as testimony to the importance of mining in the area. Towns like Osburn and Wallace were settled by miners and still retain pride in their heritage and rich history. Further east lies Kellogg, home of the Sunshine mine, the deepest mine below sea level (-3,300 feet).

A number of towns dot the rich Palouse Country south of Spokane. Rolling hills of wheat, peas and lentils exemplify some of the country's richest farmland. In the early spring, these hills are covered with a velvet greenness as new shoots push through the thick clods of rich soil. In the fall, golden wheat, ready for harvest, spans across these same hillsides.

Farming continues north of Spokane in the counties of Stevens and Pend Oreille. The Pend Oreille Valley, an hour's drive north, was formed by ice-age activity. Highway 211 follows the Pend Oreille River, one of only four in the United States to flow north.

One of the world's largest buffalo herds roam free on the Kalispell Indian Reservation between Usk and Ione. Osprey, eagles and beaver all live along the banks of the Pend Oreille River and deer and bear often can be seen from the roadway as you drive through the valley. Timber once was king along the forested slopes here. Today, some lumber is still harvested, though many small communities feel the absence of this once-thriving industry. Instead of flannel-shirted loggers thronging the neighborhood cafes, towns now see seasonal visitors who come to enjoy the pristine beauty of the many area lakes.

The Canadian border is within a two-hour drive of Spokane. Near here is Boundry Dam, one of the largest thin-arch dams in the country, with a 32-foot thick base and eight-foot thick crest. Gardner Caves, the state's largest limestone caves, are within miles of the neighboring communities of Metaline, Ione and Usk.

A flatter, drier region lies west of the Lilac City. The area is populated by large family farms and the communities which support them. Trees quickly give way to man-high sagebrush and basalt outcroppings. The acres upon acres of tilled soil make it hard to imagine the challenge faced by early pioneers who had to irrigate this dry-land area. Today decedents of these pioneers still live in towns such as Reardon, Davenport and Odessa.

Each town in each distinct region in the Inland Northwest is unique, and, for those who enjoy a slower pace of life, well worth a visit. Yet if you only have a day or two to see a slice of Americana, there are some definite must-see towns. Whether you're looking for the frenzy of a wild west rodeo or the serenity of a crystal-blue lake, you can sample life away from the fast lane in any one of these nearby communities.

Washington Communities

Cheney

At one time, the community of Cheney (population 7,600) vied with Spokane for recognition as center of the Inland Northwest. At stake was the county seat and lucrative business interests including placement of the Northern Pacific Railroad tracks. The original community of Willow Springs one-upped Spokane by renaming the town for Benjamin Cheney, a Northern Pacific Railroad board member. Mr. Cheney was so pleased, he donated $10,000 to found a small academy. Today, it's known as Eastern Washington University.

Cheney citizens did not stop there. One spring evening, when many Spokane residents were celebrating a wedding party, a group of hooded men stole the county records from Spokane and physically transported them to Cheney, making that city the de-facto county seat until further legislation mandated otherwise.

Today, Cheney combines the aesthetics of small-town living with the academic environment of a major university. Eastern Washington University contributes to the business and social fabric of this farming community with an enrollment of 8,000 students, 4,000 who reside in Cheney during the school year, the remainder commuting from Spokane and other smaller towns. Grain elevators and the Centennial Flour Mill frame the city's skyline, reminders of the rich wheat, oat, barley, beef and dairy production country surrounding the town.

Every residence in Cheney is located within 1/2 mile of a city park. The *City Parks and Recreation Department* (235-7295) schedules over 200 year-round recreation programs for all age groups. Less than a mile south of the town is the *Turnbull National Wildlife Refuge* (235-4723), covering 20 square miles. Fall is the best time to catch sight of the migratory Canadian geese and ducks that use this sanctuary for a resting ground.

The *Cheney Rodeo* (235-4848), one of the largest amateur rodeos held in the Pacific Northwest, occurs annually each July. Events include saddle bronco, calf roping, and bareback and bull riding. Local farmers and cowboys ride side by side with amateur contestants from throughout the Inland Northwest. There's dust, thrills and a fair share of spills, too. If you want a taste of real, live cowboys in action, this is a don't miss event.

With Spokane's restaurants only 20 minutes away, the local selection of eateries remain limited. However, good dining spots include the *Willow Springs Station*, 809 First (235-4420), and *DJ's Restaurant and Lounge* (235-6367) on Fish Lake Road. *The Fiesta Charra*, 505 Second (235-5679), rates great reviews for Mexican food. The only motel in Cheney is the *Willow Springs Motel*, 5 B Street (235-5138), though a *Super 8 Motel*, 11102 W Westbow (838-8800), is located directly west of town near the freeway to Spokane.

Deer Park

The rural community of Deer Park is 22 miles north of Spokane. Many of its 2,245 citizens commute into Spokane for work. Others till the rich farmland of the valley nestled at the foot of the Selkirk Mountain range.

Established in 1889, Deer Park began as a lumbering town and, as land was cleared, became one of the largest dairy areas in Eastern Washington. You'll still find many charming turn-of-the-century residences lining the quiet streets of the town.

The City of Deer Park owns and operates a municipal swimming pool, two municipal parks and two playfields. Eight fresh water lakes within 20 miles of the town also afford plenty of opportunity for leisure pursuits. For winter activities, a cross-country ski trail lies northeast of the airport and is operated by the city.

Two well-attended community events include the *Deer Park Winter Festival* in January and *Settler's Picnic* in June. The *Chamber of Commerce* (276-5900) can provide more details on these and other events, including a *Spring Dairy Show* in June and the *Deer Park Fair* held every August.

There are no motels in Deer Park, but there is a charming Victorian-style bed and breakfast called *Love's*, 31315 N Cedar Road, Deer Park (276-6939). What the area lacks in accommodations, it amply makes up in places to eat. For breakfast and lunch try *Rose's Cafe and Deli* located in the *Excell Food Store* or *Jackie's Cafe* on Main Street (276-6748). Dinner spots include *Shagnasty's Food and Spirits*, 122 W 1st (276-5073), and the *Fire House Pizza*, 3 N Main (276-7030), for great pizzas.

Greenbluff

This small district, situated on a bluff eight miles north of Spokane, is as much a way of life as it is a community. Here, only minutes from the center of Spokane, you can pick apples, peaches, strawberries, raspberries and more. Most of the area farmers and orchardists open their acres to visitors who come to pick fresh fruit and vegetables. You can also purchase pre-picked boxes and bushels or just visit for a breath of country-fresh air.

During the year, the *Greenbluff Growers Association* sponsors a number of events which draw visitors like bears to honey. They also publish a yearly produce map, describing the various farms and what they produce as well as information on the exact dates and times of the community events. The maps are available at Spokane area libraries, at each of the 37-participating farms, or by writing to the Association, E 9423 Greenbluff Road, Colbert, 99005.

Starting in the summer, when the cherries ripen on the trees, is the *Cherry Picker's Trot* (238-4709). This event includes a four-mile fun run, a tot trot for little ones 5 and under, a hamburger feed and a cherry pit spit.

In September is the annual *Apple Pickers' Volkssport Walk* (489-3198). This is a non-competitive 6.7 mile walk through orchards, country roads and newly-plowed fields. There's no fee for the walk, and the entire family is welcome to participate.

The *Oktoberfest Harvest Festival* is held in October. Every weekend in the month, many orchards have live music, pony rides, arts and crafts booths as well as fresh-baked apple pie and hot German sausages for sale. You can also pick as many apples as you like. At *Walter's Fruit Ranch* (238-4709) there's a free "fruit loop express" train, which transports visitors deep into the orchards for apple picking. *Wellen's Luscious Fruit and Antiques* (238-6978) provides the little ones a ride in a miniature covered wagon pulled through the orchard by a pony, while the adults can browse the antique store and crafts booths.

The community activities, U-pick fruits and vegetables and congenial country pace make Greenbluff well worth the visit.

Rockford

This tight-knit community (population 494), referred to by area residents as a "diamond in the rough," is located only 15 miles southeast of Spokane's Dishman Mica Road and Sprague intersection. It's old-time eaterie, the *Harvest Moon Cafe* (291-4314), serves thick, juicy hamburgers and rib-sticking large breakfasts. Rockford has one of the few bull riding arenas in the area, the *Rocking Go Arena* (291-6451). Rockford also hosts a county fair the last weekend in September. At the fair, you'll find rides for the kids, homemade arts and crafts and a sense of strong community.

Idaho Communities

Coeur d'Alene

The town of Coeur d'Alene lies 33 miles east of Spokane. It was originally called Coeur d'Alene City to distinguish it from the like-named river, mountain range, mining district, forest, military camp, lake, railroad line and Native American tribe. Today, the city is known as "The Lake City." With a population of 27,000, it's the sixth largest city in Idaho and serves as the county seat of Kootenai County.

The *Greater Coeur d'Alene Convention and Visitors Bureau* (208-664-0587) offers a wealth of information on area sites, events and activities. At the heart of many city events is lovely Coeur d'Alene Lake. The lake extends 23 miles to the south. Its 109 miles of shoreline include sandy beaches, craggy rock slopes studded with native ponderosa pine and other species of trees, as well as docks and homes.

The City Beach in Coeur d'Alene is a beehive of activity all summer long. Here you'll find swimming, boating, sailing, jet skiing and sunbathing. Rent canoes, kayaks and paddleboats on the City Dock at Independence Point, or try a seaplane ride or parasailing. *North Idaho College* (208-769-3300) rents catamarans and windsurf boards just east of the docks.

If you don't want to get wet, take a walk on the 12-foot-wide, 3,300-foot-long floating boardwalk rimming the *Coeur d'Alene Resort*. The boardwalk was constructed in 1986 and is recognized as the world's longest floating boardwalk. It's open daily to the public.

For both shopping convenience and variety, many visitors enjoy the downtown *Coeur d'Alene Resort Plaza* with its 30 boutiques and gift shops. There's also a great selection of retail spots lining Sherman Avenue between 2nd and 8th streets. *The Silver Lake Mall,* just five minutes north of downtown on Highway 95, is North Idaho's largest indoor mall and is open seven days a week.

Consider *T.W. Fisher's*, 204 N 2nd (664-BREW), for great pub food and ales, *3rd Street Cantina*, 201 N 3rd (664-0693), for traditional Mexican food or *Cricket's Restaurant and Oyster Bar*, 424 Sherman (765-1990), for family fun.

If you need a place to stay, the *Greater Coeur d'Alene Convention and Visitors Bureau* (208-664-0587) can provide you with a list of accommodations to suit any budget and preference. In addition to the standard hotels and motels, there are several charming bed and breakfast establishments. Among them are the historic *Blackwell House*, 820 Sherman (208-664-0656), or the renovated 1905 schoolhouse, *The Roosevelt Inn*, 105 Wallace, Coeur d'Alene (208-765-5200; 800-290-3358). For more information, refer to Chapter 1: Places to Stay.

Coeur d'Alene is truly a charming destination town, whether you visit for the summer sun and water fun or the winter recreational activities.

Post Falls

The town of Post Falls was named after German immigrant Frederick Post. Post originally settled in Spokane, where a street was named after him as inducement to locate his flour mill there. By 1880, Post decided to establish a mill driven by the power of the Spokane River closer to Coeur d'Alene Lake. The town of Post Falls grew up around this first business.

Today, Post Falls, located 20 minutes east of Spokane and 10 minutes west of Coeur d'Alene, is the heart of a business and residential growth boom. This is due in part to its strategic location along the I-90 corridor. Other reasons include tax incentives, room to grow and an active campaign by regional officials in advertising the positive attributes of the area. Yet despite the influx of people, the town itself retains its provincial flavor.

Within the city limits, you can visit the petroglyphs and pictographs at Treaty Rock or enjoy the view of the falls from *Q'emiln* (ka-Mee-lan) *Riverside State Park*. In early spring, the water rushes through a narrow chasm, cascading down the falls. By summer, the falls has narrowed to a trickle, but there are still plenty of boating and water activities to enjoy both at the park or through *Templin's Resort* (208-773-1611).

Rafting on the Spokane River through the
Toenail Rapid in Riverside State Park

Photo by Ron Swords

The North Idaho Centennial Trail, a 56-mile-long paved walking and biking trail, passes through the city. Golf is as near as the *Highlands Golf and Country Club* (208-773-3673).

One of the area's most highly rated restaurants, *Chef in the Forest*, 7900 E Hauser Lake Road (208-773-3654), is located here, as well as *Mallard's Restaurant*, 414 E 1st (208-773-1611), with its lovely view of the Spokane River. It's the only commercial property in the state of Idaho designated as a wild-life viewing area. Catch sight of nesting osprey in the early spring or migrating wildfowl, ducks and Canadian geese in the fall and late winter months.

Hotel accommodations are easy to find in and near this small community, including *Nendels Inn* at Riverbend (208-773-3583), which is located near the Greyhound Race Park and Factory Outlet shopping center. Or consider visiting the *Pine Squirrel Bed and Breakfast*, 300 Penny Lane and West Riverview (208-773-9310), for a relaxing stay.

For additional information and free brochures of area attractions and services, contact *Post Falls Tourism*, P.O. Box 908, Post Falls, ID 83854 (208-773-4080; 800-292-2553).

11

Annual Events
Calendar

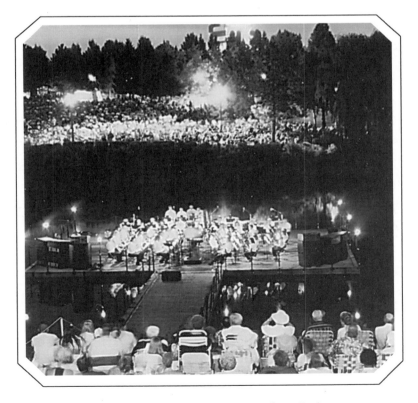

Royal Fireworks Concert at Riverfront Park
Photo by Patrice Tobler

Annual Events Calendar

S pokane serves as the hub of a 36-county region including parts of Eastern Washington, Montana, Oregon, Idaho, British Columbia and Alberta. Because of this, annual events in the Greater Spokane area and nearby communities reflect the rich kaleidoscope of background, interests and pursuits of the entire Northwest population. There are activities to suit every taste. Whether your interest is in arts and crafts, revving hot-rod engines or community basketball, you'll find a way to celebrate it in the Inland Northwest.

January

Connoisseur Concerts' Annual *Bach Festival* is widely recognized as one of the premier music festivals in the United States. For four wonderful days, the music of Bach is performed by local and internationally-known musicians. Tickets can be purchased for individual concerts (325-7321) or for the entire festival.

Spokane Ag Expo/Pacific Northwest Farm Forum (459-4108). For over 18 years, this annual event has been a social and business boon to Inland Northwest farmers. This three-day show, sponsored by the Agricultural Bureau of the Spokane Chamber of Commerce, displays enough farm machinery to fill the Convention Center, Ag-Trade Center and the Coliseum. There are over a hundred educational seminars for farmers and their families and social activities such as a horse pitching contest and an international dinner tour, where participants sample ethnic cuisine from around the world at local restaurants. Farmers and non-farmers alike are welcome.

For those interested in RV travel and camping, there are two Spokane RV shows. One is at the *Interstate Fairgrounds* (535-1766) in January and the second is at the Spokane Convention Center (353-6500) in February. Both offer a variety of recreational and camping vehicles for your perusal.

Don't let snow flurries keep you indoors, especially when there's winter fun only 20 minutes north of Spokane, at the *Deer Park Winter Festival*. You'll enjoy watching dog sled races and weight pulls, ski competition and snowshoe softball. If you're cold, warm up inside while you visit the art show.

For the truly outdoor and adventuresome types, why not experience Coeur d'Alene's *Hangover Handicap Run and Polar Bear Plunge* (208-765-5105). This annual fun run, followed by a dip into the semi-frozen waters of Coeur d'Alene Lake, will have you looking forward to a hot toddy and warm fire.

February

With spring just around the corner, hundreds flock to the annual *Boat Show* in the Convention Center (353-6500). Over 20 marine dealers display everything from cabin cruisers to speed boats. The *Home and Garden Show* (534-5380) also draws crowds with exhibits of furniture, home accessories and hundreds of home-remodeling ideas. For those ready to hit the road in a new RV, the Spokane Convention Center (353-6500) hosts one of two seasonal RV shows (see January listing).

For those who haven't experienced winter enough, there's always the *Coeur d'Alene Ice Fest* (208-667-4040). This ice-carving festival is a treat for the whole family.

March

For a truly community event, try the *Washington State "B" Basketball Tournament* (448-6967). During this four-day competition, 16 boys' and 16 girls' teams battle for the state championship. Nearby farming and logging communities literally empty during the games, while whole towns cheer on the teams. One year, the bank in Reardon was robbed while most of the residents were courtside in Spokane.

Another annual event eliciting almost as much excitement is the *St. Patrick's Day Parade.* This grass roots procession through downtown Spokane features cement trucks filled with beer and enough green decorations to cover Ireland twice over. Many of the parade's participants come from the crowds lining the sidewalk. It's loud, raucous and a great time for all.

April

Where's a good place to enjoy 10,000 screaming, laughing, running children? The annual *Junior Bloomsday* race. Participants range from ages 5 to 12, and courses are set up by age category. Everyone receives a T-shirt at the end of the race. This mad-cap scene is held each year at Joe Albi Stadium (325-9044).

Nearby Idaho communities are ablaze with activities and events. *The Annual Kite Festival* (208-263-9577) is held at Sandpoint's City Beach. Not only is the sky filled with colorful kites of all shapes and sizes, but competitive awards are given for handmade kites. In Coeur d'Alene, there's the *Spring Dash Fun Run* (208-667-2566), or for those with a more sedate bent, the *Mad Hatter Easter Stroll* (208-667-4040), highlighted by an Easter hat contest.

May

The largest and most adrenaline-raising spring event is *Bloomsday* (838-1579). Held the first Sunday of the month, this timed, 12-K fun run is the world's largest road race of its kind. Over 50,000 men, women and children participate. The whole town turns out to either run or cheer on the participants. Running or walking up the notorious Doomsday Hill at the five-mile mark creates stories and legends long after the race. Many an unwary visitor wonders why, for the week following Bloomsday, so many individuals wear the same T-shirt. The shirts are given to every participant who finishes the race and are worn as a proud show of accomplishment.

For a more cerebral event, try the all-volunteer *Spokane Music and Arts Festival* (327-7674 or 535-8274). For over 50 years, the festival has sponsored a series of musical concerts. Students in music and visual arts submit their work in a juried competition culminating in a Young Artists Concert. Tickets are available through the Spokane Symphony Box Office (624-1200) and G&B Select-a-Seat (325-SEAT).

Another traditional festival held annually for over 57 years is the *Lilac Festival* (326-3339). This is a celebration of spring and the blossoming of the lilac, a hardy, pioneer flower. Highlights of the 10-day celebration include the Armed Forces Torchlight Parade, an evening parade through the streets of downtown Spokane, a golf tournament and the Junior Lilac Parade for youngsters.

Traditionally close on the heels of the Lilac Festival is the *Fairchild Air Force Base Aerospace Day* (247-5704). Thrill to the spectacle of a variety of aircraft circling overhead, then tour the Air Force Base grounds, aircraft and a display hanger. There are also plenty of informative and interesting demonstrations. For a number of years, this event was held the same week as the Lilac Festival, but it can be held before or after. Look for it on a Sunday during the spring or summer months, or call for exact dates. This is an event you won't want to miss.

Bloomsday participants climb "Doomsday Hill" next to the Spokane River.
Photo by Ron Swords

The *Fred Murphy Pioneer Festival Parade* (208-667-1232) is held Memorial Day weekend. This festival in Coeur d'Alene pays tribute to local folk hero Fred Murphy, a long-time area resident and tugboat skipper on Lake Coeur d'Alene. *The Coeur d'Alene Marathon* (208-667-4167), a 26-mile loop run through the city center, city park, past three lakes and two golf courses, is held at the same time. Also look for the *Mother's Day Band Concert* (208-769-3415).

June

Artfest is a three-day celebration of arts and music held on the grounds of Spokane's Cheney Cowles Museum. A juried art sale, demonstrations by artists and craftspeople, food and free musical entertainment highlight this event.

If you enjoy the roar of engines and the squeal of tires, be sure to visit the *National Street Hot Rod Association Northwest Nationals* (535-1766) held each year at the Interstate Fairgrounds. If you prefer classier cars, try the *Car d'Lane* (208-667-4040) antique car show held in Coeur d'Alene.

Neighboring communities join in the fun throughout the month of June. The *Chewelah Chataqua* (935-8991) offers free musical entertainment, a parade, square dance festival, fine arts and crafts, a carnival and food. Fairfield hosts *Flag Day*, and north of Spokane, the citizens of Elk celebrate *Pioneer Days*. Post Falls (800-292-2553) honors its own pioneers in a community *Pioneer Festival*.

Another slice of the past is the annual *Moran Strawberry Social*, held at the MoranGgrange at 61st and Palouse Highway. There, you'll discover arts and crafts, a talent show, bingo and the renown strawberry shortcake. The sun-ripened strawberries are well worth the small donation requested.

For a change of pace, try *Hoopfest*. This non-profit tournament is the 5th largest basketball contest of its kind in the country and takes place on the streets of downtown Spokane. Over 2,300 teams of three each pit themselves against like-age opponents in this non-professional fun-for-all. The event nets a hefty profit for local charities.

A fun way to get exercise is the annual *Spokane River Canoe Classic* (624-8384). Known as the "Bloomsday on Water," this canoe race on the Spokane River starts in Corbin Park, Post Falls and finishes at Plante's Ferry Park in Spokane.

July

What better way to celebrate the 4th of July than with friends and neighbors at a Riverfront Park picnic? *Spokane Neighbor Day* was established just for that purpose. The one-day festival offers music, ethnic foods, parachute jumps, dancing, family activities and much more. The day comes to a dramatic close with a free, outdoor symphony concert and fireworks display near the Opera House.

Coeur d'Alene hosts its own fireworks extravaganza on the 4th, as well as an *American Heroes Parade* (208-765-1112).

For those who didn't get enough pyrotechnics on the 4th, there's always the *Royal Fireworks Concert*, held in Riverfront Park the last Sunday evening in July. The concert showcases music from the 17th and 18th centuries including Handel's Royal Fireworks Music. The performance ends with a dazzling grand finale fireworks display.

The Inland Northwest has long been a hotbed of rodeo activity, with many local events attracting farmers and ranchers who both watch and ride the bucking bulls and broncos. The *Cheney Rodeo* boasts over 28 years of rodeo fun and excitement. Information about this three-day event, which is held the second weekend of the month, can be found through the Cheney Chamber of Commerce (235-8480).

A picnic in the park highlights the *Hillyard Festival*, a "community-within-a-community" event. Now just a bend in the road on North Market Street, Hillyard was once a railroad town named after Railroad magnate Jim Hill. Though it has been swallowed up by the city, Hillyard still retains its community feeling. The area is loaded with antique and second-hand shops filled with treasures. Check billboards and local newspapers for the exact dates of this event, which is advertised well in advance.

The fun and hilarious *Cherry Picker's Trot* (238-4709) celebrates the cherry harvest in Greenbluff and includes a four-mile run, a Tot Trot for youngsters, a hamburger feed and the notorious cherry-pit spitting competition. Another decade old event as entertaining to onlookers as participants is the Kaniksu Ranch (624-6777) *Bare Buns Fun Run*. Though the 5-K run is sponsored by a nudist park, it does advertise, "clothing optional."

August

AHRA World Finals Championship Drag Races are held at Spokane Raceway Park (244-3636). Hundreds of automobiles, including top fuel cars, funny cars and wheelstanders as well as a multitude of trucks and motorcycles, entertain the spectators. Grab a hot dog and enjoy the good old-fashioned noise.

The Deer Park Fair and Rodeo (276-2444) is held in conjunction with the *Settler's Picnic* (276-5900). Together they provide for one of the largest parades in the area.

For over 45 years, the *Moran Fair* has drawn crowds to the Moran Grange located at 61st and Palouse Highway. This free three-day event is a smaller version of the Interstate Fair and includes arts and crafts, animal and agricultural displays and fun for the whole family.

Over 50,000 visitors visit *Art on the Green* each year. This three-day cultural festival is held at historic Fort Sherman on the shores of Lake Coeur d'Alene. The festival includes a juried art show, exhibits by artists and craftspeople, free music and dance exhibitions (208-667-9346). Be sure to sample the traditional mouth-watering, hot buttered corn on the cob and German sausage sandwiches.

During the festival, Coeur d'Alene merchants close off Sherman Avenue and host art displays, crafts booths, entertainment and a grand sale at the *Downtown Street Fair* (208-667-4040). Another celebration, *A Taste of Coeur d'Alene* (208-667-1232), features more entertainment and plenty of good food.

The *Coeur d'Alene Triathlon* (208-667-3589) features a 1.5-K swim in Coeur d'Alene Lake, a 40-K bicycle race to Kidd Island Bay and a 10-K run through the City Park and Tubbs Hill. *The Chinook Fishing Derby* (208-667-9304) is an opportunity to hook a salmon on Coeur d'Alene Lake. If you aren't lucky enough to catch anything, you can always create a great story about the "whopper" that got away.

Those who love music, dance and Celtic tradition should try the **Spokane Highland Games** (927-0572). This festival celebrates the ethnic heritage of the Highlands with music, dance, a games competition and ceilidh, complete with twirling plaid skirts, the strain of haunting bagpipes and the beat of Highland drums. There's even a sheep dog demonstration. Be sure to sample authentic Scottish food. The festival is held at Riverfront Park.

One area event harkening back to the days of leather chaps and long hours in the saddle is the **Omak Stampede** in Omak, Washington. This affair is famous for its Suicide Race, where horses are spurred off a ledge, down a steep grade and into a river. A three-day rodeo is only part of the annual festivities. Also offered are a Western art show, Native American dances and stick games, parades and various crafts. Tickets can be ordered ahead (800-933-6625) or bought at the gate.

The last week of August features the **North Idaho Fair and Rodeo** (208-765-4969), held at the Kootenai County Fairgrounds. This four-day event draws crowds of over 50,000 to view the traditional livestock shows, horse pulling contests, headline entertainment and circus.

Native American Encampment and Pow Wow (535-0886). Over 35 tribes converge in Riverfront Park to celebrate Native American dancing and storytelling and to enjoy cultural exhibits and crafts displays. In addition, there's a feast featuring salmon, deer, elk and other wild game. Another Native American celebration is the Coeur d'Alene peoples' **Annual Pilgrimage to Cataldo**. For over 60 years, tribal members and visitors have gathered at Cataldo Mission in Northern Idaho for a feast of corn, melon, frybread and other delicacies.

September

The **Spokane Interstate Fair** (535-1766), a five-day event, draws participants from all of Washington and neighboring states. It includes home and garden exhibits, arts and crafts, livestock events, a carnival and more food than you can consume in a lifetime. Especially delicious are the Elephant Ears. Plan on a full day to see, taste and hear it all.

For great food, and lots of it, try **Pig Out in the Park** held every year in Riverfront Park. Over one million people have enjoyed this event, sampling the delicacies provided by area restaurants, shopping the arts and crafts booths and delighting in the live entertainment.

October

Each year, the Washington State Quilters unfurl a host of antique and contemporary quilts at their annual *Quilt Show*. The Convention Center is the site of this tactile celebration, and while the quilts themselves are the highlight of the three-day event, many visitors come for the crafts and fabric dealers' booths lining the Convention floor.

Another large-scale event held in the Convention Center is *Family-A-Fair* (456-3733). Over 10,000 people crowd through the doors for this two-day family celebration. Interactive exhibits, workshops for parents (child care provided), live entertainment and more all add to the excitement.

For a taste treat, consider a meal at the annual *Greek Festival*, 1703 N Washington (328-9310). Sponsored by the Holy Trinity Greek Orthodox Church, this two-day, three-night event features a dinner of ethnic specialties such as spanakopeta, stuffed grape leaves and moussaka. A crafts bazaar and bake sale is also part of the festivities.

Greenbluff Oktoberfest Festivities (238-4031) lasts throughout the month of October. There are special events each weekend as well as homemade treats, music and apples waiting to be picked.

November

The holidays are celebrated with a triple whammy in Coeur d'Alene. *The Festival of Lights Parade* (208-667-4040), *Holiday Lighting Festival* (208-765-4000) and *Festival of Trees* (208-765-4000) combine fun with the opportunity for gift buying and viewing lights galore.

For a delicious way to ring in the season, don't miss the *Scandinavian Bazaar* sponsored by the Central Luthern Church, 309 W 5th (624-9233). There are crafts and bakery items for sale. A Scandinavian lunch is served, featuring such delights as lefse and krumkake.

December

Traditions and holidays fit hand-in-glove, and at no time of the year is this more true than during December. Both the **Nutcracker Ballet** and **Handel's Messiah** bring crowds to the Spokane Opera House (325-7328). Coeur d'Alene also offers the **Nutcracker Ballet** (208-769-3415) as well as a special **Sounds of Christmas Concert** (208-769-3415), presented by the North Idaho Symphony and Choir.

A wonderful event, which highlights artisans' one-of-a-kind creations, is the three-day **Yuletide Arts and Crafts Show**. Sponsored by the Spokane Art School (328-0900), this juried event not only funds the school's art programs, it provides a showcase for artisans around the Northwest and beyond.

While decorative lights on any area home bring ohhs and ahhs, there's a truly spectacular display at the golf course at **Qualachan**, 301 East Meadowlake Road (448-9317). Over 90,000 lights set in 27 illuminated scenes make up the largest display of its kind in Eastern Washington. There's a small donation at the front gate.

Wild Roses – a sure sign of
Spring in Spokane

Photo by Ron Swords

Index

Fireworks at Riverfront Park

Photo by Patrice Tobler

Index

.

M.E. Buckham
Author

Mary Buckham was born and raised in Spokane. Except for sojourns in Seattle, Honolulu, Washington D.C., Florence and London, she calls the Inland Northwest home. Buckham is a full-time free-lance writer. When not researching an article or writing guidebooks, she savors a good double latte.

Patrice Tobler & Ron Swords
Photographers

Patrice Tobler is a 30-something photographer, wife and mother of one who has lived in Spokane for 15 years. She is a graduate of the Spokane Falls Community College photography program. Tobler enjoys capturing special moments or telling a story through photography.

Ron Swords has lived in Spokane since he was 10. He has a photo science degree from Eastern Washington University. When not taking photos for guidebooks, he works for the Associated Press and does free-lance sports photography.